Between God & Green

How Evangelicals are Cultivating a Middle Ground on Climate Change

KATHARINE K. WILKINSON

OXFORD

UNIVERSITY PRESS

OXFORD
UNIVERSITY PRESS

Oxford University Press, Inc., publishes works that further
Oxford University's objective of excellence
in research, scholarship, and education.

Oxford   New York
Auckland   Cape Town   Dar es Salaam   Hong Kong   Karachi
Kuala Lumpur   Madrid   Melbourne   Mexico City   Nairobi
New Delhi   Shanghai   Taipei   Toronto

With offices in
Argentina   Austria   Brazil   Chile   Czech Republic   France   Greece
Guatemala   Hungary   Italy   Japan   Poland   Portugal   Singapore
South Korea   Switzerland   Thailand   Turkey   Ukraine   Vietnam

Published by Oxford University Press, Inc.
198 Madison Avenue, New York, New York 10016
www.oup.com

Library of Congress Cataloging-in-Publication Data

Wilkinson, Katharine K. (Katharine Keeble), 1983–
Between God and green: how evangelicals are cultivating a middle
ground on climate change / Katharine K. Wilkinson.
p. cm.
Includes bibliographical references (p.) and index.
ISBN 978-0-19-989588-5 (hardcover: alk. paper) —
ISBN 978-0-19-989589-2 (ebook)   1. Human ecology—Religious aspects—
Christianity.   2. Nature—Effect of human beings on.   3. Climatic changes.
4. Evangelicalism.   I. Title.
BT695.5.W566 2012
261.8'8—dc23
2011039922

1   3   5   7   9   8   6   4   2
Printed in the United States of America
on acid-free paper

This book is dedicated to the living memory of my influential teacher and mentor and treasured friend, Margaret W. "Jane" Pepperdene, who taught me to "see feelingly" and exemplified the tradition of those who so "gladly . . . lerne and gladly teche."

Contents

Preface

ON FEBRUARY 8, 2006, *New York Times* readers opened the newspaper to find a full-page advertisement announcing "Our commitment to Jesus Christ compels us to solve the global warming crisis." Readers of *Christianity Today* (*CT*) were similarly presented with this coming-out notice for the Evangelical Climate Initiative (ECI). Both audiences were likely surprised, though perhaps from different perspectives. At the time, many assumed all evangelicals marched in lockstep with the Republican Party, and President George W. Bush staunchly opposed action to ameliorate climate change. It seemed implausible for a group of senior evangelical leaders, including such high-profile individuals as megachurch pastor and best-selling author Rick Warren, to launch a national effort advocating mitigation of greenhouse gas emissions and adaptation to climate change impacts. But at the National Press Club in Washington, DC, they did just that.

As I illustrate in the text that follows, this emergence was anything but sudden, yet for me, too, it was unexpected, despite working at the time for the Natural Resources Defense Council, a leading environmental nongovernmental organization (NGO). The ECI clearly aimed to broaden the traditional evangelical Right agenda of personal morality issues—abortion, homosexuality, and pornography—to include environmental or "creation care" concerns, specifically climate change. For these leaders, the vantage point of religion seemed to endow the issue with particular significance, suggest particular courses of action in response, and animate their voices in the cacophonous, evolving chorus concerning it.

Though I had studied both religion and environmental studies and was aware of their intersections, I was struck by the particular use of language in this ad—a very different message from that of the conventional, secular environmental movement. Our communication about climate change, like any issue, mediates our understanding of it, the meaning it holds for us, and our reaction or inaction to it. How we speak about climate thus has a great deal to do with prospects for ameliorating the problem. On that front, I was convinced the environmental movement, of which I was a part, was not getting the job done. Dominated by tedious science and dry policy and resonant with too narrow an audience, our communication of climate change was not moving enough people to action. Given evangelicals' significant numbers, level of influence, and cultural and political prominence, might they be able to encourage public engagement and political will where our efforts had been inadequate?

The purpose of this book is to answer that question. The chapters that follow explore why and how a growing number of evangelicals are engaging climate change as a matter of both private faith and public life. The ECI is part of a phenomenon I call climate care. Drawing on conversations with evangelical leaders and churchgoers—unique but interconnected subsets of American evangelicalism—as well as numerous documents, I probe climate care's historical evolution, current engagements, and challenges faced. I look particularly at its implications for the American evangelical community, the broader public, and the discordant landscape of American climate politics.

When I embarked on this research as a D.Phil. candidate at the University of Oxford, I had no prior connection to the evangelical subculture and limited experience with it. I was an outsider to the community of people I hoped to learn from and about, though an insider to the particular issue of climate change. So I depended on many people's generosity to open dialogue: pastors welcoming me to their churches for discussion groups; evangelical leaders taking time out of their demanding schedules to talk with me.

I went through a process of building relationships in order to gain entry to a community not my own. I started by reaching out to my own network, inquiring about any connections to evangelical churches or to evangelical leaders engaged in creation care. Through a colleague, I made early contact with Lowell "Rusty" Pritchard, at the time national director of outreach for the Evangelical Environmental Network (EEN) and editor of *Creation Care* magazine. In the summer of 2007, Pritchard and I met to discuss the project over breakfast in Atlanta. Subsequently, he facilitated contact with Alexei Laushkin, then project manager at the EEN, among others. An invaluable aid, Laushkin not only supplied contact information for many of the leaders I hoped to interview, but in most instances he sent an email introduction on my behalf. During our conversations, leaders would often suggest other people in the climate care network they thought I should speak with, frequently offering to facilitate contact themselves. Research opportunities built on top of one another with a snowball effect.

In addition to churchgoers and leaders, I focused on the main texts of climate care, which often convey its message and mediate the two. Specifically, I analyzed in depth the ECI's foundational document, "Climate Change: An Evangelical Call to Action" and used it as a stimulus to ground, spur, and guide group discussions. I then integrated key themes from the "Call to Action" and from churchgoers' conversations into my interviews with evangelical leaders. To supplement these core sources of information, I read blogs, sermons, and newsletters, frequented church services and evening events, tracked websites, media coverage, and publications, reviewed audio and video archives, and attended conferences and talks.

I personally transcribed audio recordings of the group discussions and one-on-one interviews, generating nearly 1,000 pages of transcripts. As I read and reread them, key elements, themes, metaphors, narratives, and storylines— became apparent.[2] I siphoned and traced them throughout the transcripts, scrutinizing the texts repeatedly with particular ones in mind. In making sense of climate care, then, I emphasized patterns but also attended to outliers, dissenting voices, and things unsaid. I allowed for both ideological contradiction and consistency, both ambiguity and clarity. Areas of agreement as well as tension within this body of believers became clear. Though I set out to explore engagement with climate change within a religious community, in doing so I necessarily examined other contextual influences—cultural, social, political, historical, and economic.

In turning this research into a coherent account of climate care, I crafted a story—one marked with intricacy and incongruity and often about others' lives. From a secular perspective, environmental sustainability and climate change, in particular, may seem to be purely matters of science and policy, though perhaps also essentially issues of ethics.[3] But for many of the leaders I met and for a handful of lay evangelicals, creation care is a core part of their individual religious experience and their identity as Christians.

In this book, I try to attend carefully, fully, and with subtlety to the multidimensional aspects of this religion-environment intersection. Following scholars of American religion Marie Griffith and Michael Lindsay, I embrace the approach of critical empathy, aiming for deep yet analytical comprehension of others' experiences.[4] With clarity about where one ends and the other begins, description and analysis are woven together to produce richer results. Descriptively, I chronicle evangelicals' conceptions of climate change and their engagement with it. Seeking to communicate their story, I use direct quotation and descriptive summary to allow participants to speak for themselves. Understanding this group of evangelicals on their own terms then

The importance of these personally facilitated connections canno
stated. As an outsider to the evangelical community and someone re
time from high-profile individuals with crowded calendars, my out
leaders would surely not have been as successful without personal ir
tions, indicating my trustworthiness, and their accompanying, impli
sure to oblige an interview request. These evangelical gatekeepers ;
access to the community. Many leaders' interest in students and pas
the topic also helped open doors. Similarly, my outreach to pastors ir
to church-based group discussions was most successful when made via
acquaintances, those who could establish a personal connection.

I conducted this research over two years, from June 2007 to June
holding group discussions in the southeastern United States and
viewing leaders from coast to coast.[1] Striving to attend to the di
of American evangelicalism, the nine group discussion churches
sent a variety of denominations, church characteristics, and geogra
locations, from bustling cities to sprawling suburbs to rural towns.
churches were large and well established; others were newer, with bur
ing congregations. Some were dominated by older members, othe
younger families, and still others by a dynamic mix of the two. Arra
ahead of time and logistically facilitated by pastors or other church offi
these conversations took place after Sunday services or in place of
lar Wednesday evening gatherings. I assured pastors and participants
churches' and individuals' identities would not be revealed and every e
would be made to maintain confidentiality; their responses would nc
connected to them or to their congregations. Though I clearly rema
an interloper in their communities, three factors—having grown up
attended college in the American South; having a Christian, albeit main
Protestant, background; and having studied religion—mediated just h
much of an outsider I seemed to be.

The climate care leaders I interviewed included megachurch pastors, ev
gelical academics, college and university presidents, parachurch organizat
executives, writers and media specialists, and relief and development prol
sionals—twenty-seven individuals from across the country. (See Appendi
for key figures in this book.) Our conversations typically took place in p
son, in people's offices, though other times in houses, churches, restauran
and hotel lobbies. My interactions with interviewees were often remarkat
affable, and at times they extended warm hospitality, inviting me into the
homes, feeding me, and offering to pray for my research. They were typical
more open and more forthcoming than I had anticipated.

forms the foundation for subsequent analysis. I share others' perspectives on this material, develop my own commentary, and interpret the dynamics at work—within advocacy organizations, the evangelical community, and American public life and climate politics. As a result, this project's general direction is concentric; I ground macroevaluations and synthetic conclusions in microanalysis and empiricism, employing a kaleidoscopic lens to examine American evangelicals' engagement with climate change.

Given my roles as discussion facilitator, interviewer, transcriber, analyzer, and interpreter, this work bears my personal mark. Because I necessarily interacted with and influenced the topic as I researched and wrote about it, I felt a great deal of responsibility throughout the process. In particular, I remained always cognizant of my role as conveyor of this story and its internal variations and was particularly sensitive to the impacts it might have for the creation care movement. While working on the project, I frequently encountered people who held deep stereotypes about American evangelicals. Their comments were a regular reminder of the need to treat this topic, heavily laden with prior assumptions, with respect and care as well as the experiences of the evangelicals I met with the utmost fairness and consideration. Sharing my writing with select interviewees and receiving their feedback and validation also became a critical part of the process.

Accepting Lynn White's thesis as gospel—that Christian "dominion" is responsible for environmental degradation—many environmentalists misread Christianity as a foe to sustainability or, at best, irrelevant.[5] Sometimes they dismiss religion entirely; other times they look to alternatives perceived as "greener" or "friendlier" to the cause, Buddhism among them. But I agree with Wendell Berry, who has argued that Americans live within a Christian cultural matrix from which there is no escape. Those interested in advancing environmental sustainability would be wise to engage this religious tradition, not to escape into surrogate philosophies.[6]

Thus, in addition to writing an illuminating book for academics, their students, and generally interested readers, my aim was to produce a piece of scholarship that might benefit environmental practitioners—those within the faith community and those outside it interested in better understanding and even partnering with faith-based efforts. That is, I sought to inform both knowledge and praxis. My greatest hope is that this book may bring different communities, even those frequently dismissive of one another, into conversation and perhaps collaboration.

Acknowledgments

EVEN IN ITS most isolated form—the single-author book—academic work refuses to be a solitary endeavor. This project was no exception, and I am deeply grateful to those who contributed to the process in myriad ways.

Theo Calderara, my editor at Oxford University Press, believed in the possibility of this book when it was merely snippets of a D.Phil. dissertation. His enthusiasm, guidance, and insight had everything to do with its realization, as did the support and expertise of his assistant editor, Charlotte Steinhardt.

This topic and its treatment are a product of many years of liberal arts education. I am indebted to Ted Wesemann and Susan Tinsley Daily at the Outdoor Academy for sowing the seeds of my environmental passion; to Jane Pepperdene at Paideia and Gary Phillips at Sewanee for teaching me to work with texts carefully and thoroughly and to write with clarity and expression; and to Jerry Smith, my undergraduate adviser, for encouraging me to challenge conventional environmental thinking and to cross disciplinary lines in pursuit of meaningful insights.

At Oxford, my doctoral supervisors, Max Boykoff, Dave Frame, and Diana Liverman, gave me the academic freedom to pursue a unique interdisciplinary topic. For that independence and their expert support throughout the process, I am enormously appreciative. The Rhodes Trust generously funded my years of research, and I received additional support from the Environmental Change Institute, the Smith School of Enterprise and the Environment, and Trinity College. I am especially grateful to the Smith School, Hub Atlanta, and Morningside for providing happy and productive places to write at various stages.

This project could not have succeeded without the willing cooperation of my research participants, who shared their time and stories with me, nor without Alexei Laushkin and Rusty Pritchard's integral help facilitating contacts. At different points in the process, Ben Carmichael, John Cole, Andy Crouch, Mike Hulme, David Gushee, Laurel Kearns, Lucy Keeble, Mayur

Pater, Tom Thornton, and Janet Ward generously read and commented on my work. Their insightful, probing comments and enthusiasm for the project proved invaluable.

Numerous people, particularly my dear friends from Sewanee and Oxford, participated in clarifying and stimulating conversation and offered bottom-less encouragement and support. In particular, I would like to thank Daniel Altschuler, Alex Conliffe, Ian Desai, Marissa Doran, Sam Gill, Caroline Howe, Jeff Miller, James Morrissey, Emily Crowe Pack, Tamson Pietsch, Jen Robinson, Sarah Rudebeck, Aliza Watters, and Jeni Whalen. Candace Fowler and Ned Morse played critical roles in helping me see this project through to completion, for that I am tremendously appreciative.

Finally, to my wild and wonderful family—Lucy Keeble, Alison Wilkinson, Jack Wilkinson, Janet Ward, Peter Hess, and the McDonoughs—thank you for your unceasing counsel, sustenance, and love. To my parents, in particular, thank you for giving me an affection for the written word that has propelled my academic life. Words are inadequate to express my gratitude.

Abbreviations

ACES	American Clean Energy and Security Act
AERDO	Association of Evangelical Relief and Development Organizations
CCCU	Council of Christian Colleges and Universities
CFACT	Committee for a Constructive Tomorrow
CT	*Christianity Today*
ECCA	Evangelical Collaboration for Climate Adaptation
ECI	Evangelical Climate Initiative
EEN	Evangelical Environmental Network
ERLC	Ethics and Religious Liberty Commission
ESA	Endangered Species Act
ESUPC	Evangelicals and Scientists United to Protect Creation
ICES	Interfaith Council for Environmental Stewardship
IPCC	Intergovernmental Panel on Climate Change
JRI	John Ray Initiative
NAE	National Association of Evangelicals
NEP	New Evangelical Partnership for the Common Good
NIV	*New International Version*
NRPE	National Religious Partnership for the Environment
RGD	Resisting the Green Dragon
SBC	Southern Baptist Convention
SBECI	Southern Baptist Environment and Climate Initiative
UNFCCC	United Nations Framework Convention on Climate Change

Between God & Green

Introduction

God saw all that he had made, and it was very good.

GENESIS 1:31[1]

DURING THE AUTUMN of 2009, the global environmental community tee-
tered between optimism and angst. They anxiously anticipated negotiations
on climate change, to be held in Copenhagen that December. With the Kyoto
Protocol set to expire in 2012, if and how the international community would
tackle this pressing problem hung a question mark over the Scandinavian city.
They wondered if China and India, with their rapidly developing economies,
would be willing to compromise. They crossed their fingers that, after eight
years of foot dragging by the Bush White House, President Barack Obama
would come to the table as a facilitator rather than an obstructionist. In the
wake of eighteen years of negotiations, hopes ran high that the world's leaders
might actually reach a deal on climate change.

With its eyes turned toward policymakers, the environmental community
may not have noticed action stirring in a more unexpected realm. Preceding
the Copenhagen negotiations, two American evangelical pastors, Tri Robinson
and Ken Wilson, traveled to the United Kingdom to launch their own action
plan to combat climate change from within their religious community. They
were joined by leaders from different faith traditions around the world, all with
similar commitments to action, who filled the grand halls of Windsor Castle
with a colorful mélange of religious vestments and reverberations of prayer and
song.[2]

Cohosting the interfaith gathering with Prince Philip, Duke of Edinburgh,
United Nations Secretary-General Ban Ki-moon addressed the delegates.
"The world's faith communities occupy a unique position in discussions on
the fate of our planet and accelerating impacts of climate change," he said.
Noting stagnation among policymakers, Ban urged, "You can inspire, you
can provoke, you can challenge your political leaders, through your wisdom,
through your power, through your followers."[3]

As the events in Copenhagen unfolded the following month, high hopes were dashed. Without domestic climate policy in place, the Americans lacked a foundation from which to negotiate. The Chinese were uncooperative. Smaller states were sidelined. Barely salvaged from total impasse, negotiations resulted in nothing more than a toothless accord—more image than substance—and the future of international cooperation on climate change remained unsettled. Environmentalists expressed their disappointment. "What, then, shall we do?" was a common query. Ban Ki-moon and Prince Philip are two among a growing ensemble of scholars and practitioners who would answer: Pay heed to the religious leaders gathered at Windsor. Consider the prospect that religion might shift the debate and propel action on climate change where other efforts have failed.[4]

An Alternative Voice

In the United States, in particular, the intersection of religion and environment is crucial. Today, the political will to tackle climate change remains in short supply and the partisan divide deep.[5] The public engagement that might undergird political will is also thin, as people maintain ambivalence about the issue. Polls suggest high awareness of climate change and confidence in its reality but also indicate ongoing uncertainty about its causes, effects, and possible solutions. Low concern and minimal action in response are the norm.[6] Despite extensive advocacy, the environmental movement has not been able to adequately build engagement among policymakers and the public. If the efforts of Tri Robinson, Ken Wilson, and their compatriots are any indication, religion and its faithful followers may help turn these trends.

Religion forms a lens through which many individuals read the world, the contemporary issues facing it, and proposed solutions to those problems. As religion scholar Roger Gottlieb argues, "For hundreds of millions of people religion remains the arbiter and repository of life's deepest moral values," framing their perceptions of and interactions with the world around them.[7] More broadly, Mary Evelyn Tucker explains, religion provides an "orientation to the cosmos and human roles therein," embedding believers in a meaningful world in which they are responsible actors.[8] This overarching framework influences human beings' conceptions of themselves, their context, and themselves in context, while the specific stories, symbols, practices, norms, and structures of religion shape a sense of meaning for believers *in situ*. Religion endows significance and guides ways of thinking and acting. For environmental issues, then, it is a major source of values and beliefs that form a matrix of meaning within which scientific observations are made, policy objectives are pursued, and lifestyle choices are selected. Through its vital influence on adherents' worldviews, ethics, and practices, religion mediates human-environment relations.[9]

As environmental issues have garnered increasing public attention, a greening trend in many of the world's religions has blossomed. As Tucker describes it, in light of current crises, religions have entered an "ecological phase."[10] Both leaders and laity pay increasing attention to the environment as a matter of religious import, produce statements of concern and intent, and engage actively in environmental issues as part of religious practice.[11] Climate change has proved a particular rallying cry. Faith-based climate advocacy is swelling, and American evangelical leaders are playing a central role. Like many religious adherents, theology forms the grounding of their concern. They view the Earth as God's creation, its care entrusted to believers, and see climate change as evidence of their own failure but also as an opportunity to do better.

Author and environmentalist Bill McKibben deems the phenomenon of evangelical climate care perhaps "as important in the fight against global warming as any stack of studies and computer models."[12] Here, McKibben is referring to the Evangelical Climate Initiative—a coalition of some 250 senior evangelical leaders and their defining statement, "Climate Change: An Evangelical Call to Action," both launched in 2006. (See appendix E.) As prominent figures within a religious community that makes up 25 to 30 percent of the US population, their potential to shift political will and public engagement on climate change is considerable.[13]

American evangelical leaders wield significant public voice and political influence. In recent decades, these capacities have been most visibly exerted by the evangelical Right, particularly in partnership with the Republican Party. Forged in the 1980s, this alliance played a significant role in the 1994 Republican Revolution in Congress, when the GOP gained control of both the House and Senate during the first Clinton administration, and in securing two terms in the White House for President George W. Bush.[14] But the relationship is not predestined or eternal. Rather, the alliance between evangelicals and the political Right exists, as sociologist Michael Lindsay explains, because "Republicans have done a better job of drawing upon the expressive and institutional aspects of political action in ways that resonate with evangelical sensibilities."[15] Not simply an inevitability, this relationship was carefully crafted and deliberately, artfully solidified.

We would be remiss, however, to think all evangelical leaders deploy their influence to politically conservative ends—exclusively or at all. An evangelical Left and Center accompany and often counterpoise the evangelical Right; increasingly, a growing group of "freestyle" evangelicals display "political bivocality."[16] They may continue to hold traditional evangelical stances, disapproving of abortion and homosexuality, but also advocate for conventionally progressive causes. Such evangelicals bring fresh perspectives and advocacy to enduring issues, deploying their influence and resources in potentially transformative ways. To challenge the evangelical-Republican connection and to capitalize on this growing political plasticity, Democrats are also working to forge alliances with American evangelicals. On the issue of climate change, in particular, given their unique history and context, evangelical leaders may have access to and sway with policymakers that other environmental advocates do not and thus possess a distinctive capacity to shift partisan faultlines and to effect policy change.

Evangelical leaders' influence is also intimately tied to their constituency—a robust body of believers. As with their leaders, the relationship of the evangelical public to the political Right varies, and a full spectrum of political orientations exists among those who adhere to conservative theology. Recent Pew data indicates that among the evangelical public, 50 percent identify as or lean Republican, 9 percent identify as independent, and 34 percent identify as or lean Democratic. Similarly, 52 percent describe themselves as conservative, 30 percent as moderate, and 11 percent as liberal.[17] (In both cases, 7 percent of respondents did not know or refused to answer.) While these numbers suggest that evangelicals trend more Republican and significantly more conservative than their mainline Protestant and Catholic counterparts, they are by no means monolithic in their political beliefs.

On the specific issue of climate change, lay evangelicals represent a traditionally disengaged—or even opposed—audience that mainstream, secular environmentalism has historically failed to reach.[18] As such, evangelicals embody a substantial opportunity for heightened public awareness and engagement, with contributions to make as consumers in a capitalist society and as citizens in a democracy.[19] Like most Americans, evangelicals produce significant personal greenhouse gas emissions. Estimates suggest emissions over which US individuals have personal, direct control account for one-third of the national total.[20] Individuals further shape US emissions as citizens, supporting or opposing government action, influencing its content, and implementing solutions. As such a large portion of the American public, evangelicals ought not to be ignored in either their individual or collective roles.

Contested Terms

This book focuses on two areas—evangelicals and climate change—that are often debated and imprecisely defined. The first term, *evangelical,* derives from a simple etymological root: the Greek for "good news." As employed by early Church Fathers, it refers to the good news of the Gospel and Jesus Christ, which Christians proclaim, but the term has become "an essentially contested concept," frequently misused or employed without clarity, weighed down by a good deal of baggage, and muddled by stereotypes.[21] To understand what is or can be meant by it, one must consider both its historical roots and norms of evangelical belief and practice.

I use the term to refer broadly to theologically conservative Protestants, including fundamentalists, evangelicals, Pentecostals, and charismatics.[22] American evangelicalism traces its roots to the Protestant Reformation, but in the eighteenth century, its varied strains of influence—pietism, revivalism, Puritanism, and Wesleyanism—metamorphosed into a uniquely American religion during revivals of the Great Awakening and under the influence of Jonathan Edwards, John Wesley, and George Whitefield.

Numerous scholars have sought to identify the factors that unite the diverse religious tradition that is evangelicalism, but D. W. Bebbington's "quadrilateral of priorities" receives the most support. He outlines four pillars of evangelical belief: first, conversionism—an emphasis on being "born again" or having an individual life-changing experience of God's grace; second, activism—a requisite concern for sharing the "good news" and offering others a chance to be "saved"; third, biblicism—the authoritative role given to scripture and paramount centrality of the Bible; and fourth, crucicentrism—a stress on the crucifixion of Christ as the core of belief and sole source of salvation.[23]

Historian Mark Noll notes, "These evangelical traits have never by themselves yielded cohesive, institutionally compact, or clearly demarcated groups of Christians. But they do serve to identify a large family of churches and religious enterprises."[24] The multifaceted definitions of *evangelical* point to the tradition's complexity and patchwork nature but also denote a phenomenon that contrasts with other traditions and communities.[25]

The second term, *climate change,* tends to conjure up the science behind it or ways society might mitigate or adapt to it. This book is not primarily concerned with those issues, but I do assume as given the near global scientific consensus that anthropogenic climate change is a serious issue and would have severe impacts on the Earth's ecological and social systems if allowed to continue unabated. The leaders of the evangelical climate care movement concur, so understanding what this consensus proposes is critical.

The Intergovernmental Panel on Climate Change (IPCC) is an international body of scholars that every few years compiles the world's peer-reviewed climate research to paint a combined picture of what we know about the problem's causes, likely impacts, and possible solutions. The IPCC's Fourth Assessment Report, released in 2007, is its most recent and makes two key scientific claims. First, changes in the world's atmosphere, ice cover, and oceans show unequivocally that the world is warming. Second, greenhouse gases (carbon dioxide, methane, nitrous oxide, and fluorinated gases) produced by human activity are very likely the cause of that temperature increase.[26] (As used by the IPCC, "very likely" indicates greater than 90 percent certainty.) Fossil fuel use, land-use change, agriculture, and some industrial processes are the primary generators of these anthropogenic emissions that intensify the Earth's natural greenhouse effect, raising global average temperature and producing follow-on climate change.

Although the anticipated effects of climate change are variable based on emissions concentrations in the atmosphere, they include widespread ice melt, substantial sea level rise, coastal inundation, shifting patterns of precipitation, more frequent and intense droughts, heat waves and floods, greater storm intensity, ocean acidification, the bleaching of coral reefs, species extinctions, the spread of disease, human displacement, and permanent damage to the global economy—some of which have already been observed.[27]

The necessity of international action to ameliorate this problem and avoid the worst of these impacts is widely recognized. The earliest global agreement and foundation for the 1997 Kyoto Protocol, the 1992 United Nations Framework Convention on Climate Change (UNFCCC) calls for concentrations of atmospheric greenhouse gases to be stabilized "at a level which would prevent dangerous anthropogenic interference with the climate system."[28] Though debate continues about what that stabilization level should be, an emerging consensus suggests that it should fall in the range of 350 to 450 parts per million of CO_{2eq} to avoid temperature increases in excess of 2°C.[29]

In order to achieve this goal, global emissions reductions of roughly 50 percent below 2000 levels by 2050 will be necessary, and rich countries will have to cut their emissions by at least 70 to 80 percent.[30] Making cuts of this magnitude will require the enactment of a suite of solutions aimed at increasing energy efficiency, switching to cleaner energy sources, and reversing deforestation, among others.[31] Though implementing such measures has a substantial price tag, failure to do so and allowing full impacts to set in would ultimately be more costly for the world's economy.[32]

Despite the dire nature of climate predictions and the clear need for swift and decisive action, the United States has not adequately engaged the challenge at hand. At the federal level, the United States has lagged behind other industrialized countries in combating climate change, failing to participate in a binding international agreement or to enact national climate legislation requiring mandatory emissions reductions. Meanwhile, the American populace, comprising less than 5 percent of the world population, continues to contribute a disproportionate one-fifth of global greenhouse gas emissions.

In the absence of action at the national level, states—both as independent entities and as regional collectives—cities, individual firms, NGOs, and universities have accepted the science of human-induced climate change and established their own policies and programs to reduce emissions.[33] In isolation, however, they cannot achieve the domestic reductions needed to avoid the worst impacts of climate change—perhaps 80 percent below 2000 levels by 2050. National and global policy efforts will be essential, but those efforts continue to face a good deal of opposition in the United States.

A New Story

To better understand the intersection of climate change and evangelicals and their relevance to each another, language and discourse are central. A scholar of rhetoric, Robert Cox defines environmental communication as "the pragmatic and constitutive vehicle for our understanding of the natural world . . . the symbolic medium that we use in constructing environmental problems and negotiating society's different responses to them."[34] How we speak about the environment plays both instrumental and meaning-making roles and impacts human perceptions of and interactions with the nonhuman world, giving language real material consequences.[35]

The significance (or lack thereof) of an environmental issue such as climate change is largely established through the language we use to discuss it. Our communication can define the problem, endow it with meaning, and mobilize particular responses. Alternatively, it can neglect, deemphasize, and disable. As political scientists Maarten Hajer and Wytske Versteeg explain, "Environmental discussion can lead to a revision of rules, the enactment of laws, or the creation of institutions—but underlying these visible changes, there is the creation, thickening, or discarding of meanings."³⁶ These mean-ings and discourses can shift the boundaries of important and unimportant, right and wrong, possible and impossible.

Communication about climate change often materializes in the public sphere—a space for negotiation and debate as well as the implementation of action. Here, words become a key means for rousing political will and public engagement. Advocates and interest groups on all sides of the issue employ language strategically and persuasively, seeking to shape the conversation in their own ways and to influence environmental decisionmaking and public opinion. The support of politicians and citizens is often won or lost on the basis of communication. It is also in the public sphere, then, that the diversity of voices on climate change converge. Different perspectives on science, eco-nomics, politics, and society spawn diverse narratives about climate change, at times complementary but often in conflict.³⁷

Religion continues to gain influence in this discursive pastiche, defining climate change as a concern, with whom responsibility lies, and what solutions should be pursued.³⁸ While the language of science and policy has traditionally dominated conversations about the issue, it has not produced effective, com-pelling communication—the kind that moves policymakers and the public to ameliorative action.³⁹ Religion, on the other hand, brings morality and ethics, beliefs and values into the debate. It goes beyond what and how to why. In doing so, faith-based discourse on climate change can instill a sense of empathy and duty and cultivate empowerment and hope. The guilt-based, fear-inducing messages that have often dominated can lead to paralysis rather than action, but religion is in the business of communicating a future worth fighting for. It can generate new meanings for climate change that drive engagement.⁴⁰

Expressly tackling values, ethics, and meaning, the language of evangelical climate care contributes to a normative case for climate action and the enthu-siasm to attain it. In telling their own story about climate change, evangelical leaders are challenging the issue's conventional secular and liberal boundaries and expanding beyond dominant concerns of science, policy, and economics. Through this discourse and the advocacy it undergirds, they may integrate climate care into the vast fabric of their religious community and propel shifts within the broader landscape of American climate politics. As debates from Capitol Hill to Copenhagen rage, these leaders have the crucial capacity to engender political will across party lines and to engage a segment of the pub-lic that mainstream environmentalism has historically failed to reach. Though climate change persists as a seemingly intractable problem, this blend of God and green may break the stagnation.

I

Chronicling Evangelical Climate Care

ONE SUMMER DAY in 2002, two unlikely acquaintances strolled along a park path beneath Oxford University's "dreaming spires," absorbed in conversation. At the time, Richard Cizik was the head lobbyist and public policy guru at the National Association of Evangelicals in Washington, DC, while Sir John had recently concluded his fourteen-year chairmanship of the scientific arm of the Intergovernmental Panel on Climate Change. A steadfast British evangelical as well as preeminent climate scientist, in his modest yet evocative way Sir John spoke to Cizik of his experience at the faith-science intersection and of the particular role American evangelicals might play in moving the United States to action on climate change.[1] Sir John "[made] the case that I couldn't shirk, shrug, rationalize, or escape my biblical responsibility to care for the environment," Cizik recalls. "It changed me."[2]

Like John Wesley's famous Aldersgate experience in 1738, in the course of their exchange, Cizik suddenly felt his heart "strangely warmed" and experienced a conversion to climate change that echoed his conversion to Christ two decades earlier.[3] This feeling capped two days with a large and sundry group of scientists, policymakers, and Christian leaders, spent discussing the scientific and religious dimensions of climate change. Sensing that God had intervened in his life at this crucial moment, Cizik departed Oxford with a passionate commitment to climate care, soon to become a leading advocate for the cause across the Atlantic.

For Richard Cizik, this climate conversion was a rather abrupt and dramatic shift. In reality, three decades of evangelical engagement with environmental issues preceded this moment, paving a way to it, making it possible. Similarly, a much longer history of the shifting tides of broader evangelical engagement in the public sphere provided an essential context. The roots of climate care run deep into American evangelicalism's past, fostering its emergence and molding its contours. As one phenomenon within the patchwork of contemporary evangelicalism, climate care is affected by the community's broader dynamics and trends. It also affects them. The evolution toward Cizik's and others' interest in climate change fundamentally shaped and was shaped by moderating events within American evangelicalism that made creation care increasingly mainstream and the evangelical Center ever more prominent.

Undulating Activity

American Predominance: The 1800s

During the 1730s and 1740s and then again from the 1790s to 1840s, popular religious revivals dotted the American landscape. Such itinerant preachers as Jonathan Edwards and George Whitefield and, later, Lyman Beecher and Charles Grandison Finney gave emotional and, at times, electric sermons to crowds of hundreds, even thousands. Some 20,000 people gathered in Cane Ridge, Kentucky, for a pivotal camp meeting in 1801, steeped in religious ferment. Prompting waves of individual conversion and church expansion, the First and Second Great Awakenings and such popular revivals provided a rich breeding ground for American evangelicalism.

Thanks in large part to their widespread prominence, during the nineteenth century evangelicals sustained the dominant form of American religion and were thoroughly integrated into American culture. Relevant, respected, and influential, evangelicals held positions of leadership in the academy and were active in the public sphere, engaging issues of social reform including abolition, women's suffrage, prison reform, and child labor. As Alexis de Tocqueville noted at the time, "There is no country in the whole world in which the Christian religion retains a greater influence over the souls of men than in America," and that Christian religion was very much evangelical.[4] Guiding the timbre of American life, "they were *the* establishment."[5]

But as a new century approached, the rising tides of religious pluralism and modernism started to weaken evangelical cultural pervasiveness. As Darwinism gained acceptance, liberal theologians began to employ historical methods of biblical criticism, undermining evangelicalism intellectually. Simultaneously, evangelical social welfare efforts started to prove incapable of tackling emerging problems on the ground, indicating further inefficacy. Factions within the community responded differently to these changing, challenging circumstances, diminishing evangelical influence in the process.

Toward the Great Reversal: 1900 to 1925

In the face of these challenges, evangelicals strove to maintain their prominence into the early twentieth century. Threatened by the rise of liberal Protestantism and the Social Gospel movement in various denominations, they publicly reaffirmed their orthodox Christian faith through *The Fundamentals*—an aptly titled booklet series that lent conservative Protestants a new name.[6] Yet their control over major denominations and theological institutions continued to slip.

Disparate views about eschatology widened the divide. Christian theology of the end times concerns whether the millennium, or thousand-year age of blessedness depicted in Revelation 20, will begin with or culminate in Christ's Second Coming. In the early years of the twentieth century, liberal Protestants increasingly embraced postmillennialism, the belief that this physical return will occur after the millennium. Leaders of the Social Gospel movement promoted this eschatological view, critiquing an individualistic gospel and working toward progressive social reforms in advance of the Second Coming.

Evangelicals, on the other hand, held to the premillennial belief that this physical return will occur first and usher in the millennium. They were increasingly influenced by a specific brand of this eschatology know as dispensationalism. Premillennial dispensationalism divides history into distinct eras—"dispensations"—and suggests that the present epoch will end when world apocalypse hastens a secret rapture of saved Christians from the Earth, in advance of a seven-year tribulation, the subsequent Second Coming of Christ, and the establishment of his millennial reign. This premillennial view takes the arc of human history to be in decline, embracing cultural deterioration as foretelling the rapture and urging believers not to impede but to hasten that event.

Given this theology's dominance at the time, evangelicals were largely absent from and even rejected efforts to redeem social ills. So while their theologically liberal counterparts perceived earthly prospects in optimistic terms, generating further engagement, evangelicalism adopted a pessimistic theological stance that produced disengagement. Once aligned with mainstream American culture and public, progressive engagement, evangelicalism became a privatized faith focused on personal salvation and evangelism. Historians dub this shift the Great Reversal, in which the Scopes "monkey trial" of 1925 was a particularly decisive moment, cementing emerging trends.[7]

A science teacher in the small town of Dayton, Tennessee, John Scopes was charged with violating the state's Butler Act, which banned the teaching of human evolution in public schools. Defended by Clarence Darrow of the American Civil Liberties Union and prosecuted by William Jennings Bryan, a popular Presbyterian lawyer and politician, Scopes's trial generated media frenzy. It dominated front pages and thrust fundamentalist opposition to the idea of evolution into the limelight, due in particular to journalist H. L. Mencken's satirical reporting. Though conservative Protestants technically achieved a victory in court—Scopes was found guilty—the events were a public relations catastrophe.

Cast as anti-intellectual, due to their opposition to evolution, and having lost the battle with liberals for control in some denominations, the fundamentalists withdrew from a society that ridiculed them into their own religious communities and institutions. They constructed bible schools, missionary societies, radio programs, and publishing houses as insulation against mainstream America, whose culture and theology they rejected. By the 1940s, they had created their own vibrant national subculture. Nonetheless, their loss of dominance within wider American society was clear: They went from having a prominent place in the public square to seeing that influence collapse.

A Time of Transition: 1925 to 1975

Between 1925 and 1975, conservative Protestantism was in transition. While many fundamentalists adopted a separatist, militant stance during this period, expanding and strengthening their own organizations, another group, largely of a younger generation, became disillusioned with this hostile, socially disengaged approach and determined to reform it. At the behest of Boston pastor Harold J. Ockenga, a number of leaders interested in reentering American religious, public, and intellectual life convened in 1942, birthing a self-designated neoevangelical movement. They set out to achieve no small task: "A new tradition, a new subculture, a new vision, and new goals would have to be envisioned, organized, and promoted."[8] While preserving a strong commitment to orthodox theology, this group envisioned a radically different way of engaging in American life.

Drawing on their nineteenth-century heritage, the neoevangelicals formed a broad-tent coalition and founded core institutions to advance their cause: the National Association of Evangelicals (NAE) in 1942, Fuller Theological Seminary in 1947, and *Christianity Today* magazine in 1956, among others. Also in 1947, Carl F. H. Henry published a manifesto for the movement, *The Uneasy Conscience of Modern Fundamentalism*, and the following year Billy Graham started his contemporary revivals, or crusades, becoming neoevangelicalism's most public face.[9] These events, leaders, and organizations—particularly their attitude and style—established a clear break from separatist fundamentalism. Modern American evangelicalism was born.[10]

Though the neoevangelical movement was interested in engaging in the public square, it remained relatively obscure during the 1950s and 1960s. But changes were under way that would lead to "the political rebirth of American evangelicals" in the 1970s, as the boundaries of evangelical morality were redrawn to include public as well as private concerns.[11] While cultural liberalization advanced, in the early 1960s the Supreme Court issued rulings that banned state-sponsored prayer in schools, and a decade later its *Roe v. Wade* decision legalized abortion—events that concerned and politicized evangelicals. Simultaneously, Henry, Graham, and their compatriots continued to build a robust and extensive infrastructure of neoevangelical institutions. Eventually, their movement dropped its prefix, becoming simply evangelicalism.

Active (Re)engagement: 1976 to the 1980s

Nineteen seventy-six was a watershed moment. After his polling research revealed that 34 percent of Americans claimed to have had a "born again" experience, George Gallup Jr. deemed it the "year of the evangelical." *Time* and *Newsweek* followed suit.[12] Born-again Baptist Jimmy Carter was elected president the same year, an event followed by the rise of Jerry Falwell's influential and more conservative Christian Right organization, the Moral Majority, in 1979.[13] Alongside the debut of Henry's and Graham's revised evangelicalism, another public face of conservative Christianity, with more fundamentalist roots, was also emerging.

Following these decisive events, the 1980s proved a decade of growth for American evangelicalism in its various strains. Following Falwell, a group of Christian Right leaders "entered politics with a vengeance," marshaled support for President Ronald Reagan, and received key posts in his administration.[14] Pat Robertson's 1988 presidential bid further mobilized the evangelical grass roots, leading Robertson to found the Christian Coalition to continue channeling this political influence. Through these efforts, issues of importance to conservative Protestants, including abortion and homosexuality, were pushed to the fore. Meanwhile, with strong organization and communications, evangelical leaders combated perceptions of preceding generations that political involvement was "unbiblical."

Though a faction of separatist fundamentalists remained, a widespread "reversal of the Great Reversal" took place.[15] Evangelicals became aware of their potential for public influence and embraced what sociologist of religion Christian Smith calls an "engaged orthodoxy."[16] They began offering their own approach to social and political issues, "taking the conservative faith beyond the boundaries of the evangelical subculture, and engaging the larger culture and society."[17]

Engaged Orthodoxy: The 1990s to the 2000s

John Green, an authority on American religion and politics, has identified an evangelical "continuum of civic engagement" that details this engaged orthodoxy. On one end of the continuum lies the view that believers have "*no public role* in solving social problems," while its opposite is the perception that Christians should seek "*political solutions*" to them. Between these extremes are two intermediate approaches: "*helping individual fellow believers* solve their personal problems, and *helping individual non-believers* solve theirs."[18] That is, a spectrum of approaches is at work. While some evangelicals perceive religion to be a wholly private matter, the majority are quite open to civic engagement. For many, however, this engagement has a particularly individualistic bent: Evangelicals see conversion and interpersonal support as efficacious strategies for tackling social problems.

This engaged orthodoxy continued throughout the 1990s and into the present. For most of that period of time, the Christian Right was the most prominent, visible force among evangelicals in the public sphere, extending a relationship forged with the Republican Party in the 1980s. The combined efforts of the movement's leaders and activist corps, alongside a GOP voting base of conservative Protestants, made possible the 1994 Republican Revolution in Congress and George W. Bush's two-term presidency. Though less high profile during this era, moderate and liberal evangelicals have embraced a publicly engaged modus operandi as well.

The presence of evangelicals in the public sphere has ebbed and flowed over the past two centuries. The history of these private-public fluctuations evidences and underlies the different strains within evangelicalism—not infrequently in tension with one another. While civic engagement to tackle social problems was common among evangelicals in the nineteenth and early twentieth centuries, it subsided between the mid-1920s and mid-1970s, before resurfacing once again. American evangelicals today continue to debate the style and content of an engaged orthodoxy, with differences of opinion among the Left, Right, and Center. Those ongoing debates and this general history of civic engagement together form an important context and backdrop for evangelicals' involvement in environmental issues.

Evangelical Ecotheology

Despite a flood of recent media attention in regard to evangelical interest in climate change, the phenomenon of climate care did not arise suddenly or *ex nihilo*.[19] Rather, it developed out of more than three decades of evangelical engagement with broader environmental issues. While evangelicals have often been cast as antienvironmental, mainstream evangelical leaders and scholars long displayed receptivity to the concerns of environmentalism—though to different degrees and at different points in time.[20] This history has two main axes: first, the process of building a theology of creation care and, second, the process of putting that ecotheology into practice.[21]

Spurred to Thought: The 1970s

American evangelicals' engagement with environmental issues began in the late 1960s, amid a general environmental fervor in American culture and specifically as a response to Lynn White's 1967 publication, "The Historical Roots of Our Ecologic Crisis," in *Science*.[22] In this noted article, White identifies Western science and technology as the drivers of environmental degradation, the cultural roots of which can be traced back to the "Judeo-Christian" creation story and the "dogma of man's transcendence of, and rightful mastery over, nature." The biblical doctrine of human dominion over nature, drawn from Genesis 1:28, appears central to his interpretation: "God blessed them and said to them, 'Be fruitful and increase in number; fill the Earth and subdue it. Rule over the fish in the sea and the birds in the sky and over every living creature that moves on the ground.'" In White's estimation, "We shall continue to have a worsening ecologic crisis until we reject the Christian axiom that nature has no reason for existence save to serve man."

Though this argument was primarily historical and not a critique of contemporary Christians, it prompted many religious thought-leaders to come to Christianity's defense nonetheless.[23] In contrast to the dominion interpretation cited by White, for American evangelicals this defense rested in a Genesis-based doctrine of stewardship, following the call of Genesis 2:15 for human beings not to use God's creation profligately but to tend it carefully: "The Lord God took the man and put him in the Garden of Eden to work it and take care of it." Attempting to defend their faith and demonstrate the compatibility of Christianity and environmental concern, many conservative Christians began to construct a uniquely evangelical environmental ethic.

Francis Schaeffer, a prominent and respected evangelical intellectual, published one such rebuttal to White's argument in 1970. Titled *Pollution and the Death of Man*, it was the first full-length book on evangelical ecotheology and reprinted White's essay.[24] In the work, Schaeffer rejects the notion that pantheism and Buddhism offer workable alternatives to "antienvironmental" Christianity and criticizes Platonic forms of Christianity for their body-soul dualism that denies the value of the material world. Instead, he contends Reformed Christian theology is the only adequate basis for an ecological ethic, grounded in the biblical doctrines of creation, incarnation, and bodily resurrection that endow physical matter with inescapable worth. As God's creation, nature is imbued with "value in itself," Schaeffer argues, and as creatures made in God's image, human beings have a moral responsibility to exercise careful dominion over it.[25]

In 1970 and 1971, the NAE responded to the debate with two resolutions on ecology that call for stewardship in the face of critical environmental problems. They made clear, strong claims: "Today those who thoughtlessly destroy a God-ordained balance of nature are guilty of sin against God's creation," declared the first statement.[26] The second urged action: "We pledge our cooperation to any responsible effort to solve critical environmental problems, and our willingness to support all proven solutions developed by competent authorities. We call upon our constituency to do the same, even at the cost of personal discomfort or inconvenience."[27] *Christianity Today* also published a series of editorials on the topic. Beyond putting words on paper, however, evangelicals' environmental engagement during this period was limited, and, following trends of declining interest within broader American culture, it waned as the decade wore on.

Expanded Engagement: The 1980s

Evangelical engagement with environmental concern entered its next significant phase in the 1980s, primarily in the form of intellectual undertakings and promotion of the issue within evangelical higher education. A small but dedicated group of scholars, including philosopher Loren Wilkinson and biologist Calvin DeWitt, continued to build the body of ecotheological literature initiated in response to White's essay—a development that marked the beginning of "pronounced and remarkable expansion" in this area.[28]

This group spent the 1977 and 1978 academic year conducting research at Calvin College in Grand Rapids, Michigan, and subsequently published *Earthkeeping: Christian Stewardship of Natural Resources* in 1980.[29] The book quickly became "an important resource for Christians concerned with the relationship between their faith and the planet's health."[30] It emphasizes rereading the Genesis creation accounts as an attribution of inherent value to God's creation and as a call to dominion in the form of stewardship—as serving God's creation. This focus on creation endows human-environment relationships with a rich cosmological context, giving human beings certain divinely ordained rights and responsibilities as both part of creation as an integrated whole and other than creation as its special rulers and caretakers. These pioneering scholars and their covenantal understanding of stewardship laid the groundwork for the first evangelical environmental organization under the directorship of DeWitt.

The Au Sable Institute of Environmental Studies was founded in 1979, its mission to blend ecological knowledge with biblical principles and, through that integration, to help Christians gain better understanding of the creator and creation stewardship. To those ends, Au Sable implemented educational programs in partnership with evangelical colleges and began hosting annual forums on ecotheology, which "established Au Sable as the most consistent and fruitful source of evangelical reflection on environmental issues during the 1980s."[31] These forums led to the publication of such seminal texts as Wesley Granberg-Michaelson's edited volume, *Tending the Garden*, in 1987, which continued the maturation and expansion of evangelical ecotheology.[32]

This early ecotheology established a number of core principles. Reinterpreting the dominion passage as a call to stewardship, it exhorts Christians to recognize the sinfulness implicit in environmental destruction and the intrinsic value of divinely created nature beyond utilitarian assessments. Challenging an otherworldly religious orientation that focuses its gaze vertically to heaven at the expense of taking in a horizontal earthly view, it urges believers to move beyond a singular focus on individual salvation and to reject a material-spiritual binary that implicitly devalues the physical world. Looking to the future, it calls Christians to embrace an eschatology that envisions the redemption of all creation rather than its destruction at the end of days. Articulating the injustices of environmental degradation and their disproportionate effect on the poor, it integrates social justice into creation care.

This work of dedicated evangelical scholars in the 1980s formed a sophisticated theological launching pad for environmental engagement outside the ivory tower. As the decade came to a close, notions of creation care began to spread beyond this academic group, taking greater popular hold and preparing the way for subsequent developments in evangelical environmental advocacy. The foundational role of these tenets and interpretations of scripture remains paramount in climate care today.

From Theology to Activism

Onward to Action: The Early 1990s

In the 1990s, more direct environmental action in the public sphere emerged—again following broader trends of American culture—and a series of events activated evangelical ecotheology and increased the public visibility of creation care. Further publications were central to this flowering of environmental engagement. With an eye to popular audiences, creation care texts helped move the issue beyond its academic stronghold. In synergy with ongoing ecotheological efforts, evangelicals also established advocacy organizations to carry out creation care efforts on the ground.

In 1990, a catalyzing event transpired at the Global Forum of Spiritual and Parliamentary Leaders Conference in Moscow, Russia. A group of scientists, spearheaded by astronomer Carl Sagan and including thirty-two Nobel laureates, presented an "Open Letter to the Religious Community."[33] Its signatories emphasized the centrality of both religion and science to environmental protection: a common cause that should be taken up jointly by scientists and believers. In response to this "Open Letter," the Joint Appeal in Science and Religion was established later that year as a collaborative effort by scientists, religious leaders, and politicians to engage American religious communities on environmental issues.

As a tide of environmental engagement rose within religious communities generally and within broader American culture—spurred by the discovery of an ozone hole in the atmosphere and the 1989 Exxon Valdez spill and marked by outpourings of support on Earth Day in 1990—uniquely evangelical advocacy also materialized. In 1990, after a twenty-year lull, the NAE passed another resolution, its title echoing an established shift in theological language: "Stewardship: All for God's Glory."[34] The work of DeWitt, Wilkinson, and others appeared to be gaining traction outside the academy.

Meanwhile, scholarship efforts continued. In 1992, the World Evangelical Fellowship cohosted a forum with Au Sable on evangelicalism and the environment that explored the intersections of creation care theology and sustainable development. The gathering resulted in a special edition of the *Evangelical Review of Theology* and the establishment of the International Evangelical Environmental Network—a precursor to the US-based Evangelical Environmental Network initiated a year later—with the aim of offering a uniquely evangelical alternative to other Christian environmental groups.[35] Also in 1992, a *Christianity Today* editorial announced: "The time has come for evangelicals to confront the environmental crisis."[36]

Developing a Body and a Voice: The Mid-1990s

These early seeds of creation care advocacy soon took lasting root. In 1993, the Joint Appeal evolved into the National Religious Partnership for the Environment (NRPE), founded under the leadership of Paul Gorman with Jewish, Roman Catholic, mainline Protestant, and evangelical representation. Finding the latter was an early challenge for the NRPE, as the other religious traditions had existing advocacy bodies. At Gorman's request, theology professor Ron Sider developed the Evangelical Environmental Network (EEN) as part of his activist group, Evangelicals for Social Action, to represent the conservative Christian community in this new consortium.[37] Nearly two decades later, the EEN continues to work in concert with the Coalition on the Environment and Jewish Life, the National Council of Churches of Christ, and the US Conference of Catholic Bishops to forward the NRPE's mission: "to encourage people of faith to weave values and programs of care for God's creation throughout the entire fabric of religious life."[38] Efforts across these faith groups have driven the evolution of religious environmentalism in the United States—at times through deliberate cooperation, at others through separate but synergistic activities.

In its first major initiative, the EEN advanced the development of eco-theology by launching "An Evangelical Declaration on the Care of Creation" in 1994. (See appendix A.) In addition to its theological end, the declaration was also designed to establish the EEN's credibility to speak as a collective evangelical voice on environmental issues—a role secured with nearly 150 original signatories from the evangelical establishment. Asserting "that this Earth belongs to God and that we are responsible to him for it," the document poignantly commits its signers "to work vigorously to protect and heal that creation for the honor and glory of the Creator." The declaration also makes clear that such efforts intrinsically include care for the poor and those suffering the injustices of environmental degradation.

At the same time, the EEN also began to reach out to the evangelical public through a quarterly magazine—now called *Creation Care*—and congregational awareness-raising materials, such as "Let the Earth Be Glad: A Starter Kit for Evangelical Churches to Care for God's Creation," sent to some 30,000 churches.[39] (The other NRPE partners sent similar materials to their own constituencies.) As the EEN grew, it outstripped the administrative capacities of Sider's organization, prompting the hiring of Baptist minister Stan LeQuire as its first full-time director. But despite this institutional expansion and the declaration's support, in the early 1990s creation care advocacy remained "confined to the left wing of evangelicalism," while environmental concerns "failed to galvanize [most] evangelicals in any serious way."[40] Though the EEN had clearly had some early successes, the organization was not reaching evangelicals across the board—and certainly not the community's more conservative wing.

Gaining National Presence: 1996

Shortly thereafter, however, the EEN was thrust onto the national political stage, as the antienvironmental efforts of the 104th Congress roused heightened religious-environmental advocacy. The 1995 and 1996 Republican assault on the Endangered Species Act (ESA) of 1973 presented the EEN with a challenge and opportunity to flex its activist muscles, garner media attention, and impact public policy. At a press conference in Washington, DC, Calvin DeWitt declared the ESA "the Noah's Ark of our day" and accused "Congress and special interests [of] trying to sink it."[41]

In DeWitt's act of engaged ecotheology, the scholar-cum-advocate deployed a clear Christian perspective on a particular environmental policy issue. The biblical story of Noah's Ark and the Flood functioned as a moral statement on the value of individual species and a mandate to conserve them. Running starkly counter to the dominant conservative messages at the time, DeWitt's contrarian allusion generated a good deal of press coverage and ultimately public support, making a significant evangelical contribution to the eventual defeat of the ESA attack. In the process of achieving this policy and public relations victory, the EEN successfully cut its activist teeth and proved its efficacy, making clear that the evangelical creation care movement had established its presence.[42]

Meanwhile, since passing its third resolution in 1990, the NAE had again been dormant on stewardship issues. But, in March 1999, the association moved past making statements and hosted a conference on the campus of

Malone College in Ohio. The aim of "Compassion and the Care of Creation" was to explore the intersections of environmental issues and poverty, as well as their place within Christian discipleship. Jo Anne Lyon, then chair of the NAE's Social Action Commission, remembers the restrained, cautious nature of the gathering. Though the EEN funded it, she said, the "NAE at that time was so paranoid of EEN, they would not even allow me to have a sign that said NAE and EEN co-sponsor this. It could only be NAE."[43] Lyon recalled that climate change was not part of the discussion because many were "just so fearful to talk about it." Despite the EEN's success with the Noah's Ark campaign, creation care's marginal position within evangelicalism persisted; and although the EEN's umbrella organization, the NRPE, periodically engaged the issue of climate change, widespread perception cast it as a volatile issue. Given the unreceptive conditions reflected in Lyon's comments, the changes that took place from 1999 to 2006 and the dynamic debut of climate care are all the more striking.

Warming Up

As the 1990s came to a close and a new millennium began, the scientific consensus on global climate change strengthened, heightening its dominance as an environmental concern. Following their secular counterparts, creation care advocates turned their focus to this increasingly pressing issue, soliciting a good deal of public attention along the way. Simultaneously, creation care continued to inch inward from the periphery of the evangelical agenda and to gain greater traction among evangelical leadership. In many ways, the two concurrent, punctuated processes were mutually supporting.

Emerging Leaders: The Early 2000s

In 1999, Jim Ball was hired to replace LeQuire as head of the EEN, and he brought in tow a prior interest in both policy and climate change. While a Ph.D. student at Drew University—where the conversation about Christianity and the environment was already quite active—Ball had read then-Senator Al Gore's *Earth in the Balance* (1992). It "crystallized in my mind" the issue of climate change, he said, not just as an environmental issue but as a national security, justice, and human concern.[44] Ball wrote his dissertation on evangelical theology and the ecological crisis, and after graduating he first engaged his interest in climate change and public policy at the secular, nonprofit Union of Concerned Scientists in Washington, DC. Although employed within mainstream environmentalism for some three years, Ball remained involved in creation care efforts as well.

When he transitioned to the EEN in 2000, Ball knew the organization had a fairly broad environmental focus. "The community wasn't really ready yet...for just climate," he recalled. "And so I knew I had to do some other things and kind of bide my time a little bit....I didn't automatically go to climate."[45] Yet climate change remained his calling—one he engaged to some degree through the NRPE's public policy work but answered more fully a couple years into his presidency.

Two years later, in July 2002, Au Sable and the UK-based John Ray Initiative (JRI) jointly hosted Climate Forum 2002 at Oxford University. Calvin DeWitt and JRI's founder Sir John convened the event, bringing together more than seventy climate scientists, policymakers, and Christian leaders for an empirically grounded discussion of climate change. The group produced the "Oxford Declaration on Global Warming," drawing on the ecotheology outlined above but applying it specifically and with clear scientific grounding to the issue of climate change. (See Appendix B.) Called to care for creation and for the poor, the declaration asserts that Christians have a particular obligation to recognize and respond to the reality and urgency of this global problem. Looking beyond the forum itself, it urges religious, business, and government leaders to join participants in their recognition of climate change as a moral issue and in their commitment to take immediate action.

Although the declaration was the publicized upshot of Forum 2002, a far more significant outcome resulted from the interaction of Cizik and Sir John, chronicled at the beginning of the chapter.. Through their conversations, Cizik came to experience a self-described "conversion" on climate change that sparked his role as a key climate care advocate. Also present at the Oxford gathering, Ball believes a newly energized Cizik was "the real tangible thing that came out of that conference."[46] David Gushee, a professor of Christian ethics at Mercer University in Atlanta, deems Cizik's climate conversion "one of two major developments that have moved creation care from the evangelical Left to the evangelical Center." The other is Ball's work "to engage a widening circle of evangelical leaders in addressing climate change."[47]

As part of those efforts and again in synergy with the other NRPE organizations, Ball initiated an educational campaign about fuel consumption later in 2002. Playing off the popular Christian motto "What Would Jesus Do?"—or WWJD—he dubbed it "What Would Jesus Drive?" and scheduled a hybrid car tour through the heart of the Bible Belt.[48] From Austin, Texas, to Washington, DC, Ball stopped and talked to church leaders, government officials, and the lay public about the moral implications of personal transportation choices and transportation policy. The campaign proved another media success for the EEN, generating more than 4,000 press hits and further heightening the public profile of creation care efforts.[49]

Cementing Commitment: 2004

With its genesis in Forum 2002, the EEN and cosponsors *Christianity Today* and the NAE hosted a subsequent creation care meeting for American evangelical leaders on the Chesapeake Bay in June 2004. According to Ball, the Sandy Cove conference "was a major step for EEN." "We'd always [wanted] to get into the center of the community and hadn't been successful," he said. But thanks to the supportive leadership of Cizik at the NAE and *CT* editor-in-chief David Neff, the EEN was able to cohost the event with "two flagship organizations at the center of the community," encouraging broader attendance than they might have otherwise had.[50]

Participants included Barrett Duke from the Ethics and Religious Liberty Commission (ERLC)—the public policy arm of the Southern Baptist Convention (SBC) and a powerful evangelical Right organization—and then NAE president Ted Haggard. (Later in 2006, Haggard's leadership at the NAE and New Life Church in Colorado Springs, CO, ended abruptly when Mike Jones, a former male prostitute, alleged that the two had a sexual relationship. Haggard later admitted to "sexually immoral conduct.")[51] Sir John, again in attendance, served as the key scientific messenger, making a persuasive presentation on climate science.

This gathering also produced the "Sandy Cove Covenant and Invitation." (See Appendix C.) This document articulated an American evangelical commitment to creation care, including a key phrase: "We covenant together to engage the evangelical community in a discussion about the question of climate change with the goal of reaching a consensus statement on the subject in twelve months." Although Ball had hoped they might achieve such a statement at the Sandy Cove conference itself, the group departed the Maryland shore with a clear objective in hand. Putting the prospect of an evangelical climate accord in writing prefigured its eventuality.

A second moderating event occurred in October 2004 when the NAE board of directors decisively approved "For the Health of the Nation: An Evangelical Call to Civic Responsibility."[52] The declaration outlines the intent to harness American evangelicalism's size and power to the ends of "biblically faithful" public policy, presenting a broader agenda than that of the evan-gelical Right and including creation care as one of its principles of Christian political engagement. (See Appendix D for the full creation care excerpt.) "We labor to protect God's creation," the text states, because:

> God gave the care of his Earth and its species to our first parents. That responsibility has passed into our hands. We affirm that God-given dominion is a sacred responsibility to steward the Earth and not a license to abuse the creation of which we are a part. We are not the owners of creation, but its stewards, summoned by God to "watch over and care for it."

Employing ecotheology initiated by Francis Schaeffer more than three decades before and in conjunction with Sandy Cove's joint institutional sponsorship, this inclusion transformed creation care. Once an issue affiliated with the evangelical Left, it became a decidedly centrist one—"mainstreaming" that laid an important foundation for further action.[53]

Launching Climate Care: 2006

In the context of this shift and growing climate advocacy across Christian traditions, the Sandy Cove meeting and covenant served as precursors to a formalized group of leaders, dubbed the Evangelical Climate Initiative, and its founding statement, titled "Climate Change: An Evangelical Call to Action."

Working with Jim Ball, Richard Cizik, David Neff, and Ron Sider, David Gushee, then at Union University, drafted the text. Once finalized, the "Call to Action" was bundled with supporting materials and sent out to senior evan-gelical leaders under influential letterheads: Cizik wrote to all the NAE board members; Robert Andringa, president of the Council of Christian Colleges and Universities (CCCU) at the time, reached out to member institutions' presidents; Michael Nyenhuis, president and chief executive officer (CEO) of MAP International, and Richard Stearns, president of World Vision, contacted executives of groups affiliated with the Association of Evangelical Relief and Development Organizations (AERDO).

This extensive outreach effort garnered eighty-six original signatories for the "Call to Action," including key figures of the evangelical Center. Duane Litfin, then president of Wheaton College in Illinois—commonly termed the "evangelical Harvard"—lent his name to the effort, as did Leith

Anderson, former NAE president at the time. (Anderson soon stepped back into that position after Haggard's resignation and currently leads the organization.) Influential megachurch pastors also joined, including Joel Hunter of Northland, a Church Distributed, in Longwood, Florida, and Rick Warren of Saddleback Church in Orange County, California, and best-selling author of *The Purpose-Driven Life*.[54]

With signatories confirmed, on February 8, 2006, organizers formally launched the initiative at the National Press Club in Washington, DC. A significant break from the Bush administration's climate antagonism at a time when many assumed an implicit alliance between the Republican Party and American evangelicalism, the ECI's debut generated significant media attention, and the group maximized the public relations opportunity with print, radio, and television advertisements. In a television spot, Hunter proclaimed, "As Christians, our faith in Jesus Christ compels us to love our neighbors and to be stewards of God's creation. The good news is that with God's help, we can stop global warming, for our kids, our world, and for the Lord."[55]

This event further asserted the position of climate change and creation care within the evangelical Center. At the same time, it played a role in shaping the broader dynamics of American evangelicalism—less dominated by the mighty evangelical Right, a narrow Christian agenda, and immutably conservative politics. Thus, the ECI launch was a defining event for evangelical creation care and for the growing presence and strength of the evangelical Center.

Inescapably Embedded

With the formation of the ECI, climate care was enshrined in the evangelical establishment, though it was still far from a consensus issue. The development was climactic and attracted the rapt attention of many. Climate care inherited an engaged orthodoxy from the history of American evangelicalism, while a twofold process of developing ecotheology (in the 1980s) and activating that theology through advocacy efforts (in the 1990s) preceded it. Then, in a concurrent, synergistic process, creation care crept toward the core of the evangelical agenda, while creation care leaders became increasingly attuned to climate change. These shifts, alongside the rise of religious environmentalism more broadly, paved the way for evangelical climate advocacy in the first decade of the twenty-first century.

To make sense of this phenomenon, we must understand the broader contexts in which it sits, both past and present, and attend to the wider trends that molded and were molded by its emergence. The history of American evangelicalism and its contemporary landscape are inescapably complex. Their multiple strains and factions intersect with and influence evangelical climate advocacy as one phenomenon among many. In the following chapters, its place within the patchwork becomes increasingly clear.

The shifting currents of evangelical engagement in the public sphere also illuminate the status of climate change as a matter of both private faith and public life for evangelical climate advocates. Simultaneously a religious and civic issue, leaders attend to it as such. Embracing an engaged orthodoxy, they apply an evangelical perspective to understand, evaluate, and offer solutions to this social problem. I subsequently probe how this application takes place.

Ultimately, the events recorded in this chapter form not just a historical context for climate care but also a discursive one. Evangelical climate advocates participate in an ongoing conversation. When speaking about climate change, they are inescapably in dialogue with historical trends and events as well as contemporary realities. Climate care leaders are embedded in the multifarious landscape of American evangelicalism. This religiocultural backdrop shapes the way they construct and take action on the issue, as it does for their opponents and for people in the pews.

2

Beginning with the Word

IN JANUARY 2007, Barbara Boxer became chairwoman of the Senate's powerful Environment and Public Works Committee. During her decade and a half representing California in the upper house of Congress, Boxer, a Democrat, had been a passionate advocate for environmental protection. When she assumed her post as chairwoman, she directed that passion to the issue of climate change. Over the coming months, her committee held numerous hearings on the topic, gathering testimonies of various experts, including, on June 7, 2007, those of religious leaders. Inside a large, wood-paneled room in the Dirksen Senate Office Building, committee members heard from representatives of Jewish, Catholic, mainline Protestant, and evangelical groups—among them Jim Ball of the Evan selical Climate Initiative.[1]

"My name is the Reverend Jim Ball," he opened. "I am an evangelical Christian who professes Jesus Christ to be my personal Savior and Lord." On behalf of the ECI and its signatories—a new generation of evangelical leaders—Ball spoke passionately about the scientific consensus on climate change, its anticipated impacts on the world's most vulnerable populations, scriptures that command a response, and the details of what that response ought to be, especially from national policymakers. At the close of his testimony, Ball returned to scripture: "Moses, the great lawgiver, in his farewell address to the Hebrews, set before them the paths of life and death; life, by loving God and doing His will, and death, by forsaking God and His commands." Quoting Moses (Deut. 30:19), he issued a plea: "'I call heaven and Earth to witness against you today that I have set before you life and death, blessings and curses. Choose life so that you and your descendants may live.' *Let us choose life this day by addressing global warming.*"[2]

Like many witnesses in the months before him, Jim Ball drew on his own perspective to address climate change. A distinguished scholar on the subject,

Mike Hulme explains that climate change is not simply a physical phenomenon but an idea with currency in our global society. "Depending on who one is and where one stands," Hulme says, "[that idea] carries quite different meanings and seems to imply quite different courses of action."[3] Ball constructed that idea in a particular way, emphasizing certain aspects, deemphasizing others. Ultimately, he couched the multifaceted issue within an evangelical moral and theological framework—perhaps the defining element of who he is and where he stands.

More broadly, Ball's testimony shows that evangelical climate advocates share a distinct point of view on climate change, one that the ECI's seminal "Call to Action" poignantly illustrates.[4] A manifesto for action on the issue, the twelve-page statement weaves science, theology, ethics, and policy to define the problem, touching on its anthropogenic causes, global consequences, normative dimensions, and appropriate responses. It is key to probing how climate care leaders construct the idea of climate change and what should be done to address it. The "Call to Action" also provides fruitful fodder for understanding the ECI's intrinsic link between language and advocacy.

Clearly, then, the "Call to Action" is an important document, but why should it merit our extended attention? Evangelicals are people of the Word. At the core of their faith lies the Bible: as they conceive it, the inspired, infallible, authoritative word of God. The gravitational pull of scripture holds together evangelical believers, institutions, and communities. Just as the Bible forms the heart of evangelical faith, so, too, does the "Call to Action" lie at the heart of the ECI, cementing the network of signatories, speaking as their unified voice, and fueling evangelical climate care advocacy. Without it, the ECI would not, could not, exist. Given this central role and the core climate care story it contains, understanding the document is revelatory.

Bearing Witness

A call to action is a summons, an invitation, a bidding. In American history, such summonses have often been calls to serve one's country: FDR's call to arms, JFK's call to service, MLK's call for justice. The Bible, too, is full of calls—to Abraham; to Moses; to Aaron, Elisha, Joshua, and Samuel; to John the Baptist; to Paul—calls by God, calls to be an apostle or saint, calls to fellowship, obedience, wisdom, and holiness. Today, Christians speak of callings as divine promptings to salvation or to faithful service. Other times callings are simply experienced as inner summonses to a principled course of action.

By setting itself up as a call to action, the ECI's core statement on climate change echoes both the bugle call and the church bell, summoning its readers to patriotic, religious, and moral duty. It is not merely a thought piece or a public relations ploy but a manifesto with desired ends—fervent engagement on climate change.

A Moral Argument: "Yes, We Are Witnesses"
(Joshua 24:22)

From the start, the ECI engages contested questions of values and ethics. These self-proclaimed "American evangelical Christian leaders" intend "to offer biblically based moral witness" with a particular goal and context in mind: to "shape public policy" through religious discourse in the public sphere. Like Ball, they highlight the religious identity fueling their witness, and given language's central role in the modern agora, they focus on biblically informed communication.

The ECI also positions evangelical climate care in a broader religious context by drawing on "For the Health of the Nation." As outlined in the preceding chapter, in October 2004, the NAE board of directors approved this seminal statement. It asserts boldly: "Never before has God given American evangelicals such an awesome opportunity to shape public policy in ways that could contribute to the well-being of the entire world. Disengagement is not an option." By reference, the ECI leaders convey a particular stance on civic engagement—engaged orthodoxy—and a clear, unapologetic focus on public policy.

They also take a stance on debates about the evangelical agenda. "For the Health of the Nation" presents a broader inventory of issues than the contemporary evangelical Right has typically advocated. While affirming a "longstanding commitment to the sanctity of human life" and the keystone issue of abortion, the ECI also commends nontraditional evangelical concerns, including sex trafficking, genocide, and HIV/AIDS. These leaders embrace an expansive issue agenda and reject the notion of "single-issue" evangelicalism—a stance they suggest is rooted in faith. Guided by a higher authority rather than suspect political motives, the sacred, not the profane, sets the agenda, and the leaders follow. "We seek to be true to our calling as Christian leaders," they assert in the "Call to Action," "and above all faithful to Jesus Christ our Lord."

Mention of "For the Health of the Nation" and its parent, the NAE, implies this group is moderate—well within the center of the evangelical community in terms of both subject matter and style of engagement.

This positioning fends off possible criticisms, bolsters the ECI's active engagement in civic life and public policy, and protects climate care from being written off as a fringe anomaly or singular obsession. Yet turning to the specific issue at hand, the leaders further hedge their stance. They have not, they make clear, taken up the issue in haste or been easily persuaded. Rather, they have "engaged in study, reflection, and prayer" and "required considerable convincing…that climate change is a real problem and that it ought to matter to Christians."

Having issued disclaimers and asserted that the group is both judicious and faithful, both reasonable and moderate, the ECI then makes its stand:

> But now we have heard and seen enough to offer the following moral argument related to the matter of human-induced climate change. We commend the four simple but urgent claims offered in this document to all who will listen, beginning with our brothers and sisters in the Christian community, and urge all to take the appropriate actions that follow from them.

Echoing Jesus's call in Mark 4:23—"If anyone has ears to hear, let them hear"— the leaders suggest something ultimate is at stake here: Climate change is morally wrong and must be remedied.

Target Audiences: "Whoever Has Ears to Hear, Let Them Hear" (Mark 4:9)

But whose ears is the ECI trying to reach? Whom does it call to action? The "Call to Action" emphasizes that these are American evangelical leaders who want to shape public policy in the United States, "the most powerful nation on Earth." It also underlines their identity as evangelical Christians who want to influence their own faith community. This band of climate care advocates speaks with an overtly national bent to those within the evangelical fold as well as to policymakers—some of whom are evangelicals themselves, many of whom have evangelical constituents. Aware of their sway as elite evangelical leaders, they target these dual and, at times, overlapping audiences.

These are not the sole audiences of the "Call to Action," however, for others will unintentionally overhear or deliberately eavesdrop on the message. Though the ECI leaders want to begin "with our brothers and sisters in the Christian community," they extend this argument "to all who will listen." Those attentive to the messages generated in the evangelical community are not only evangelicals themselves nor only politicians for whom they may vote. Evangelical discourses are important threads in the wider public exchange, as just a brief survey of media coverage on evangelicals makes clear. Because their social, political, and cultural clout may extend to, challenge, or be synergistic with broader trends and dynamics, the ECI places no limits on its potential "hearers."

Most importantly, the leaders implore all these audiences, direct and indirect, to hear and then do. Pursuant to their moral argument, they "urge all to take the appropriate actions that follow." The ECI intimately links talk and action, discourse and advocacy, and this emphasis on call and response is accented throughout its treatment of climate change.

Confronting the Evidence

Consensus Science: "I Am Going to Confront You with Evidence" (1 Samuel 12:7)

Though theology might be the anticipated opening claim, the first building block of the ECI's construction of climate change is science. The leaders put it decidedly: "human-induced climate change is real." They continue: "Because all religious/moral claims about climate change are relevant only if climate change is real and is mainly human-induced, everything hinges on the scientific data." The entire "Call to Action" is meaningless without empirical support for two essential adjectives: *real* and *human-induced*.

The existence of anthropogenic climate change has remained a contested question in the United States, and even when recognized as a bona fide phenomenon, its cause may remain under debate. But climate care advocates reject such dissent on the basis of mainstream scientific consensus. They draw on prevalent scientific documents, claiming:

> Since 1995 there has been general agreement among those in the scientific community most seriously engaged with this issue that climate change is happening and is being caused mainly by human activities, especially the burning of fossil fuels. Evidence gathered since 1995 has only strengthened this conclusion.

Released in 1995, the Second Assessment Report of the Intergovernmental Panel on Climate Change found that the "balance of evidence suggests a discernable human influence on global climate."[5] The point of citing it is clear: The ECI's stance is not a new or radical one. The majority of the global scientific community judiciously shares it.

Drawing additionally on the Third Assessment Report—the most recent IPCC report at the time—the "Call to Action" cites documentation of the increase in global temperature, projections that the trend will continue, and attribution of "most of the warming" to human activities.[6] Concurrence from the US National Academy of Sciences and equivalent bodies in all other G8 countries buttresses the claims of what the ECI calls "the world's most authoritative body of scientists and policy experts on the issue of global warming." Leaders' reliance on mainstream climate research is clear, closely echoing the scientific claims conventional, secular environmentalists might make.

Negotiating Skepticism: "Stop Doubting and Believe" (John 20:27)

Yet, as above, the leaders are careful to point out they have not accepted the science quickly or easily. "As evangelicals we have hesitated to speak on this issue until we could be more certain of the science of climate change," they admit. The link between hesitation and identity as evangelicals is a nod to issues of scientific distrust in the community, for the climate care leaders know all too well this claim is thorny and a likely tripping point for fellow evangelicals, as well as conservative policymakers.

To further allay doubts, the ECI points to two key figures. First, George W. Bush—a president many evangelicals supported but whose administration showed deep "hostility to climate policy" and repeated "misuse and abuse of climate science."[7] Despite this, the "Call to Action" grants that, by early 2006, Bush had "acknowledged the reality of climate change and the likelihood that human activity is the cause of at least some of it." By citing this shift on climate change, however small, these leaders speak to their audiences' awareness, perhaps even support, of Bush's longstanding climate opposition and seek to sway them with this changing tide. It is an attempt to break down a liberal-conservative, Democrat-Republican divide and depoliticize the issue.

The other key figure is Sir John, longtime leader of "the IPCC's assessment of the climate science" and "a devout evangelical Christian." As discussed in the previous chapter, Sir John was a core scientific messenger to Richard Cizik at Forum 2002 and to other evangelical leaders at the Sandy Cove conference. Including Sir John's name here indicates his significance within evangelical climate care but also, strategically, lends credibility to the IPCC's findings. The inclusion implicitly challenges any notion that the science of climate change and evangelical faith are incompatible. Sir John is living proof that faith and reason can be mutual and complementary, rather than irreconcilable and divisive, and that the IPCC is not comprised solely of atheist scientists who reject religion and embrace theory and inquiry as its substitute. Sir John embodies the marriage of devout evangelicalism and expert science.

Having outlined the science of the problem at hand and attended to likely detractors, the ECI leaders again beat the drum of duty: "[E]vidence demands action." The signatories "are convinced that evangelicals must engage this issue without any further lingering over the basic reality of the problem or humanity's responsibility to address it." They do not make a case for absolute certainty but argue that existing knowledge is sufficient to necessitate action; evangelicals must move from debating the existence and cause of climate change to ameliorating it.[8]

Climate Impacts: "As Heat and Drought Snatch away the Melted Snow" (Job 24:19)

Science delineates the nuts and bolts of climate change, but it is a problem, evangelical leaders suggest, because of its likely impacts. "The consequences of climate change will be significant and will hit the poor the hardest," they argue in the "Call to Action." Again, this claim draws on mainstream consensus research for an inventory of the effects of climate change: sea level rise and inundation, more intense and frequent weather events, agricultural damage, and the spread of disease.

The ECI frames these predicted events within a broader perspective that avows interdependence between human beings and the natural world and rejects a clear binary in favor of innate relation. "The earth's natural systems are resilient but not infinitely so," the leaders caution, "and human civilizations are remarkably dependent on ecological sustainability and well-being." To their mind, the Earth is moderately fragile; there are limits to its resistance to disturbance and capacity for renewal. But ecological stability and well-being are not goods in and of themselves. Rather, their importance lies in support of the earth's human inhabitants.

But what of nonhuman inhabitants? The "Call to Action" adds an aside: "…not to mention the various negative impacts climate change could have on God's other creatures." For climate care leaders, human beings are patently more important than nonhuman life—a perception bolstered by theological undercurrents that denote a hierarchy within the created order, with human beings at the apex. In contrast to the Noah's Ark discourses of the ESA defense efforts, outlined in the previous chapter, what might be termed ecocentric or biocentric concerns are sidelined in this treatment of climate change. An overtly anthropocentric creation care takes their place. Because some Christians criticize secular environmentalism for inverting the ranks of creation and equalizing incommensurate beings, the ECI leaders err on the side of caution, only hinting at the potential for species loss and the antici-pated impacts on biodiversity wrought by climate change.

From their developed and specifically American perspective, the leaders also worry about the national security implications of climate change. Each of the impacts mentioned, they explain, "increases the likelihood of refugees from flooding or famine, violent conflicts, and increasing international insta-bility, which could lead to more security threats to our nation." Climate and security concerns such as these are increasingly gaining traction, even in the halls of the Pentagon.[9] In 2003, scenario-planning specialists Peter Schwartz and Doug Randall published a report for the Defense Department detailing the geopolitical destabilization that might result from abrupt, nonlinear cli-matic shifts and the resulting implications for US national security.[10] By raising such concerns, the ECI may resonate with security hawks in their audiences, though doing so also risks inflaming anxiety around immigration and casting vulnerable human beings, especially refugees, as "security threats."

Yet the climate care leaders' ultimate appeal is not pragmatic but emo-tional. Looking beyond America's borders, they fix their gaze on the develop-ing world:

> Poor nations and poor individuals have fewer resources available to cope with major challenges and threats. The consequences of global warming will therefore hit the poor the hardest, in part because those areas likely to be significantly affected first are in the poorest regions of the world. Millions of people could die in this century because of climate change, most of them our poorest global neighbors.

By repetition, their emphasis is on the poor—a focus that calls up indirect but poignant theological implications and concerns about the unequal burdens created by climate change. The ECI primarily stresses intragenerational jus-tice—the harmful effects of climate change are spatially dispersed from their causes—but also hints at intergenerational justice—those effects are also tem-porally dispersed, with consequences for those not yet born.[11]

This perspective on the impacts of climate change, like its causes, is based on mainstream documents and discourses, interpreted with a uniquely evangelical thrust and an anthropocentric approach. "The consequences of climate change will be significant," the leaders claim, and the measure of this significance is the impact on human beings, particularly "our poorest global neighbors." Yet while they focus on the unequal distribution of impacts and the varied capacity to cope, who exactly bears the brunt of culpability, also disproportionate, remains unclear. Precisely how those responsible should address the problem is equally murky. And though the ECI answers one important question—Do these evangelical leaders believe in climate change?—a more pressing one is left lingering in evangelicals' minds: What does the Bible say?

A Matter of Faith

The most critical and unique building block of the ECI's construction of climate change is theological. "Christian moral convictions demand our response to the climate change problem," the "Call to Action" proclaims. The leaders' stance is framed by religion and grounded in scripture. They locate concern about and action on climate in three powerful biblical tenets: love of God, love of neighbor, and the demands of stewardship.

Love of God: "This Is the First and Greatest Commandment" (Matthew 22:38)

First, the ECI leaders argue, "Christians must care about climate change because we love God the Creator and Jesus our Lord, through whom and for whom the creation was made. This is God's world, and any damage that we do to God's world is an offense against God Himself." This particular portrayal of the natural world and clear expression of its value is rooted in the creation account of Genesis 1. "In the beginning God created the heavens and the Earth," it opens. After depicting the pointillistic stages of the creation process, the account concludes with divine admiration: "God saw all that he had made, and it was very good" (Gen. 1:1–31).

Drawing on this opening chapter of the Bible, the ECI insists on the Earth's unique status as the praiseworthy product of a powerful creator God. In Genesis 1, God is the singular maker of all things, from their "formless and empty" start to a complete, complex, and carefully structured creation—what the ECI calls "God's world." This divine role establishes an intimate relationship between the creator and creation but also an essential distinction; the two are connected but not one and the same.

While in process, God repeatedly evaluates the creation as "good" (Gen. 1:4, 10, 12, 18, 21, 25, 31), and on the sixth day, when God creates human beings, this assessment shifts simply but profoundly to "very good" (Gen. 1:31)—an undeniable appraisal. Though the addition of human beings in the final stage of this multilayered process transforms creation from "good" to "very good," only creation in its entirety merits ultimate approbation, and the value of non-human creation is clear.[12] As environmental philosopher Max Oelschlaeger argues, this conservative Christian theology implies "nature has *intrinsic value* because God made it, not simply instrumental value for human beings."[13]

Climate care leaders further bolster this conception of Earth as creation, and thus its inherent value, by citing Psalm 24:1: "The Earth is the Lord's, and everything in it, / the world, and all who live in it." According to this unequivocal statement, creation and its creatures do not belong to human beings but, rather, to their creator. No aspect is irrelevant or insignificant to God, and because everything, all that exists, is part of the creation, damage to any aspect of it is an offense against God as the maker. On the other hand, caring for creation and all its inhabitants is an act of love and an expression of honor. It glorifies God.

The ECI augments these Old Testament passages with an accompanying New Testament reference from the book of Colossians: "For in him all things were created: things in heaven and on Earth, visible and invisible...all things have been created through him and for him" (Col. 1:16). Through him, Christ, all things came into existence; Christ is the creator. But all things also exist for Christ; Christ is the aim of creation. In some sense, then, Christ is both benefactor and beneficiary, artist and beholder, in whom all things hold together and through whom all things are redeemed (Col. 1:15–20). Thus, the ECI suggests, on the issue of climate change, evangelicals should seek to align themselves and their actions with the creating, sustaining, and reconciling work of their savior Jesus Christ and echo his love.

Love of Neighbor: "Love Your Neighbor as Yourself" (Leviticus 19:18)

The ECI makes a second claim: "Christians must care about climate change because we are called to love our neighbors, to do unto others as we would have them do unto us, and to protect and care for the least of these as though each was Jesus Christ himself." The leaders return to impacts on the poor and cite the Gospel of Matthew to imbue climate care with a dimension of justice. When pressed by the Pharisees, Jesus identifies the first and greatest commandment, "Love the Lord your God with all your heart and with all your soul and with all your mind" (Matt. 22:37), and the second, similarly, "Love your neighbor as yourself" (Matt. 22:39). The ECI underscores the point with another passage from Matthew: "[I]n everything, do to others what you would have them do to you" (Matt. 7:12). The value one holds for oneself should extend to all human beings, and the moral considerability one desires should be reflected likewise in the treatment of others. These two core pillars of Christian faith, the leaders assert, apply profoundly to climate change.

Reference to the final parable recounted in Matthew implies the gravity of these precepts. In it, Jesus evokes the Day of Judgment: "Truly I tell you, whatever you did for one of the least of these brothers and sisters of mine, you did for me... [but] whatever you did not do for one of the least of these, you did not do for me" (Matt. 25:40, 25:45). Commonly cited to advocate consideration of the poor, this excerpt suggests that on the basis of believers' actions, eternal consequences hang in the balance and will be accordingly determined. Love of one's neighbor has greater gravity than a mere suggestion. For the ECI, this precept of justice should be enacted on climate change with the care Christians would have for "Jesus Christ himself."

Stewardship: "Every Deed Prompted by Faith" (2 Thessalonians 1:11)

Third, the leaders advocate: "Christians, noting the fact that most of the climate change problem is human induced, are reminded that when God made humanity he commissioned us to exercise stewardship over the Earth and its creatures." This last aspect of climate care theology returns to the Bible's opening chapter to explore human beings' place within the created order, their role as stewards:

> Then God said, "Let us make mankind in our image, in our likeness, so that they may rule over the fish in the sea and the birds in the sky, over the livestock and all the wild animals, and over all the creatures that move along the ground."
> So God created mankind in his own image,
> in the image of God he created them;
> male and female he created them.
> God blessed them and said to them, "Be fruitful and increase in number; fill the Earth and subdue it. Rule over the fish in the sea and the birds in the sky and over every living creature that moves on the ground."
> (Gen. 1:26–28)

Following Lynn White's essay, many have read this passage as establishing a hierarchy and dominance of human beings over nature, thus encouraging environmental exploitation.[14] But the ECI demurs, interpreting it as a call to stewardship instead.

According to this passage, the role of steward is grounded both in human beings' actions and in human beings' being. Humans are created *imago Dei*, in the image and likeness of God. This unique quality distinguishes them from other creatures, and because of it God assigns them a responsibility and a particular role: to rule. Though it may seem vague in isolation, when read in light of other biblical uses of dominion language, including that attributed to Jesus in the Gospel accounts, it becomes clear that this command is not meant to imply domination or abuse but rather just and responsible tenancy.[15]

Although the "Call to Action" does not cite Genesis 2, evangelical leaders often use the scripture to ground humanity's responsibility to creation.[16] According to this creation account, "The Lord God formed a man from the dust of the ground and breathed into his nostrils the breath of life, and the man became a living being" (Gen. 2:7). Dirt and breath together create Adam—a combination of the physical and the transcendent that emphasizes the inescapable earthliness of human beings. Moving again from being to doing, the account continues: "The Lord God took the man and put him in the Garden of Eden to work it and take care of it" (Gen. 2:15). This passage amends and expands the call to conscientious dominion with an unmistakable call to service. Tending the earthly garden must benefit not only human beings but also creation itself.

Taken together, these scriptures endow human-earth relationships with a cosmological context, giving human beings certain divinely ordained rights and responsibilities as both part of creation as an integrated whole and other than creation as its special rulers and caretakers. They are both a part and apart.[17] The idea of creation, in which people are integrally embedded, overcomes stark human-nature binaries but also preserves human beings' unique place within it—a position with attendant obligations.

Yet Christians have often failed to heed this biblical responsibility. In the "Call to Action," climate care leaders call their community to task for habitual "failure to exercise proper stewardship," of which climate change is only "the latest evidence." They also insist that it "constitutes a critical opportunity to do better." By identifying the theological significance of the Earth, human beings, and proper human-creation relations, the ECI locates this "critical opportunity" within the purview of faith and casts concern about climate change within a larger framework of religious adherence. Ultimately,

Christians are enjoined to respond to the problem "with moral passion and concrete action." The leaders call them to be active believers, linking faith and feats on issues of creation care, even if, in the past, they have failed to do so. Theological conviction should, indeed must, beget engagement.

Multifaceted Solutions

What then, one might ask, should the solutions be? Linked with the science of climate change, its likely impacts, and its normative dimensions, the final segment of the ECI's construction of climate change concerns how best to reduce greenhouse gas emissions, the responses through which word and deed should be linked. "The need to act now is urgent," the leaders argue. Impacts are already materializing; time lags between the release of greenhouse gases and shifts in the climate system ensure changes yet to come; and many decisions made now will shape emissions well into the future. Because the consequences of our current emissions "will be visited upon our children and grandchildren," they urge, "governments, business, churches, and individuals all have a role to play in addressing climate change—starting now."

Accountable Actors: "Give Back to Caesar What Is Caesar's" (Mark 12:17)

Of these four actors, the ECI's first and most insistent emphasis is on the US government. The group's stance conforms to a pervasive call: "To pass and implement national legislation requiring sufficient economy-wide reductions in carbon dioxide emissions through cost-effective, market-based mechanisms such as a cap-and-trade program." To further specify what legislative solutions it advocates, the ECI released "Principles for Federal Policy on Climate Change" a year after the "Call to Action." (See Appendix G.) Following the IPCC's recommendation, the principles assert that by 2050 emissions should be cut 80 percent from year 2000 levels, aiming for the stabilization goal of the UNFCCC: preventing "dangerous anthropogenic interference with the climate system."[18] The ECI document contends cap and trade would "harness the power of the market" to this end by putting a price on greenhouse gas emissions and creating economic incentive for their reduction. At the same time, such a system would minimize government interference, restrictions on individual freedom," and economic cost but also maximize the protection of life, property rights, and national and energy security.

Despite allowing that international coordination is necessary given the global scope of the problem, references to the Kyoto Protocol, an agreement to succeed it, or the United Nations are conspicuously absent from both ECI documents. The policy principles refer only to the FCCC, omitting its UN prefix. The ECI obviously knows its target audiences. Those with conservative political orientations may well harbor staunch opposition to Kyoto as an infringement on American sovereignty. Adherence to fundamentalist eschatology may make others wary of transnational or "one world" governance as a tool of the Antichrist, a character sometimes portrayed as the UN secretary-general.

But regardless of international cooperation to tackle climate change and participation from developing country emitters, particularly China and India, the policy principles beseech, "America must do the right thing." Historically, the United States has "contributed by far the most CO_2 to the atmosphere," and this historical responsibility requires action, even if unilateral.[19] This stance challenges core arguments against American participation in Kyoto, forwarded in the Senate's 1997 Byrd-Hagel Resolution and later by the George W. Bush administration. In the "Call to Action," the ECI pairs dissidence with an upbeat note, commending senators who voted in favor of the 2005 Domenici-Bingaman Resolution, which acknowledges the human role in climate change and the need for federal response and encouraging "them to fulfill their pledge."[20]

The leaders additionally applaud businesses that "have moved ahead of the pace of government action through innovative measures." By citing select companies' support for cap and trade and the "timely leadership" of voluntary actions from the private sector, the "Call to Action" indicates that climate change is an increasingly mainstream issue and that mitigation can be pursued within a probusiness framework. Climate change need not raise fears of economic ruin, the leaders imply, but should be seen as a possible boon. The policy principles countenance only as much government intervention as is needed to ensure "prices are right" and to provide firms with "long-term regulatory certainty." Climate care leaders harbor no anticapitalist sentiment. They also offer no critique of the system that might be implicated in causing climate change.

The "Call to Action" also insists that churches and individuals have roles to play in the mitigation enterprise. As with businesses, it highlights voluntary efforts—the use of energy-efficient light bulbs or hybrid cars, for example—and praises "pioneers [who] are already helping to show the way forward." Focusing on individuals as consumers, the ECI gives little indication of their potential roles as citizens and what contributions they might make beyond singular purchasing decisions. Nonetheless, churches and the public are clearly perceived as important actors.

Across the board—for government, businesses, churches, and individuals—the solutions the ECI advances are nothing out of the ordinary. Pushing rather moderate actions that do not challenge established orthodoxy, climate care is measured in terms of advocacy. Moreover, while the leaders demonstrate an international outlook concerning the impacts of climate change, when it comes to enacting solutions, their focus is domestic. The "Call to Action" clearly speaks both to policymakers and individuals and prescribes both governmental regulation and voluntary action. The ECI's strategy is twofold: primarily, to effect change on Capitol Hill by deploying a unique voice in the push for federal climate legislation and, secondarily, to engender a shift among the broader evangelical public. One prong is directed at top-down structural change, the other at bottom-up individual change, though the narrow articulation of the latter suggests lesser interest in generating a grassroots movement. Ultimately, the leaders convey, from Main Street to Wall Street, from church aisles to West Wing corridors, action to address climate change is under way. Change is not simply up for consideration but has already begun, they urge. Bystanders, get on board.

Leading the Charge: "I Will Fulfill the Oath" (Jeremiah 11:5)

By signing the "Call to Action," the ECI leaders position themselves at the forefront of this tide within the evangelical community. "We will not only teach the truths communicated here," they pledge, "but also seek ways to implement the actions that follow from them." Again, the core theme of the interlinking of word and deed emerges. The leaders will begin with words and continue the conversation begun in the "Call to Action" but will also implement pursuant actions. "In the name of Jesus Christ our Lord," they commit themselves: May this language and action be supported by religious conviction, conducted in the interest of Christian faith, and blessed by God.

The "Call to Action," of course, would mean little in the absence of its accompanying list of signatories. Their names lend necessary credibility to this effort within a religious tradition that, in contrast to Catholicism and mainline Protestantism, lacks institutional hierarchy. The original list of eighty-six signatories has now grown to some 250.[21] So in addition to its discursive advocacy effort, the ECI is a network of leaders with various spheres of influence in American evangelicalism—from megachurches to universities, parachurch organizations to relief and development NGOs—whose names, titles, and affiliations assert the elite nature of the ECI. (While their signatures bring with them institutional weight, the leaders sign only as individuals, not on behalf of their organizations.)

From Language to Action

The landscape of ideas and discourses about climate change is thick and varied.[22] With its particular way of describing the issue—its causes, consequences, and solutions—evangelical climate care adds a unique voice to this cacophonous chorus. This construction of climate change weaves a number of different threads or story lines, some of which could easily have been plucked from the mouths of secular environmentalists, others of which have a distinctly evangelical tenor. Treatments of the science and impacts of climate change and the solutions to it are, essentially, nothing new. The ECI's special contribution is what, in the eyes of its leaders, gives the material realities of climate change meaning: the theological interpretation, particularly with support from high-profile signatories.

In this sense, the ECI is largely a discursive effort. It deploys language deliberately and strategically to shape others' conceptions of climate change and to mobilize engagement. To this pragmatic end, the "Call to Action" functions as a product for public consumption, a lobbying and outreach tool in the public sphere. It is equipped for battle in the contested space around climate change, and, following its 2006 release, the "Call to Action" was indeed launched into the broader landscape of American climate politics. Through the text, trustworthy, credible messengers deliver a targeted message to particular audiences whose values and beliefs, predispositions and idioms the leaders know well and speak to and with. A persuasive messaging endeavor is at work, recasting this environmental issue in evangelical terms and telling its story using biblical language and central theological tenets—love of God, love of neighbor, and the demands of stewardship. Evangelicals are people of the Word, and here the word seems to work well.

But the efficacy of climate care discourse lies not just in its strategic dimensions but in its complementary constitutive ones as well. The "Call to Action" plays a mediating role, shaping the attribution of meaning to climate change, engaging with why it matters. With grounding in scripture, the ECI locates this current issue facing humanity within an ongoing religious narrative of creation and its care. Christians are cast at the dramatic intersection of biblical history and current climate challenges, giving them agency in writing the story's next chapter through their actions and implicitly imploring them to take a particular role.

Beginning with creation, the biblical narrative establishes a meaningful, linear progression of time and the significance of past, present, and future. As Max Oelschlaeger explains, "The most important function of a creation story is to legitimate the present by locating it in sacred time," situating "human beings in a cosmic continuum...that gives direction (meaning, purpose, significance) to existence."[23] This is an unfolding drama. Creation care continues to be revealed, and believers take part in its revelation. It is this generative narrative that imbues climate change engagement with profound import.

Ultimately, though, this construction of climate change and the messages of climate care do not exist in isolation. Word is connected with the people who speak and write, hear and read it. It is embedded in their world. Climate care leaders and evangelical believers interact with these discourses, and their interactions shape and are shaped by their institutional, cultural, social, and political contexts. How climate care advocates link word and deed and how willing evangelical churchgoers are to join in the effort are crucial questions. Though the "Call to Action" is a watershed document, its capacity for impact is tied to these issues of human reception and response. Without active engagement from evangelical leaders, the ECI statement loses its meaning; without support from the evangelical public, its traction wanes. In the presence of these actors, this poignant call for climate care becomes either language in action or merely words on the page.

3

Advancing Climate Care in Word and Deed

RICK WARREN IS, perhaps, the most prominent figure in American evangelicalism today. He is pastor to a congregation of 22,000, leads a network of churches in some 160 countries, wrote one of the best-selling nonfiction books in history, and hosted a forum for the 2008 presidential candidates—the only time John McCain and Barack Obama appeared together during the campaign outside the debates. Given his enormous influence, obtaining Warren's signature on the "Call to Action" was a critical goal for the Evangelical Climate Initiative. Various climate care leaders reached out to him, requesting his support, but as the 2006 launch drew nearer, organizers had not received a response. Perhaps Warren was simply not interested. Perhaps engaging climate change seemed too radical. Perhaps their messages were not even reaching him. Racking his brain for alternative strategies, Jim Ball had an epiphany as to who to contact: John Stott, the British would-be "pope" of global evangelicalism, with a passion for birdwatching.[1]

Stott's combination of evangelical faith and zeal for birding had made him a keen supporter of A Rocha, a Christian conservation association with initiatives around the world.[2] Without a doubt, he could gain audience with Warren, and as a friend to creation care efforts, he might just want to. Ball immediately emailed Stott's fellow countryman and Richard Cizik's converter, Sir John, asking him to enlist Stott. Within twenty-four hours, Ball received a reply: "John Stott is going to be seeing Rick Warren on Friday. Draft up a letter. Send some materials." He felt chills and sensed the Holy Spirit at work. Within the week, Stott met privately with Warren at Saddleback and read him Ball's letter about the ECI. "I'm in," Warren said on the spot. "I'll sign it."

This story is unambiguous: the ECI is a statement, but it is also people—the leaders who commit their names to it. The "Call to Action" is central to evangelical climate care, yet signatories lend the document crucial clout and credibility—an essential role given evangelicalism's lack of a formal institutional hierarchy. Ultimately, the ECI forms the basis of an evangelical climate care coalition. The leaders who take part are located throughout the United States, holding various professional positions and principally invested in other organizations—circumstances that limit their in-person collaboration. Hence, physical interactions and shared institutions are not the central links between these diverse and diffuse actors. How they conceive of and speak about the issue cements them as a group, as a network.[3]

While the signatories are crucial to the "Call to Action," its story lines and construction of climate change also do something important for them. They extend the conversation started in formal ECI communications and bring it to life in their advocacy, which is often comprised of discrete actions, not highly coordinated across leaders' organizations. But as this opening story shows, relationships and religion are equally as important as discourse. They both act as a kind of glue and fan the flames of engagement. My conversations with leaders revealed that existing bonds within the evangelical community help connect them and foster trust, that shared belief cements them, and that a sense of ultimate meaning lights their way, individually and as a coalition. Climate care is an expression of faith and community.

A Net Cast

Gathering Signatories: "Gathered up One by One"
(Isaiah 27:12)

As the history of evangelical creation care shows, some seeds of a climate care network were sown well before Jim Ball, Richard Cizik, and others began to develop it concretely, but the process of building one began in earnest once they had the "Call to Action" in hand. The roots of their network were in the statement itself. The ECI organizers' goal, Professor David Gushee explained to me, was "to draft a statement that [could] be embraced by as wide a spectrum of evangelical leaders as possible."[4] Obtaining signatures that could not be dismissed as "liberal" was imperative, as was composing "a sober, non-inflammatory, consensus-building" document around which a climate care coalition could cohere. At the same time, producing a document of substance was vital. Ball insisted on including a call for "a mandatory market-based approach" to climate mitigation. "Without that, the statement would have been nice but not very meaningful," he said—little more than tokenism.[5]

Given the text's policy teeth—a stance conventionally associated with the Left—the organizers knew they had to make signing it feel safe for evangelical leaders. To do so, they looked to trusted names and organizations and used preexisting networks within the community—the AERDO, the CCCU, and the NAE—to pull in initial signatories and build the original ECI group. Cizik, CCCU's Robert Andringa, MAP International's Michael Nyenhuis, and World Vision's Richard Stearns asked people in their respective networks "to consider the issue carefully, consider signing, and get back to us."[6] According to sociologist of religion Michael Lindsay, evangelical leaders frequently employ this convening process to bring together elites and recruit them to their causes.[7] By drawing on their convening power, these men were not merely leveraging their address books but also tapping into trusted connections. "This is the key to all this," Ball told me. "You've got to have these trusted relationships."[8]

So the ECI leaders capitalized on other evangelical elites' trust in established networks, organizations, and interpersonal relationships. In his interview, Cizik noted that deploying a "leader-to-leader strategy" has been a mainstay for the ECI. He personally engages senior figures within American evangelicalism; likewise, various "opinion makers in the evangelical world approach others to join them."[9] With an evangelical witnessing style, webs of existing relationships and affiliations were and continue to be engaged and a new one developed. The story of John Stott and Rick Warren poignantly demonstrates this process and the persuasive power of leader-to-leader witnessing to reach even the most prominent individuals.

Peer outreach succeeded in bringing many signatories on board, but the process was often arduous. During this founding period, Rusty Pritchard directed national outreach for the EEN with a focus on climate change. "It's a lot of work to build this kind of network," he explained, "especially because it's not just a no-brainer for folks. They have to be convinced about the issue and then be convinced that they have the capital—cultural and social capital within their networks—to pull off a signing and not be attacked too much or destroy the other great work they're already doing."[10] Preexisting affiliations can help facilitate a new coalition like the ECI, but the attendant expectations and demands that come along with them can also be an impediment.

Pritchard's comment also points to two complementary processes in which fellow evangelicals played key roles. First, in educating leaders, Sir John became an important messenger. A key presence and speaker at the Oxford and Sandy Cove gatherings, he subsequently made a presentation to the NAE board of directors in March 2005 and had intimate meetings with some of the target signatories.[11] In addition, a DVD featuring Sir John was included in the "Call to Action" packets the ECI sent out. He gave the science of climate change a conservative Christian voice.

Numerous climate care leaders spoke to me about the sway Sir John's combined intellectual clout and devout faith hold for them. Speaking of the Sandy Cove conference, David Neff noted Sir John's presence was "very important" because "he was able to lend the kind of credibility to the discussion that almost nobody else on the face of the globe could lend to it."[12] But Neff was not only moved by the atmospheric physicist's scientific credentials. "It was interesting for me to learn that the former head of the Met in the UK and the co-chair of the scientist half of the Intergovernmental Panel was an evangelical Christian and that I had this kind of background in common with him," he said. As Christians they were able to communicate on a more meaningful level. Sir John epitomizes the link between evangelical Christianity and climate concern, which makes him a persuasive envoy who shares a religious identity with and speaks the language of his audience.

Second, for moving from education to a willingness to expend leadership capital by signing the "Call to Action," safety in numbers was essential. As more and more leaders came on board, more and more felt able to do the same. Those involved in building the coalition could point to high-profile leaders as proof that engaging with the ECI was sensible and within the evangelical mainstream. They sought Warren's signature to demarcate their middle-of-the-road position, and due to the connecting work of Ball, Sir John, and Stott, that addition solidified the ECI and its "Call to Action" and empowered the early climate care enterprise.

Experiences of Enlisting: "Wisdom Will Enter Your Heart" (Proverbs 2:10)

Beyond the centrality of peer outreach, leaders traveled a variety of different pathways to becoming signatories. For those involved with creation care from its early days or already engaged in social justice advocacy, the ECI was a natural progression from past engagement. The roots of Professor Ron Sider's interest began with his 1977 book, *Rich Christians in an Age of Hunger,* and grew through his work with Evangelicals for Social Action, the initial evangelical partner of the NRPE.[13] Similarly, Scott Sabin's experiences as executive director of Plant with Purpose, a Christian nonprofit organization, drew him to climate care. "Seeing the impact of deforestation and environmental degradation on the poor, seeing hillsides and people trying to farm bedrock are what really have made me into an environmentalist," he told me.[14]

For others, the "Call to Action" tapped into a longtime passion for the environment—often rooted in childhood experiences or primed by conventional environmental thinkers—and offered an opportunity to link it formally with their faith. John Phelan, president of Chicago's North Park Theological Seminary at the time, explained to me: "From reading the work of Wendell Berry, Ed Abbey, and a lot of other environmental writers, I came well prepared to the conversation. So when the evangelical side began talking about this, this was nothing new to me—not something I had to think about. It was already very much rooted in my own understanding."[15] He welcomed the coming together of the two.

Theological reflection informed many leaders' decisions to become ECI signatories. Early in his tenure as president of Trevecca Nazarene University in Nashville, Tennessee, Dan Boone received a letter from Ball and a copy of the "Call to Action."[16] "I reviewed it, read it, and felt very strongly about signing it," he recalled, attributing that instant conviction to his own theological education at Trevecca and then Nazarene Theological Seminary in Kansas City, Missouri. "I think that theology across many years has kept my heart warm and ripe toward the environmental movement." For Boone, theology paved the way for action.

Looking across a dramatic Idaho landscape one morning, Tri Robinson felt stirrings of creation care, but because the topic seemed so far outside his purview as senior pastor of Vineyard Boise, he proceeded cautiously.[17] He spent the next six months in intensive scriptural study and contemplative prayer, before giving his first sermon on creation care in April 2005. The process was transformative. "I got my heart broken," Robinson told me. He went on to embed creation care into the fabric of his congregation and write two books on the topic: *Saving God's Green Earth* (2006) and *Small Footprint, Big Handprint* (2008).[18] In his experience, as with Boone and so many others, the intellectual and the empathic were intimately connected.

Like Robinson's moment looking out on the Idaho butte and Cizik's moment in Oxford, a number of leaders described experiences of "epiphany" and "conversion" in relation to climate change. Ball explained: "I came to this in a very evangelical way."[19] While pursuing a Ph.D. in the early 1990s, a fellow student, Bonnie Gisel, challenged him to read the

Bible with an eye toward environmental concern. Reluctant and skeptical, he did and by reading with these "fresh eyes" found himself "totally turned around," "totally convicted." Suddenly, Ball's faith gave him a new, zealous sense of vision and mission—the precursor to his advocacy on creation care and public policy.

For Matthew Sleeth, then an emergency room doctor, his wife, Nancy, prompted his environmental revelation.[20] While vacationing on an island off the coast of Florida, the two sat out on their balcony and talked. "What is the biggest problem facing the world today?" she asked pointedly. Sleeth paused, reflecting on his experiences inside and outside the emergency room, then answered solemnly: "The world is dying." Well then, she wanted to know, "What are you going to do about it?"

At the time, Sleeth had no answer. He returned to the hospital and emergency care but continued to wrestle with the question, seeking answers. After looking to a number of humanity's great texts, he eventually found satisfying answers—and a call to service—in the Bible. Sleeth was unsure how to describe his new calling—"green doctor? Creation care minster? ecoevangelist?"—but "felt certain that the call was from God."[21] Moved by conviction, he left medicine, made drastic, simplifying lifestyle changes with his family, and started the nonprofit Blessed Earth, speaking at hundreds of churches and publishing *Serve God, Save the Planet* (2007) and *The Gospel According to the Earth* (2010).[22] For Sleeth and his whole family, God and green went hand in hand and paved the way to climate care.[23]

In the fall of 2006, the NAE and Harvard's Center for Health and the Global Environment cohosted a meeting at bucolic Melhana Plantation in Thomasville, Georgia. Amid sprawling live oaks draped with Spanish moss, the meeting brought together climate scientists and evangelical leaders, including Ken Wilson, senior pastor at Ann Arbor Vineyard in Michigan.[24] During the gathering, Wilson interacted with James Gustave "Gus" Speth, then dean of the Yale School of Forestry and Environmental Studies.[25] A veteran secular environmentalist frustrated with his movement's piecemeal approach to change, Speth spoke of the need for a spiritual and cultural transformation and for religious leaders' help.[26] In that moment, hearing his plea, Wilson had a spiritual awakening. "The Holy Spirit came upon me," he recounted. "I felt a chill over my body, the hair on my arms went up, and I had that fullness in my throat and water behind my eyes. That's when I had my awakening to environmental concern."[27] Like Cizik four years prior, Wilson felt mobilized to return home and get busy—specifically with a collaborative initiative, Evangelicals and Scientists United to Protect Creation (ESUPC). Conversion again gave rise to engagement.

All of these accounts might be interpreted simply as evangelical descriptions of a generic experience, but "conversion" seems to be both a powerful metaphor and an evaluation of what these leaders actually underwent: an intellectual and emotional transformation with a transcendent element. These encounters—with a text or an individual—led not just to a change of mind but to a change of heart, which for those involved indicates a religious occurrence. Described in this way, the leaders link concern about climate change to a core evangelical conviction—being born again—asserting the gravity and significance of the experience. When they speak, as Cizik did in his interview, of converting to the science of climate change, they express the coterminous nature of faith and reason even more explicitly.[28] Ultimately, these statements aver the profundity of the experiences that propelled them into climate care advocacy.

Advocates on the Ground

The Supportive Many, the Active Few: "The Harvest Is Plentiful but the Workers Are Few" (Matthew 9:37)

Although the climate care network continues to grow, both in size and depth of engagement, the coalition is constituted by degrees of commitment. A small, core group of leaders does the bulk of the advocacy work—typically those with the most profound conversion experiences—while the majority is less involved. Because signatories have previous commitments in numerous other organizations and networks, this engagement differential is not surprising. It may be an inevitable problem when working with elite leaders who are already overcommitted or have other issues on which they would rather expend their finite leadership capital. When I interviewed Jim Jewell, then campaign director for the ECI and chief operating officer of the EEN, he put it simply: "They have institutions to run, and they have churches to lead. Lots of issues, lots of demands."[29]

"I signed the document. I get their materials. I read the stuff that they send," North Park's John Phelan said of the ECI, but he was blunt about his role therein: "I keep tabs on what they're doing and support and encourage people to look at it, but I've not been heavily involved."[30] Others, such as David Neff, offered explanations: "So, will I lend my name to this? Yes. Am I eager to see it's broadly supported? Yes. Do I have time to roll up my sleeves and do publicity work alongside Jim Ball? No."[31] The demands of other responsibilities also pressed on Duane Litfin, president of Wheaton at the time.[32] "Ball and others, I think, would like to have people like me have a more high profile, public, out-there, on-the-frontline [presence]," he admitted. "But my first responsibility is giving leadership to *this* community." Sympathetic and concerned, these leaders are contributing to the extent they feel they can but are clearly constrained by prior and principle commitments.

Though these limitations on time and energy for climate advocacy are understandable, some core organizers bemoan them nonetheless. One spoke anonymously about the signatories: "They didn't turn out to be everything that we hoped they would be. They certainly didn't turn out to be everything that our funders hoped they would be. Our funders and, I think, some of our inside team to a lesser extent, hoped that this group would become zealots, would kind of be a new army for the community, and would really marshal the troops to this new height. The number of them that have done that is really small. It's a handful actually."

Ball noted the difficult balance between prodding ECI leaders to take action on the pressing problem of climate change and recognizing the risk and possible backlash they face engaging "a controversial issue."[33] "I'll push people," he said, "but I won't shove them under the bus." The core organizers know all too well how thin that line can be in the evangelical community. They also value signatories' work on other important issues, often vital to the agenda of the evangelical Center, and do not want climate advocacy to derail those efforts or harm leaders' standing in the community.

So, at times, the signatories remain nothing more than just that—names on paper. For some, the beginning was the Word, and that was all. But their names remain significant nonetheless. As Andy Crouch, author of *Culture Making* (2008), put it: "I'm just part of the shimmering penumbra of signatures that makes people say, 'Well, there's credibility to calling this an evangelical initiative because people who represent evangelical institutions are behind it. So it has some legitimacy.'"[34]

The example of Rick Warren is again instructive. Though he has remained on the periphery of advocacy, his name alone—a word with few deeds—holds immense power, appearing frequently in the media and suggesting the prominence and centrist nature of the ECI. Pastor Ken Wilson offered a concise summary: The "ECI to me is a set of signatures and the work of Jim Ball. And the signatures support his work."[35] The signatures give gravitas to the message and advocacy of the core organizers, without which they would have significantly less influence among their target audiences of policymakers and the evangelical public.

Faith in Action: "I Will Show You My Faith by My Deeds" (James 2:18)

Despite advocacy gradients within the group, many of the ECI leaders are engaged with climate care beyond lending their name to the initiative. Not surprisingly, having arrived as signatories via different avenues, they deploy their resources and efforts with different means and to different ends. They tend to work within their own spheres of influence and often perceive those areas to be the key sites of change. And though signatories do not sign the "Call to Action" on behalf of their organizations, their institutional weight has practical application. In addition to reflecting their different locations within the evangelical community, the leaders' diverse visions of and strategies for change echo the different foci in the "Call to Action."

Some emphasize the importance of engendering change at the individual level. Former doctor Matthew Sleeth is perhaps the most visible proponent of this approach, epitomized in *Serve God, Save the Planet*, with its focus on individual action and personal responsibility and suggestion that the locus of environmental change is the family unit. "I think that's part of the tradition of evangelical theology," he explained to me, "that we have a personal responsibility, a personal relationship with the world."[36] Pastor Tri Robinson detailed a similar "personal responsibility" perspective at the core of *Small Footprint, Big Handprint*: People must downsize the material aspects of their lives in order to "make a difference."[37] "It's not just about you making your life smaller," he said. "It's also about making your life bigger. But you've got to be less encumbered. You can live on less so that you can do more."

In order to make this case effectively, Sleeth, Robinson, and others believe they need to be examples. According to Sleeth, who dramatically simplified his life after his creation care awakening, "You can make films of people saying the right theology. Whether or not they do it is the most powerful sermon that they'll give. If I were to give a sermon about having a good marriage and you knew I was getting divorced, it kind of discounts what I say. So the sermon becomes your life."[38] For him, this is part of following the example of Jesus—living out one's words, the beliefs one professes. Similarly, Robinson noted that people, and specifically evangelicals, "are looking for genuine stuff," so what makes his creation care advocacy effective is that people "see my brokenness over it" and have a sense that "I'm sincere about it."[39] These leaders emphasize practicing what they preach. If their environmental witness is to have integrity, they must also.

Others, particularly the ECI organizers, focus on policymakers to effect legislative change. Ball, Cizik, and their compatriots have actively lobbied on Capitol Hill and encourage fellow signatories to do the same. "Often we have our leaders connect with their members of Congress to share with them their concerns and educate them on why this is an issue for evangelicals," said Alexei Laushkin of the EEN.[40] The ECI has also had a more formal presence in Congress, as with Ball's 2007 testimony to the Senate Environment and Public Works Committee. In addition, the organization has hired government relations firms to support its work. These leaders echo what Jim Jewell called the ECI's major goal: "comprehensive climate policy on a federal level."[41] To achieve that goal, the ECI signatories must reach out to conservative policymakers who have not historically been reached by conventional, secular environmentalists. Along with Ball and others, Paul Corts, current president of the CCCU, expressed the central need for legislative structural change to shape choices and actions at the individual level.[42]

Ultimately, a number of leaders suggested, grassroots and "grasstops" strategies must complement each other to create widespread cultural change and to engender an evangelical climate movement—an aim many shared. World Hope's Jo Anne Lyon succinctly disputed a dichotomy between the two: "I believe we can lead on this whole issue in our behavior and what we do *and* in public policy."[43] Pastor Joel Hunter explained his integrated view by describing "three realms in which the church needs to respond."[44] The first is individual: "each congregant, each church person should know what they can do as an individual—just the list of practical things." Second, each church should audit its own "carbon footprint" and work as an institution to reduce it. Third, evangelicals must "be a voice in local and state and federal policymaking because part of the Christian responsibility, part of rendering to Caesar what is Caesar's, is to voice and vote your values." Together, Hunter urged, efforts focused on individuals, churches, and policymakers should form a comprehensive, tripartite approach—one he seeks to activate in his own congregation.

Sharing this perspective, a number of signatories worry that engagement with climate change has emerged mainly among the evangelical elite and want the ECI and other climate care organizations to focus more on the grass roots.

Scott Sabin thought the ECI's greatest accomplishment had been its political impact—what he called "an impact from these leaders up."[45] "But I would love to see it have an impact from these leaders down," he added, suspecting their constituencies "are probably either unaware that their leaders have signed the ECI or kind of just shake their heads at it....ECI leaders, we speak only for ourselves. It'd be nice if there was more representation."

Though doubtful that individual lifestyles changes can make a substantial contribution to mitigation, Andy Crouch expanded on the essential importance of reaching the evangelical grass roots to "create the cultural environment within which politicians can change policy."[46] In *Culture Making*, he describes the role of culture as defining "the horizons of the possible and the impossible."[47] He told me:

> We have this horizon around us, and within it is what we can envision and do, and outside of it is what we can't envision and do. Those horizons move over time, and things that were possible become impossible; things that were impossible become possible. The old adage is politics is the art of the possible, right? So politics has to happen within that valley of culture.

Thus, in the aggregate, individual change "moves the horizons in such a way that the policy becomes visible and possible."

Wilson, too, asserted the requisite need for sweeping change within the evangelical community: "[Evangelicals] are mainstream American culture, you know? They define it, and so trying to do anything without them is like trying to do it without Americans."[48] Hence, he concluded, "I think our only real hope is that there's actually a serious tipping point on this thing for evangelicals." Given the bounds of culture and the size and influence of the evangelical community, reaching this tipping point may well be decisive for how the United States and, indeed, the global community deal with climate change.

Two Key Nodes: "Devote Yourself…to Preaching and to Teaching" (1 Timothy 4:13)

To reach the evangelical grass roots and create this cultural change, a number of leaders pointed to two key roles: one for pastors, as the link between elite leadership and the people in the pews, and the other for evangelical youth, as future leaders in the community.

Trevecca president Dan Boone explained to me that high-profile pastors are crucial: They serve as models for other pastors, giving them "courage to step out and preach."[49] As megachurch leaders do so, Paul Corts of the CCCU explained, their "message will flourish out and encourage many other pastors of smaller churches. In a sense, they will mentor the other churches to go out and move in that direction."[50] Joel Hunter, Tri Robinson, and Ken Wilson embody models for that kind of pastoral leadership. Hunter noted, "That's really my niche. I care about getting this movement into the grass roots of evangelical Christianity, and the gatekeeper is really the pastor."[51] Robinson similarly suggested the need for people to see that a "normal" pastor is "making it."[52] "I've got a legitimate, discipling, Bible-believing church that's not getting fanatical or weird but that's balancing all this ministry," he explained. "I think that's a big piece of it—having the prototype."

Because they believe, as Wilson put it, that pastors are "where all the action is" and, in Robinson's words, "that the hope is in the local church," these leaders focus the bulk of energies in that direction. In Wilson's mind, penetrating local churches is "phase two" of the movement.[53] Most of the advocacy to date has occurred at the parachurch level, where creation care leaders have been "prophets out in the wilderness." For him, the key question is: "How do you make the transition from that out-in-the-wilderness phase of the change process to getting something happening through the evangelical church? Because that's the key to social transformation on this issue. You know, it's not until evangelicals who are in evangelical churches start hearing sermons from the pulpit and seeing their churches do things for the environment that their worldview on environment's going to shift."

So in addition to communicating these issues and demonstrating church-based advocacy, they also work to develop materials "written to pastors by pastors" to equip others in their efforts. ESUPC and its Creation Care for Pastors program, which evolved from interactions at the Melhana Plantation, are one such resource. In addition to a booklet, "Creation Care: An Introduction for Busy Pastors," which thousands of pastors in the Vineyard, Willow Creek, and NAE networks have received, a website offers a host of relevant materials.[54] Similarly, Robinson developed a web resource for his Let's Tend the Garden ministry. Such support aids pastors, who have the ability to deliver custom-tailored messages to their congregations.

Although not a pastor himself, Sleeth, too, increasingly directs his energies toward pastors as "the leaders of the flocks." In his work with Blessed Earth, he tries to provide them with the biblical connections and creation care education most have not received in seminary.[55] Boone also addressed this educational problem, which underlies what he deemed "a lack of informed preaching that forms and shapes the congregations, that connects the dots" on these issues.[56] In his opinion, neglect of creation care issues in seminaries has created "a crisis of imagination in the evangelical pulpit."

Here, the key role for pastors intersects with the importance of evangelical colleges and universities—the other key focus for climate care leaders. Evangelical institutions of higher education train future leaders in the community, especially its churches. Reflecting their positions and commitments, college and university presidents—a substantial fraction of ECI signatories—emphasize this significance.

As Steve Timmermans, president of Trinity Christian College outside Chicago, told me, he and other higher education leaders are trying to integrate creation care into the operations, pedagogy, religious life, and scholarship of their institutions, expanding their prospect to "inform and lead the broader evangelical world."[57] Green buildings reduce campuses' environmental impact. Environmental studies programs educate students. Campus chapels allow for theological reflection. Institutes specializing in sustainability research contribute to academic dialogue.[58] But most important, a number of people pointed out, is the capacity for higher education leaders to influence younger generations through their words and deeds, especially through participation in such highly visible initiatives as the ECI. Similar to the role for megachurch pastors, according to Corts, their involvement "can be a real witness and a good role model for the students."[59] If they step out, others may follow. Engendering institutional leadership on climate care is essential.

These senior figures at evangelical institutions of higher learning also recognize an opportunity to capitalize on a generational fissure. Creation care has greater resonance with evangelicals under 30 than with their older counterparts, so college and university presidents often find receptive audiences within their student bodies.[60] As John Phelan put it, "I think among younger evangelicals, like a lot of our students here, it's, well, *of course*, this is clearly an issue."[61]

Many leaders support student engagement, such as participation in Renewal, a national organization aimed at supporting and connecting "students caring for creation."[62] While recognizing they can encourage students, however, a number of them see the need to let young evangelicals pursue their own passions. Corts explained, "I'm a huge believer that student things need to bubble up [from] students, and if you try to artificially bubble it up as an administrator, it's going to fail fundamentally."[63] He and others realize the issue of authenticity in student advocacy is a real one.

Just as key figures within the ECI made it possible to talk about climate change, these two spaces—local churches and institutions of higher education—are key for the broader effort to transform the conversation among evangelicals at various levels. Alexei Laushkin views the pastor as a "convening table" around which evangelical churchgoers can gather to discuss environmental concerns.[64] Evangelical colleges and universities can facilitate dialogue among the movement's youth. Across the spectrums of American evangelicalism, from powerful elite networks to churches of only a few dozen members, leaders desire to open space for dialogue—and subsequently action—and in doing so, they deploy some of the same methods that were used to build the ECI network.

Theological Mortar

As descriptions of "witness" and "conversion" suggest, these leaders are not only linked by their concern about climate change or their advocacy activities and goals. Fundamentally, they are linked by faith. Shared religious narratives and metaphors evidence what Michael Lindsay calls "salient religious identity" and what Peter Berger deems a "sacred canopy," imbuing their work with meaning and providing them with guidance and motivation.[65] "Shared spiritual identity builds cohesion among leaders who are separated geographically and institutionally," Lindsay notes. "Evangelicalism provides a moral framework through which these public leaders make sense of their lives and endow their work with special meaning." In this way, theology and belief meld the climate care coalition.

A Human Issue: "In the Image of God He Created Them; Male and Female He Created Them" (Genesis 1:27)

Echoing and extending the theological claims of the "Call to Action," climate care leaders frequently employ language of stewardship, creation care, and neighbor care. In particular, most see climate change as a human issue, related to concerns of justice and the sanctity of human life—both more established concerns among American evangelicals and the latter a defining issue for the movement.[66] It is not surprising that leaders tie climate care to prior passions. Doing so also sends a powerful message, casting climate and environment as "prolife" matters. At a January 2005 antiabortion march in Washington, DC, Ball and Cizik carried a banner that read "Stop Mercury Poisoning of the Unborn" and handed out fliers criticizing Bush administration legislation that would have allowed more mercury pollution from coal-burning power plants.[67] The EEN continues to pursue "Mercury and the Unborn" as one of its key campaigns.

Considering this human-environment connection, Jo Anne Lyon reflected on the condition of the Earth: "With any of this we don't just let it decay, as we don't let a child decay. See, I see the interdependency, interconnectedness between the Earth and people.... It's all about pro-life."[68] For her, a robust ethic in regard to the sanctity of human life does not end at the womb. Ecological systems are essential to sustaining life and must be treated as such. Phelan put it simply, "environmental concern is one part of the consistent ethic of life."[69] David Gushee noted that interweaving "a sanctity of created life ethic into a sanctity of human life ethic" should be a core theological underpinning of climate care.[70] In his eyes, the topic demands concerted scholarship as efforts move forward.

This human focus, implicit, some argued, in the notion of creation care, serves also as a theological corrective. According to Joel Hunter, "The whole language of creation care reminds us that there is a creator and that we are honoring him by taking care of this great gift of creation. It also keeps us out of the realm of the extreme egalitarian approach where the frog is as important as the person," which is a stance conservative Christians have often attributed to secular environmentalists. The term *creation care,* as opposed to *environmentalism* or *sustainability,* engenders concern for God's creation but also maintains a hierarchy within it.

Eschatology: "Renewal of All Things" (Matthew 19:28)

Although not addressed explicitly in the "Call to Action," many climate care leaders see eschatology as a core theological issue. As detailed in chapter 1, according to premillennialists, Christ will return and usher in the millennium, while postmillennialists hold that his return will follow it. (Amillennialists believe a symbolic millennium has already begun and will conclude with the Second Coming.) Hence, while orthodox theology perceives a four-part plotline of history—the Creation, the Fall, redemption, and consummation/restoration—beyond these pillars of the biblical narrative, evangelicals can hold very different eschatological convictions, which shape perspectives on the future and thus the attribution of meaning to the present.

The book of Revelation "is patient of widely differing views of the end of history," explains theologian Harry Maier, as some passages depict the destruction of creation while others suggest its transformation from old to new.[71] So eschatological views inform the meaning of the physical world, painting the Earth as either a "temporary stage" for or integrated with this biblical drama.[72] In other words, views diverge on the basis of disjunction or continuity between the material present and the future—whether the present creation can be discarded or must be restored. These leaders typically embrace a particular "eschatology of renewal," and paired with a sense of beginnings rooted in Genesis, their views on the end of time frame creation care, bookending the stewardship story in which they cast themselves and other evangelicals as actors.

Apocalyptic premillennial dispensationalism is a view they are consciously and actively working against.[73] This strain of evangelical (often fundamentalist) theology was shaped by the work of John Nelson Darby, Cyrus Scofield, and Dwight L. Moody in the late nineteenth and early twentieth centuries. Its popular representations include Hal Lindsey's *The Late Great Planet Earth* (1970) and Tim LaHaye and Jerry Jenkins's best-selling *Left Behind* series (1995–2007).[74] Dispensationalism holds that the current creation will be wholly destroyed and replaced by a new heaven and a new Earth.

"I think there is still a small group of evangelicals who are opposed to [creation care] for what I would call eschatological reasons," Phelan told me.[75] He summarized the perspective: "Jesus is coming soon. The world's going to hell in a handcart, and there's nothing you can do about it. And, in fact, environmental degradation is one of the signs of the end, and if we're fighting against that, we're in some perverse way fighting against God." In other words, dispensationalism takes the arc of human history to be in decline, embraces societal and environmental deterioration as foretelling the rapture, and urges believers not to impede but to hasten that event. The only real hope is in Christ's return.

As such, dispensationalism can engender fatalism, for the Earth has no relevance to the future and creation care is but a distraction, especially from the Great Commission of converting people to Christianity. It constructs a vertical cosmological orientation, focusing away from Earth onto heaven and away from community onto individual salvation. In Phelan's eyes, the group that adheres to this "perverse eschatological view" is not large but "sometimes noisy"—a reality with which climate care leaders must contend.

Dan Boone went a step further and argued that dispensationalism has prevented concern for creation and advocacy in its interest. "I truly believe that the environmental crisis we're in has been caused by lack of a good biblical eschatology," he said.[76] What is missing? Understanding "God's desire to restore all things" and "humans as partners with God in the care of this wonderful creation." "For lack of those two pieces," he explained, "the Christian faith has been sidelined on the issue and left it to the Sierra Club and groups like that.…Christians just couldn't get their arms around it, so as a result, we said nothing." Instead, Boone called for a different, "informed eschatology," which is not "about the trashing or burning or blowing up of the Earth but all things being made new…a hopeful eschatology that does not leave behind that which is earthly or material but fully restores and redeems it."

To make their case for an eschatology of renewal, leaders draw on biblical texts. Many, like Larry Lloyd, then president of Crichton College in Memphis, Tennessee, echoed Romans 8:22: "[C]reation is groaning and moaning for the final redemption in Christ Jesus."[77] That is, creation shares human beings' sinful condition and the need for and promise of salvation and renewal.

For Ball, Colossians 1:15–20 is at the core of his creation care ethic.[78] Intermittently quoting and commentating, he explained this centrality:

> *He is the image of the invisible God, the firstborn over all creation. For in him all things are created: things in heaven, things on Earth. All things have been created by him and for him.* All things! By him, for him! *And all things have been reconciled by his blood shed on the cross.* It's not just about human beings; it's about all things, *all things.* And to make sure that we get it, the text says, *All things, things in heaven and things on Earth*—the Hebraic way of saying all things.

For Ball, like most evangelicals, "It's about Christ. It's about his blood being shed on the cross, which is at the emotional heart of my faith—that he died for my sins." But, he appended, "not just mine. He died to reconcile all things."

Trinity's Steve Timmermans shares Ball's belief that all things—human and nonhuman—will be the beneficiaries of renewal and salvation, grounded, for him, in John 3:16: "For God so loved the world that he gave his one and only Son, that whoever believes in him shall not perish but have eternal life."[79] "For God so loved the *world*," Timmermans reiterated passionately. "It doesn't say God so loved the *people*."

As these leaders see it, the whole of creation, currently groaning, shares in the redemptive hope of Christ's crucifixion. Just as in the beginning the entirety of creation was divinely constructed, in the end all will be restored through the redemptive power of Jesus. Eschatology, then, is not about rapturing saved souls but bringing all of creation into harmony with God. Even beyond radical dispensationalism, this eschatological perspective amends the subtler but more pervasive narrative David Gushee identified as "we leave here and go *up* to heaven."[80] Instead, for climate care advocates, "this is where it all ends, with a renewed heaven and a renewed Earth."[81]

By shaping notions of the Earth's worth, an eschatology of renewal also defines proper human-creation relations. According to Tri Robinson, it implies responsibility: "We're called to stewardship to the last minute."[82] Similarly, Matthew Sleeth maintained that a call to action is embedded in the theology: "For me, the faith of Abraham is having a faith that there's going to be another generation and another generation and another generation. In the beginning of the Book of Acts, the angels show up and say, 'Get to work. You've got work to do.' And so my eschatology is if I go tomorrow, I want to be doing the right thing for all those generations to come."[83]

Moreover, Cizik believes that on the Day of Judgment, Christians will be held accountable: "When we die, God isn't going to ask us how old the Earth is or, for that matter, how it was created. He's going to ask us, What did you do with what I created?"[84] If they have failed to fulfill their stewardship responsibility, he said, "There will be an account to pay."

Revelation 11:18 addresses this accountability with gravity: "The nations were angry; and your wrath has come. The time has come for judging the dead, and for rewarding your servants, the prophets, and your saints and those who reverence your name, both small and great—and for destroying those who destroy the Earth." For many climate care leaders, that last phrase bears paramount significance. They read the book of Revelation as a transformation of creation rather than its replacement and thus view it as a call to a different mode of engagement in the here and now. The eschatological vision they share does not imply an escape from earthly duties but rather a deeper meaning of human responsibility for creation given this cosmological context and the sweep of the biblical drama.

Green in Spirit

Divine Direction and Hope: "My Hope Comes from Him" (Psalms 62:5)

Scripture gives leaders a sense that they are fulfilling a God-given job—the commission or mandate issued to the first human beings. But beyond biblical commands, many leaders sense being called or told by God to become involved in creation care or approach climate advocacy in a particular way. Sleeth said succinctly, "I get my marching orders from God."[85] Ball expressed that God directed him to begin his creation care career in conventional environmentalism: "I just felt the Lord was saying to me, 'Your path is to go into this secular environmental world and, you know, learn that.'" Similarly, Robinson told me divine guidance shifted his advocacy focus to the specific issue of sustainability: "About a year ago, I felt the Lord told me. He said, 'Make the shift and really start talking a lot about sustainability because that's the key to people's hearts and it makes sense to people.'"[86] Cizik finds ongoing encouragement and a feeling of rectitude in divine direction.[87] "We're going to be doing what we believe God calls us to do," he said. "We believe he has called us in this fashion, to say and say again what we've said. We're going to continue to do that, without apology." According to Michael Lindsay, this legitimating narrative is common among evangelical elites across a range of fields, framing their efforts with explicitly religious language and pointing to the greater meaning those efforts hold for them.[88]

A sense of guidance from and partnership with God, along with the other theological underpinnings of their advocacy, offers these leaders a deep source of hope. Jo Anne Lyon finds sustaining hope in "the power of the Holy Spirit."[89] She explained, "You keep seeing it move and you know that you're doing God's work." Interweaving eschatology, Dan Boone noted, "the thing that undergirds all of this is a radical hope that when humans have done our worst, there is still the theology of resurrection, that God has one more move to make beyond any death dealing thing we can do and somehow will make all things new."[90]

Others articulated the power of God to effect change when human beings seem utterly impotent—an immensely important source of hope when working on problems as intractable as climate change. Discussing pessimism about the issue, Ball said:

> Even if, God forbid, there are some really horrific things that happen, the Lord is the Lord, and as much as I fight for creating a better world, this is penultimate. And we are called to be faithful in this life, but there is going to be God's future. That's not an excuse for inactivity. It's actually the prod to activity, properly understood, but at the same time we are not bereft of hope. We have another hope. We have a hope that we will be with the Lord.[91]

Similarly, Duane Litfin articulated a theological foundation for pushing forward in light of the uncertain outcomes of climate care advocacy.[92] "Whether or not whatever we do succeeds in stopping global warming—I don't know if it will or won't—it's still what we ought to be doing. [Are we] really going to make any difference in global warming?" he wondered. "I have to say I don't know. But it's still worth doing as Christians. We should be doing this." For them, the work in and of itself is good, even if worldly outcomes fail to match aims. They are not called to success but to faithfulness.[93]

Faithful Distinction: "Worship the Lord Your God and Serve Him Only" (Luke 4:8)

For Scott Sabin, this hope is the distinguishing factor between faith-based efforts to address climate change and those of secular environmentalism.[94] "I mean, we could all just be too late," he admitted. "And that's when I have to turn to my faith and remind myself that God's in control. I think that's an area where we, as evangelicals, have something to offer because if you get too buried in the science and too buried in predictions, there's only two options, denial or despair—unless we have the hope."

Leaders sense that theological elements differentiate their work from that of conventional environmentalists, including creation care's human emphasis and the way in which it is a religious act, a means of honoring God. In contrast, a number of them described secular environmentalism as simply "self-preservation" and "pragmatic." John Phelan expressed that creation care adds another dimension to advocacy efforts.[95] "[While] the outcome may look the same," he said, "one person does it out of enlightened self-interest, and the other does it out of self-interest *and* out of a desire to love God and serve God's purposes in the world. So it becomes an act of worship, an act of service of God as well as something that's active, enlightened self-interest." Creation care goes beyond stopping harmful activities; it engages people in furthering Christ's reconciliation of all things to God.

Given the theological dimensions of their work, most leaders prefer the language and label of "creation care" or "steward" to "environmentalism" or "environmentalist." Because their relationship with God is at stake, creation care has immense repercussions for their identity. For them, this advocacy is not just about changing the world but also about living out their deepest beliefs. Even in small acts, as Paul Corts told me, climate care advocates express "who I am" and "what I believe."[96] So the judgments of other people matter little, as the definitive appraisal will take place when they stand before their maker.

Ultimately, then, the leaders' ends are not environmental or human centered; instead, they are religious. As Ball put it, becoming "climate-friendly transformation champions" is a "spiritual goal."[97] For them, a deep and power-ful link exists between being faithful and caring for creation or, as Matthew Sleeth's book title suggests, between serving God and saving the planet. In this evangelical context, *save* is laden with multiple meanings. Through acts of creation care, the Earth can be literally rescued from environmental crisis and protected as a natural resource. It can also be redeemed as a holistic cre-ation, in the more transcendent sense of salvation. Sleeth personifies the link between these two possibilities, as he concurrently converted to Christianity and became a committed environmental advocate. For him, the two identities are profoundly interwoven.

Thus, while the ECI network may function as an advocacy coalition, that description is an incomplete account. Given their ultimate motivation, these leaders are not just linked by their words and deeds but also by the faith that underlies their actions and their shared religious identity. Religion forms a powerful glue among climate care advocates, which Corts identified when he labeled his fellow signatories "kindred spirits."[98] Their evangelical faith engen-ders connection and cooperation, a "swirl of relationship," as Robinson deemed it, and a deep sense of community among these "allies and comrades."[99]

While relationships, faith, and story lines cement climate care leaders and fuel their advocacy, the same things have also provoked a backlash from the evangelical Right. A more conservative faction of evangelical leaders dispute the theology, politics, ethics, and collaborative strategies of the cli-mate care coalition. They see a newer brand of moderate, environmentally inclined evangelicalism as the disconcerting threat—not a warming planet. Additionally, whether those unifying beliefs, precepts, and narratives can extend to and envelop churchgoers remains equally unclear. So while climate care receives broad backing, its network of supporters represents only a por-tion of American evangelicalism. The ability of leaders to stand firm against their opposition and woo converts is decisive for its future development and expansion.

Negotiating Climate Care's Opposition

EACH SEPTEMBER, JUST as the summer heat and humidity breaks, the Family Research Council hosts its annual Values Voter Summit in Washington, DC. It is the preeminent event for conservative Christians and Republicans, boasting such sponsors as the right wing Heritage Foundation and Jerry Falwell's Liberty University. With a smorgasbord of high-profile presenters, from pundits Ann Coulter and Bill O'Reilly to politicos Newt Gingrich and Mike Huckabee, the summit puts the relationship between the evangelical Right and the political Right on patent display.

The speaker roster for 2009 included Calvin Beisner, spokesperson for the Cornwall Alliance for the Stewardship of Creation. If climate care can be said to have a primary opponent, Beisner is it. As his breakout session approached, summit attendees packed into a room at the historic Omni Shoreham Hotel, pushing aside chairs to create more space.[1] The billing promised a provocative talk: "Global Warming Hysteria: The New Face of the 'Pro-Death' Movement." The program declared, "Ultimately, climate change hysteria rests on an unbiblical view of God, mankind, and the environment. Come and hear how the Cornwall Alliance is pushing back...against the hype. Learn why policies to fight alleged man-made global warming will instead cause hundreds of millions of premature deaths throughout this century, and how human liberty, responsibility, and flourishing are the key to a healthier environment."[2]

Calvin Beisner's presentation is but one instance of the opposition evangelical climate advocacy faces from more conservative members of the community. Each development—of creation care generally and of climate care specifically—has sparked further backlash from the evangelical Right: competing campaigns, opposing groups, and efforts to unseat leaders. But what drives this opposition? Though, on the surface, it appears to be grounded in a skeptical view of climate science and mitigation, the conflicts that orbit this

particular issue actually extend far beyond the greenhouse effect and emissions reduction. Sustained attention to the tensions between the evangelical
Right and climate care advocates, as well as to the developments of organized
climate change skepticism, suggest this backlash is partially a denial of the
fact of climate change. At a deeper level, however, the debate is emblematic
of broader contests between the moderate and conservative wings of evangelicalism; the more extended forces of economics, politics, and ethics are
ultimately at work. Climate care leaders fall on a distinct side of the debates
about the appropriate role of government, the profits and perils of political
alliances, and religion's proper ethical orientation and place in the public
sphere. As the billing for Beisner's Values Voter presentation indicates, for
both camps, something larger is at stake.

Conservative Backlash

Growing Resistance: "The Assembly Gathered in Opposition" (Numbers 16:42)

Throughout creation care's history and owing to its successes, the movement
has endured attacks from the evangelical Right, often led by Beisner and
with support from politically conservative actors and organizations. When
the EEN sought signatories for the creation care declaration in the early
1990s, Beisner assailed the document in *World*, a conservative evangelical
periodical.[3] The Acton Institute, a conservative think tank, subsequently
published his book, *Where Garden Meets Wilderness* (1997), as well as other
attacks on Christian environmental efforts, which were distributed to congregations and individuals across the country.[4] Together, Beisner and Acton
founded the Interfaith Council for Environmental Stewardship (ICES) as a
competing organization—specifically with an eye to evangelical creation care
but using an interfaith slant to contest the NRPE and faith-based environmentalism generally.

The founding document of the ICES was the "Cornwall Declaration on
Environmental Stewardship," and its release in 2000 was a pivotal event in this
backlash.[5] Authored by Beisner and Acton staff, the document distilled arguments put forth in *Where Garden Meets Wilderness* and functioned as a belated
retort to the 1994 creation care declaration Beisner had vehemently criticized.
While the "Cornwall Declaration" recognizes "the moral necessity of ecological stewardship," it endorses free markets as the solution to environmental problems, rather than government action, and emphasizes human beings' unique

capacity to manage and "enrich" creation. Crucially, it deems a number of issues to be trumped up and unfounded, climate change among them.

Alongside conservative Catholic and Jewish leaders, key powerbrokers of the evangelical Right lent their support to Beisner's initiative. Notable signers include Chuck Colson, founder of Prison Fellowship Ministries, Focus on the Family's James Dobson, and the late televangelist D. James Kennedy. Aiming to raise the profile of creation care's conservative detractors, Beisner and a group of advisors formed another group, the Interfaith Stewardship Alliance, in 2005. Two years later, they rebranded the organization the Cornwall Alliance for the Stewardship of Creation to better reflect the guiding document of their coalition. (Hereafter, I refer to this group simply as the Cornwall Alliance.)

Tensions were long set between Beisner's camp and that of climate care, so leading up to the launch of the ECI in early 2006, its organizers tried vigilantly to maintain secrecy. Despite best attempts, word of the "Call to Action" spread beyond the original signatories. Among those who caught wind of the impending debut: the Cornwall leaders, who were particularly riled by Richard Cizik's central role in the burgeoning coalition. Attempting to undermine the ECI, they swiftly exerted pressure on him via the NAE board of directors—a pressure Cizik registered. To their satisfaction, though Cizik's name appeared as an original signatory, he removed it shortly thereafter.

Cizik explained to me that the decision was a strategic choice rather than a coerced act.[6] "I took my name off the ECI in the spring of 2006, not because I didn't agree with the contentions of the document," he clarified, "but because I understood tactically it would be helpful." Focused on enlarging the climate care coalition, Cizik hoped he could "reach out to those who [weren't] yet persuaded" and be a "broker" between believers in climate change and others more skeptical. Though this rationale may have seemed ambiguous to onlookers, one thing was clear: The Cornwall efforts kept the ground between these camps thorny and made their divergence impossible to ignore.

Absent Cizik's signature, the ECI went ahead nonetheless. In part because of eighty-six high-profile supporters, it made headlines across the country. "God's Green Soldiers." "And on the Eighth Day, God Went Green." "Strange Bedfellows—evangelical Christians, Fortune 500 execs, and environmentalists band together to curb global warming."[7] Incited by this public attention, the Cornwall leaders redoubled their response, this time more concretely.

In July 2006, Beisner and Kennedy, as well as Barrett Duke of the ERLC, Family Research Council president Tony Perkins, and others, penned an open letter to the ECI signatories and anyone else "concerned about global warming."[8] "Whether or not global warming is largely natural," they wrote: "(1) human efforts to stop it are largely futile; (2) whatever efforts we undertake to stem our small contributions to it would needlessly divert resources from much more beneficial uses; and (3) adaptation strategies for whatever slight warming does occur are much more sensible than costly but futile prevention strategies." Instead, they proposed, "it is far wiser to promote economic growth, partly through keeping energy inexpensive, than to fight against potential global warming and thus slow economic growth."

In concert with this letter, the group endorsed a document markedly different from the "Call to Action" and clearly intended to challenge it. "A Call to Truth, Prudence, and Protection of the Poor: An Evangelical Response to Global Warming" lays out their full counterargument to climate care.[9] Again spearheaded by Beisner, one of the text's four authors was noted climate-contrarian scientist Roy Spencer of the University of Alabama, Huntsville.

As with initial efforts to thwart the "Call to Action," this general opposition to the ECI again evolved into focused opposition to Cizik. As the NAE executive continued to utilize his prominent platform and press for evangelical action on climate change, Dobson retaliated on his daily radio show. "Evangelicals taking on the issue of environment will divide evangelicalism and destroy the US economy," he railed.[10]

Yet even as hostility mounted, Cizik decided to recommit his name to the growing list of ECI signatories, appearing in the second printing of the "Call to Action." He also began working with an unlikely partner, Eric Chivian of the Center for Health and the Global Environment at Harvard Medical School. The two sought to bridge a longtime gap between evangelical leaders and secular scientists and to facilitate partnerships between these camps, long suspect of each other. From the Cornwall perspective, such acts only made Cizik a more suspicious, disconcerting character.

In 2007, Dobson, Perkins, and twenty-three other leaders of the evangelical Right took a more aggressive step and wrote a widely distributed letter to the NAE board of directors—though many of them were not themselves members of the association. The missive asserted that Cizik's "relentless campaign" on climate change was attempting to "shift the emphasis away from the great moral issues of our time," defined as abortion, homosexuality, and abstinence. Moreover, the group claimed, Cizik's advocacy was "dividing and demoralizing the NAE and its leaders."[11] They called on the trustees to censure him:

We implore [you] to ensure that Mr. Cizik faithfully represents the policies and commitments of the organization, including its defense of traditional values. If he cannot be trusted to articulate the views of American evangelicals on environmental issues, then we respectfully suggest that he be encouraged to resign his position with the NAE.

The board, however, did not fulfill the request of this conservative faction. Instead, at its March 2007 meeting in Eden Prairie, Minnesota, the NAE reaffirmed "For the Health of the Nation," thereby asserting its independence from the evangelical Right, supporting Cizik, and keeping creation care on the evangelical issue agenda.[12]

Playing Politics: "With One Mind They Plot Together; They Form an Alliance Against You" (Psalms 83:5)

While Cornwall's staunch opposition to climate care is unmistakable, its drivers often remain nebulous. Observers contend four main factors are at work: theology, science, economics, and policy.[13] First, though Cornwall leaders may employ the language of stewardship, they maintain a theology of dominion, emphasizing "rule" and "subdue" (Gen. 1:28) rather than "tend" and "keep" (Gen. 2:15). Additionally, they frequently defer to God's sovereignty over such affairs as climate change and thereby displace human responsibility.[14] Second, Beisner and his collaborators distrust mainstream climate science. Rejecting the consensus reports of the Intergovernmental Panel on Climate Change, they argue that change is due to "natural causes." We should expect moderate rather than catastrophic effects, they underscore, claiming some will be beneficial.[15] Third, given this scientific assessment, the Cornwall leaders suggest that reducing greenhouse gas emissions would have an "insignificant impact" on climate change while inflicting vast economic damage. They advocate for free markets, unhampered by government regulation, to promote economic growth they allege would benefit the poor and finance adaptation to any "natural" climate change.[16] Fourth, tied to their economic viewpoint, this group rejects regulatory solutions, especially any measures international in scope.

These pro–free market, antiregulation stances suggest a particular ideology is at work. These two elements—"staunch commitment to free markets and disdain of governmental regulation"—define "the conservative political ideology that is almost universally shared by the climate change denial community."[17] In conjunction with leaders' concerns that climate care is "dividing" the evangelical community and Beisner's presentation at the Values Voter Summit, the ultimate driver of Cornwall's opposition crystallizes: politics. For three decades, the evangelical Right fostered a dynamic partnership with the Republican Party that increased the power of both. Leaders successfully purported themselves as speaking for American evangelicalism in its entirety, wielding the weight of that constituency. But the divisive issue of climate change threatens to expose American evangelicalism's true heterogeneity. In addition to challenging a foundational political ideology, it could burst the evangelical Right's inflated public influence, destabilize its conservative alliance, and irreparably undermine its political power.

In 2008 the Cornwall Alliance and the Acton Institute collaborated with two evangelical Right organizations, the ERLC and the Family Research Council, to extend their resistance to climate care efforts. Together, they launched the We Get It! campaign. "We face important environmental challenges," the We Get It! declaration concedes, "but must be cautious of claims that our planet is in peril from speculative dangers like manmade global warming."[18] In addition to attempting to impeach the science of climate change, it again positions mitigation and poverty alleviation as antithetical: "With billions suffering in poverty, environmental policies must not further oppress the world's poor by denying them basic needs. Instead, we must help people fulfill their God-given potential as producers and stewards." Alongside religious leaders, notable conservative political figures also gave their support, including Senator James Inhofe, the Oklahoma Republican who once dubbed climate change "the greatest hoax ever perpetrated on the American people."[19]

Most recently, the Cornwall Alliance has worked with another conservative think tank, the Heritage Foundation, on a new initiative called Resisting the Green Dragon (RGD). According to RGD's website, "Without doubt, one of the greatest threats to society and the church today is the multifaceted environmentalist movement."[20] The response? A twelve-part DVD series aimed at educating evangelical churchgoers. In the series' trailer, Beiser and James Tonkowich of the Institute for Religion and Democracy—a conservative Christian think tank where Beisner is an adjunct fellow—cast Christianity and environmentalism as incompatible. They decry the "false doctrines" of the environmental "worldview" and the green movement's ultimate quest for power, supposedly control of the economy and the population. Images of the Eye of Sauron underscore this perceived danger, linking environmentalism with the principal villain in J. R. R. Tolkien's *The Lord of the Rings*. Other visuals imply connections to the contentious issue of abortion. Citing James 4:7, RGD's assessment of environmentalism and a concomitant call to Christians are manifest: "Submit therefore to God. Resist the devil and he will flee from you."[21]

The RGD initiative points to even deeper ties between Cornwall and the conservative political machine.[22] The Cornwall Alliance falls under an umbrella nonprofit called the James Partnership, run by Republican operative Chris Rogers.[23] Those two groups and Rogers's PR firm, CDR Communications, share a Virginia address to which the RGD website is also registered. Among its clients, CDR Communications claims a suite of evangelical Right organizations—Dobson's Focus on the Family, Colson's Prison Fellowship Ministries, Kennedy's Coral Ridge Ministries, Perkin's Family Research Council—as well as the Council for National Policy, a secretive forum for conservative activists founded by Tim LaHaye.[24] Rogers also collaborates closely with David Rothbard, president of the Committee for a Constructive Tomorrow (CFACT). Established by conservative philanthropist Richard Mellon Scaife, the Washington, DC–based CFACT actively works to discredit climate science and mitigation strategies. The think tank has been called one of the "particularly crucial elements of the denial machine," responsible for funneling extractive industry wealth to contrarian scientists and oppositional front groups.[25] In addition to common funding sources that link these organizations, Beisner serves on CFACT's board of advisers.[26] Thus, though he provides Cornwall's public face and voice, Rogers and Rothbard appear to provide critical leadership behind the scenes, and financial backing appears tied to the corporations and family foundations that fuel climate skepticism, the undisclosed links to conservative politics briefly made public at the Values Voter Summit.

Of course, political maneuvering in the name of religion is nothing new in American public life. The connections between Beisner, Rogers, and Rothbard, and to actors and organizations of the evangelical Right and the conservative political machine, simply indicate this collaboration continues in the climate care backlash. It is what gives the resistance legs. Are power, politics, and the promotion of conservative political ideology the Cornwall leaders' true interests? Perhaps. Or they may simply be capitalizing on political alliances to further their own religious cause. In any case, this particular installment of evangelical Right–Republican collaboration has established a definite opposition. Cornwall's efforts function as a foil to evangelical climate care and fuel the contested space surrounding the issue in the evangelical community.

Leadership Shifts

Under Fire: "But They…Despised His Words"
(2 Chronicles 36:16)

As Cizik persisted with climate care advocacy, his notoriety grew. He and Eric Chivian organized a weeklong trip to Alaska for five scientists and five evangelical leaders, to see firsthand the impacts of climate change. The Arctic expedition provided fodder for a PBS documentary, and Chivian and Cizik's novel collaboration compelled *Time* magazine to name them among the top 100 most influential people of 2008.[27] That same year, Terry Gross invited Cizik on National Public Radio's *Fresh Air*, in part to discuss his passion for integrating environmental concern into the evangelical agenda and the ensuing resistance of the evangelical old guard.

During the December 2 interview, Gross posed a pointed question: "Are you waiting for some of the evangelical leaders who have opposed you on issues like your concern about the environment and climate change, are you waiting for them to retire and leave the stage?"[28] "I'm not waiting," Cizik replied assuredly. "I would want Jim Dobson to join us because this is about creation care. It's what the Bible teaches. It's godly, it is right. So I'm not waiting for him to leave the scene at all. I want him to join us. In other words, I'm always looking, Terry, for allies, not adversaries. Always allies."

But the interview did not win Cizik any additional friends or collaborators. It ultimately only made his adversaries more determined, supplied them further ammunition, and brought others to their ranks. In his conversation with Gross, Cizik insinuated that he voted for Barack Obama, despite the president's support for abortion rights, and suggested government should supply contraception. He also admitted his opinion was "shifting" on gay marriage and willingly shared his support for civil unions. NAE members—both leaders and laity—responded critically. They could not brook this combination of stances nor the way Cizik flagrantly stepped outside his role as representative and spokesperson. Under pressure, Cizik tendered his resignation three days later.[29]

According to NAE president Leith Anderson, "His credibility as spokesperson for the NAE was irreparably compromised."[30] But Anderson was explicit when speaking with *Christianity Today* that Cizik's comments on the environment were not the cause for his departure. Though Cizik was discharged, the NAE maintained support for creation care.[31]

Lingering Uncertainties: "What Is to Come?"
(Ecclesiastes 8:7)

This abrupt and unexpected series of events was a blow for climate care. Cizik had been the ECI's most active high-profile signatory and the most vocal and influential evangelical climate advocate on Capitol Hill.

After two years of rapid growth, climate care's future suddenly seemed uncertain.

Following his resignation, Cizik went offline for some five months and retreated from public view. After this indeterminate period of quiescence, he reemerged in April 2009 to give the fifth annual Snowdon Lecture, "Hearing Each Other, Healing the Earth," at the Interfaith Conference of Metropolitan Washington.[32] Along with Chivian and Hunter, he then participated in a briefing at the US Senate on November 17, 2009, to make the case that "scientists and evangelicals share concerns about climate change."[33] As he gradually reentered the public eye, rumors started to circulate that Cizik was "making plans for a new evangelical organization [to] address issues 'as broad as God's concerns are broad.' "[34] Then, in early 2010, Cizik, David Gushee, and evangelical pastor and filmmaker, Steven Martin, officially launched the New Evangelical Partnership for the Common Good (NEP).[35] Among the core issues of concern for the new nonprofit? Climate care.

Clearly, then, Cizik has no intentions of abdicating his advocacy work in Washington, DC, or of retreating from the issue of climate change. Freed of spokesperson responsibilities and constraints, he might be able to do so more passionately. At the same time, however, his clout among evangelicals without the NAE's organizational weight remains unclear. Though he was often well out in front of the NAE's constituency, Cizik is now primarily a prominent individual without clear followers. To what degree can his charismatic leadership and authority continue without them? No doubt the nascent NEP will be significant for the future of climate care, but exactly what role it will play remains unclear.

Despite Anderson's assurances, questions also persist about if and how creation care will feature in the NAE's ongoing efforts without Cizik there to drive the issue. Given this uncertainty, a number of climate care leaders are working to ensure environmental issues remain central. Following the interview and subsequent departure, they sent a letter to Anderson commending Cizik's advocacy of "a broad, whole-gospel agenda," including "protecting God's creation," and urged that this broad vision should "remain an enduring contribution to the evangelical public witness in America."[36]

The NAE has since selected Galen Carey, formerly with the association's aid and development arm, World Relief, to replace Cizik.[37] Creation care has not been a central part of Carey's work in the past, and he does not seem to share Cizik's zeal for the issue—a discrepancy Anderson has addressed. "Creation care is Richard's passion and area of expertise," the NAE president observed. "It should not be perceived that less visibility for the NAE on creation care is less concern. However, in all probability, there's not going to be the level of visibility that Richard has had and will continue to have."[38] The days of popular documentaries and magazine profiles were over.

Nonetheless, Pastor Ken Wilson reported that the NAE has started a creation care task force meant to play an advisory role for the organization in support of stewardship issues.[39] But, he qualified, it will also "back off…full-bore advocacy" in the interest of developing a "real movement." At present, Wilson suggested, creation care is primarily leader driven: "We've got a sharp tip to the spear but no shaft." If and how the NAE will attempt to develop this shaft, and with what degree of zeal, remain to be seen. While creation care will likely stay solidly on the NAE's agenda, though perhaps at a lower tier, retaining climate change as a central focus is improbable without Cizik at the helm of governmental affairs.

Breaking Away, Building Anew

The title of Cizik and Gushee's new organization—the New Evangelical Partnership for the Common Good—points to climate care leaders' markedly different styles and modes of engagement. In contrast to the evangelical Right, the outlook of evangelical climate advocates is broader. Geographically, they see beyond solely American concerns and domestic politics. Topically, they care beyond a narrowly construed Christian agenda. Theirs is a wider conception of moral community and moral concern, with less partisan identification—what theologian Peter Heltzel deems "prophetic politics."[40] In this dynamic moment for American evangelicalism, then, the efforts of climate care leaders feed into a divergent trajectory of evangelical engagement in the public sphere. As they activate their theology, they embrace, embody, and extend a new kind of evangelical politics, partnering with some unexpected allies in the process.

Pious Politics: "No One Can Serve Two Masters" (Matthew 6:24)

Though the evangelical Right has not traditionally displayed the willingness to collaborate that Cizik and others have, it has maintained a key alliance with the Republican Party since the late 1970s. Many climate care leaders spoke frankly to me about their desire to break away from both the evangelical old guard and its political collaborator, the GOP. This alliance, they fear, impairs their capacity to be politically efficacious and to fulfill Christian obligations.

"We cannot be prophetic to any administration if we're in bed with them," Jo Anne Lyon explained with religious overtones.[41] "And we were really in bed with the Bush Administration. And Bush before that and Reagan before that." Cizik commented that his number one objective is to follow Christ.[42] "Number two," he went on, "lead the evangelicals in a way that is more independent from either political party, in order to be in a position to challenge both. If we truly become a community whose votes are up for grabs, from a political point of view, that makes us all the more influential, not less." The ability to speak as visionary contrarians is paramount.

Other leaders lamented the way in which American evangelicalism lost itself in the religious-political alliance. John Phelan called it a "very unfortunate wedding" that resulted in evangelicals being "used by people who did not have their interests at heart and did not have the interests of the world at heart."[43] Brian McLaren, a prominent evangelical pastor and public intellectual, articulated the situation even more forcefully.[44] American evangelicalism has been marked, he said, by a "mindset of not messing with the powers that be…the sign of a domesticated religion that knows who butters its bread and won't bite the hand that feeds it." To his mind, a political alliance trumped religious purpose, and Christian responsibility was subordinated to party politics. A trend in the past, climate care leaders do not accept it for the future.

Consequently, many of the signatories reject partisanship in and a political approach to their work. Rather than being "subject to every political whim," Cizik insisted evangelicals must follow Christ rather than politics.[45] Matthew Sleeth urged that theirs should be a "moral role" in the public sphere as opposed to a "political" one.[46] Tri Robinson called his advocacy approach "biblical" rather than political.[47] They believe such a tack will be more persuasive, more effective, and, most importantly, more righteous. By decoupling evangelicalism from politics and by taking a less antagonistic approach, they hope to advance unity. "I try to be as magnanimous as possible to those who disagree with me," Cizik explained.[48] In his effort to build allies rather than adversaries, he uses a "non-argumentative, winsome approach." "In the long run," he said, "I want everybody on board." Hence, long-term strategic thinking aligns with an approach perceived as more "biblical."

This shift away from the GOP should not, however, be understood as a move toward the Democratic Party. As Peter Heltzel and sociologist Robin Rogers argue, this "retreat from the Republican Party is better understood as a retreat from party politics rather than Republican politics."[49] Similarly, because leaders' priorities do not align with the conventional liberal-conservative binary, Michael Lindsay terms this shifting trend "political bivocality."[50] Increasingly, priorities, partnerships, and advocacy often cross party lines. We may see more evangelical-Democratic cooperation than in decades past, but it will not become the new norm.

In concert with the changing style of their approach, creation care leaders also speak of a desire to expand the evangelical Right's narrow agenda. They seek to move beyond the trifecta of personal morality issues—pornography, abortion, and same-sex marriage—embracing instead what Lyon called a "public morality."[51] In their eyes, climate care is one among a number of connected social justice issues—part of an integrated agenda—and many leaders sense that their manifold engagements pursue a single purpose.

Robinson's RE:FORM initiative is, perhaps, the best example of this integration. Based out of his Boise, Idaho, church, the ministry has seven focus areas: (1) poor health and disease, (2) environmental decline, (3) world hunger, (4) human injustice, (5) illiteracy and lack of education, (6) immoral and corrupt leadership, and (7) confusion and spiritual deadness. Because, as Robinson sees it, all of these issues are linked in "the ministry of Jesus" and "the heart of God," RE:FORM seeks to bring together "the body of Christ" and disparate efforts to tackle them.[52] The spiritual, social, economic, and environmental are all of a piece in this enlarged Christian perspective.

Ultimately, by breaking down the stereotypes and boundaries of what is and is not evangelical, climate care advocates hope to renew the moral standing of the church and increase its credibility in a world that questions it, and rightly so, some said. On climate change specifically and social justice more generally, Cizik alleged, "The very integrity of the witness of the church is at stake."[53] Elaborating on the importance of these issues, Duane Litfin said, "I think one of my motives is the awareness that the more we move in this direction, the more faithful to the Lord we are, the more contribution we will make, the more credibility we will have."[54] He worries about evangelicals' current "lack of moral credibility in society." "We have no voice," he told me, "a voice that isn't heard, that's dismissed, that's seen just as moralistic." Thus, climate care leaders are interested in the particular issue of climate change, but with their new politics they also hope to promote broader change within American evangelicalism and, through it, the world.

Forging Alliances: "Two Are Better Than One"
(Ecclesiastes 4:9)

For most evangelical elites, commitment to their theologically conservative faith and commitment to engagement in the world beyond their subculture are coterminous—a tendency Christian Smith calls "engaged orthodoxy."[55] Building on that approach to public engagement, climate care leaders demonstrate what Lindsay calls an "elastic orthodoxy."[56] Simply put, "in order to engage pluralistic society, evangelicals have learned the importance of forming alliances and working with others."[57] Elastic orthodoxy allows evangelicals to engage in supple coalition building and "to retain its core principles but still change with the times"—the adaptability that makes it "a durable faith."[58]

Reflecting trends within the community, collaboration is becoming routine for many climate care leaders, as with Cizik's work on the 1998 International Religious Freedom Act and the genocide in Darfur. They extend this general approach in their climate advocacy. A number of leaders expressed to me their willingness to work with people with whom they may disagree theologically or politically to achieve a common purpose. For them, the strategy of alliance building starkly contrasts the evangelical Right's method of identifying and defeating an enemy, often unilaterally. The "new and growing way of doing things," Joel Hunter explained, "is building coalitions of people who can agree on issues along a spectrum."[59] These collaborators need not see eye to eye on all issues, but they can work together constructively on mutual areas of concern, in the interest of the common good. "We can work with groups that we haven't usually worked with before because they help us in the expression of the gospel we want to spread," Hunter added.

This megachurch pastor finds a great source of hope here. "There's just this wonderful, wonderful shift that isn't about compromising what we believe," Hunter told me. "It's about cooperating in order to achieve what we believe. And climate change is one of *the* issues that is, I think, at the forefront of enabling different groups to work together for a common interest, for the good of all people." Cizik, too, articulated the value of collaboration that "allows us to retain our authenticity and our uniqueness and the voice that we have," while also advancing the issue of ameliorating climate change.[60] David Gushee called it simply "coming out of the ghetto."[61]

To bolster their efforts, climate care leaders have built a variety of alliances. Through groups such as the NRPE, they work with leaders from other religious communities. Jim Ball deemed this interfaith collaboration a new ecumenical approach of "walking together separately, so that each group reaches out to its own community based on its own beliefs and values."[62] That is, the coalition adheres on "common action interests" without "denying each others' particularities" of doctrine and belief.

Climate care leaders have also worked with evangelicals from the secular environmental world. The ECI, for instance, periodically collaborates with

Larry Schweiger, president and CEO of the National Wildlife Federation, who addressed the Sandy Cove gathering and has been an important ally. That said, formal partnerships with environmental groups have been relatively few, as these leaders attempt to establish separate, faith-based ownership of the issues, in distinction to the conventional environmental movement.

As collaboration with Sir John evidences, partnerships with scientists, even those who do not profess belief in God, are not uncommon. Evangelicals and Scientists United to Protect Creation and the Friendship Collaborative are two such examples.[63] Both born of the Melhana Plantation gathering and influenced by the overtures of Pulitzer Prize–winning biologist E. O. Wilson, they evidence fruitful alliances between secular scientists and evangelical pastors.[64] The first initiative draws on a shared sense of moral obligation and the respective expertise of each group—scientific and theological—for a unified effort to "protect creation." Eric Chivian has been the key science partner, but ESUPC enjoys the support of numerous scientific luminaries, all of whom agreed at Melhana to refer to the Earth as "the creation" because they recognize that tackling global environmental problems will require a spiritual and cultural transformation.[65] (See Appendix F for "An Urgent Call to Action," jointly authored by these scientists and evangelical leaders.)

The Friendship Collaborative grew out of the affable relationship that Ken Wilson and marine ecologist Carl Safina share. "We just hit it off at the retreat," Wilson told me.[66] "Afterward I read his book and said, 'Carl, you're a flaming mystic!' And he said, 'What are you talking about?'" Wilson went on to quote sections of the book in which Safina describes mystical experiences out on the ocean. "I'm saying, 'Dude, I have that when I pray, you know? We've got something in common here,'" Wilson recalled. The two decided to try to replicate their experience at the Georgia retreat in a smaller format they could take to college campuses. The aptly named Friendship Collaborative aims to engender conversation across traditional divides and break down silos of concern. Wilson, Safina, and their partners do so through structured workshops, at times conducting this bridge-building dialogue onstage to illustrate genial, fruitful discussion others might emulate.

Finally, climate care advocates have quietly partnered with secular organizations to finance their work. For example, the ECI's funders have included the Energy Foundation, the Pew Charitable Trusts, and the Rockefeller Brothers Fund. Though not faith-based, these foundations help evangelical leaders advance what they see as religious work. Ball explained, "Anytime anybody wants to give me money to talk about what Jesus said we ought to be doing and the lordship of Christ, I'll take it."[67] For him, the ends of the work rather than its funding sources carry weight. These alliances, however, have not infrequently generated criticism, for the foundations' nonclimate objectives do not always align with other evangelical priorities. Differing stances on abortion are particularly charged.[68]

Regardless of criticisms, strategic and discursive alliance building has been and will remain a key practice among climate care leaders. At the same time, they will continue to assert distinct identity and values. While the trends outlined here point to the presence and possibility of coalition building, they also suggest the limitations of such partnerships. Leaders will continue "breaking down walls" to further climate care, but they will not transgress fundamental matters of belief to do so.

Harkening Back, Moving Forward

Climate change, then, is a critical piece of the new evangelical politics emerging in American public life. Gushee argues that it is central to the battle for the evangelical Center or, put differently, for the heart and soul of American evangelicalism.[69] But this battle goes beyond politics. The fissure between climate care leaders and the evangelical Right, in terms of issues as well as approaches, is ultimately tied to a deeper ethical shift. In light of contemporary challenges, climate care leaders look back to the history of evangelicalism to develop a vision for moving forward. In doing so, they weave together moral relics with contemporary perspectives, yielding a (re)new(ed) ethics that encompasses climate care.

Critical Reorientation: "Making Amends for Sin"
(Proverbs 14:9)

American evangelicals' engagement in public life has ebbed and flowed through the decades. These shifts have often revolved around a longtime tension in the community, between personal salvation and social justice—between what Peter Heltzel calls "the poles of rugged individualism and social transformation."[70] This core tension emerges again here, swirling around climate change, and leaders look to historical figures and movements for guidance as to how best to negotiate it.

For many climate care advocates I spoke with, abolitionism is at the center of this historical reflection. A number of leaders pointed to two key evangelicals whose work and thought influences them: John Wesley (1703–1791) and fellow British abolitionist William Wilberforce (1759–1833). In their eyes, both men illustrate the powerful link between Christian faith and zeal for social reform, and the movement they led highlights religion's role in advancing the common good. (For those whose denominations are part of the Holiness movement, including the Wesleyan Church and the Church of the Nazarene, Wesley's concept of social holiness as a complement to personal holiness is particularly important.)

Looking to American history, climate care leaders draw inspiration and guidance from their nineteenth-century heritage—the heyday of evangelical social reform efforts on issues including women's suffrage, prison reform, child labor, and abolition—and from its grandchild of the mid-twentieth century, neoevangelicalism. Again, Cizik and Gushee's *New* Evangelical Partnership echoes this latter link. Contemporary leaders explicitly hearken back to bygone eras of evangelical engagement in the public sphere and the link between soul and society they evidence. These historical models represent the kinds of movements they want to be part of, the kinds of leaders they want to be.

In addition to reviving positive models of social change, some leaders expressed a desire to redress the failings of white evangelicalism during the American civil rights era. Speaking on the topic of racism, Ball explained, "I have personal shame because…everything that I love about my faith I was taught by people who didn't do anything on this issue that's such a key issue."[71] That shame makes him all the more convicted in his creation care advocacy. "I want some evangelicals to be on the right side of [climate change]," he shared, wishing he had had more progressive leaders to look up to as a young believer. "I think hopefully there'll be some people to point to for younger evangelicals today, but in the future as well." In 2006, Ted Haggard, then president of the National Association of Evangelicals, said something similar: "The environmental crisis is the new civil rights issue of our day."[72] Because of evangelicals' negligence and even hostility on civil rights, Haggard committed himself to a different path (though one he was unable to pursue before his presidency came to an abrupt end). For these leaders, the challenge of climate change fits into the larger arc of the American evangelical story, past, present, and future. Climate care offers a chance to redeem historical inaction or injustice and to engender hope and further endeavors in the future, a chance to be better Christians.

These comments signal a more substantial shift, from a lens focused on the individual to one that encompasses the communal and systemic as well. Jo Anne Lyon pointed out the reality of "institutional" or "systemic evil," which must be addressed.[73] Similarly, John Phelan emphasized that "injustices are rooted in particular systems of society or politics."[74] Brian McLaren expressed a parallel sentiment: Justice requires that "you deal with the systemic issues that throw people into misery."[75] These are the more intractable elements of sin.

"If you hang out on the individualistic end of [evangelicalism]," Steve Timmermans told me at Trinity, "then the solutions that you strive for are individual solutions. We can change people's behavior, perhaps. And those are all good. But you have to be on the other end of the continuum too. How do we change the structures, you know? It's a both-and."[76] Moreover, he noted, these structures do not lie outside the bounds of Christ's redemptive power. "In all things, Christ rules. The structures, these things that we have created—economic structures and political structures and the like—those too need to hear the call of renewal and redemption." In other words, the tension between personal salvation and social justice is a false one. The two are intimately connected.

Here, leaders' fundamental reorientation is evident. Their evangelical vision has recalibrated from the purely vertical—gazing from Earth to heaven—to include the horizontal, taking in the here and now. Moreover, as Robinson put it, while they once focused on the self, they are becoming increasingly "other-centered."[77] Beyond specific advocacy work on climate change or poverty or human trafficking, they hope to imbue evangelicalism with this steady gaze on the globe and its inhabitants—to render it a worldly religion.

Matter Matters: "Dust of the Ground... Breath of Life" (Genesis 2:7)

In his work on the early history of Christianity, biblical scholar John Dominic Crossan identifies "a profound fault-line in Western consciousness" that is instructive here.[78] Two sensibilities, he argues, function within the Christian tradition: *sarcophobia* and *sarcophilia*. The first suggests a dualism of flesh against spirit, emphasizing the spirit's transcendence over the body and the flesh's irrelevance to the soul. Sarcophilia, in contrast, indicates a monism of enfleshed or embodied spirit. That is, spirit and flesh are inextricably linked with no conflict between the two. Each sensibility, and the spectrum that runs between them, impacts the believer's perception of and relation to the material world. Sarcophobia denies the importance of the earthly, leading to a disconnect from reality; sarcophilia, on the other hand, affirms the world, emphasizing one's fundamental relation to it.

Today, climate care leaders are negotiating this very fault line. Their periodic mentions of Martin Luther King Jr. suggest how they are doing so. On April 12, 1963, eight white Alabama clergymen sent a statement to King, rebuking his civil rights advocacy as "unwise and untimely." Merely one instance of white evangelicals' relentless criticism, the correspondence made its way to King within the iron confines of the Birmingham city jail.[79] He crafted a reply on April 16—a striking articulation of a sarcophilic perspective, a scathing rebuke of a sarcophobic one.

In this "Letter from Birmingham Jail," King criticizes the white church for its shortcomings and shortsightedness on civil rights.[80] Too many Christian leaders, he writes, "have been more cautious than courageous and have remained silent behind the anesthetizing security of stained-glass windows." King goes on:

> In the midst of blatant injustices inflicted upon the Negro, I have watched white churchmen stand on the sideline and mouth pious irrelevancies and sanctimonious trivialities. In the midst of a mighty struggle to rid our nation of racial and economic injustice, I have heard many ministers say: "Those are social issues, with which the gospel has no real concern." And I have watched many churches commit themselves to a completely otherworldly religion which makes a strange, unbiblical distinction between body and soul, between the sacred and the secular.

This distinction and its vertical, heavenward orientation lead to a fixation on personal salvation and to extreme individualism, allowing Christians to distinguish between personal religiosity and social ethics.

But, for King, there is an absolute connection between social and religious life. Believers' relationships with other human beings are utterly, inextricably connected to their relationships with God. "We are caught in an inescapable network of mutuality," he explains, "tied in a single garment of destiny." When confronted with injustice, then, Christians must not remain silent behind stained glass windows but become "co-workers with God." In King's eyes, the former response would be blasphemy, for the just act is the ethical act is the religious act. Redemption is reciprocally linked with social change. Using sarcophilic analysis to address the moral failings of a sarcophobic mode of thinking and being, King makes clear that there is no dualism of flesh and spirit but rather a deep and abiding unity.[81]

Sharing King's critique of the white church during that era and hoping to forge another course, climate care leaders are also reevaluating sarcophobic versus sarcophilic sensibilities and resisting spirit-flesh dualism—a reevaluation that resonates with their views on justice, eschatology, and social sin. Though rarely addressed overtly, allusions to these notions ran throughout their comments. They are under consideration though perhaps unsettled. In this sense, then, leaders are engaged as much in a hermeneutical struggle—a battle of interpretation to set out a biblically based evangelical social ethic—as they are in a struggle to ameliorate climate change. "[T]he judgment of God is upon the church as never before," King warned in 1963. "If today's church does not recapture the sacrificial spirit of the early church, it will lose its authenticity, forfeit the loyalty of millions, and be dismissed as an irrelevant social club with no meaning for the twentieth century." His counsel rings poignantly true for climate care advocates today. In their sarcophilic, here-and-now approach, neighbor and creation matter, undeniably and transcendently.

Beyond Leadership

Ultimately, climate care is but one piece of a larger shift moderate leaders are fueling within American evangelicalism away from the evangelical Right to a broader, more inclusive agenda, greater, more varied collaboration, and (re)new(ed) social ethics. As David Gushee puts it, "few contemporary moral/policy issues offer a more trenchant demarcation of the left/center versus right boundary line in American evangelical Christianity."[82] The contours of broader debates between the two camps shape realities on the ground for climate care advocates.

Significantly, though, most of them do not see a backlash from the evangelical Right as the major difficulty they face. They perceive the opposition's influence to be waning, both on this particular issue and in American evangelicalism more generally. A number of prominent evangelical Right leaders have converted on the reality and severity of climate change, even if they have not subscribed fully to climate care. In fact, in 2006, Pat Robertson declared himself a climate change "convert" on *The 700 Club*.[83] In 2008, he appeared in advertisements with liberal Baptist minister and civil rights activist, Al Sharpton, for Al Gore's Alliance for Climate Protection.[84] Conservative pastor Harry Jackson Jr. attended Cizik's and Chivian's expedition to Alaska in 2007. Having observed the effects of climate change firsthand, Jackson subsequently included a chapter on "The Environment and Global Warming" in his book, *Personal Faith, Public Policy*, coauthored with Tony Perkins.[85]

What, then, do climate care leaders see as the major challenge? As Ken Wilson indicated to me, their advocacy is, at present, primarily limited to evangelical elites. The cause has high-profile champions but lacks common presence at the pulpit or in Sunday school classrooms. To grow a true movement that can influence both the public and policymakers, leaders need to cultivate grassroots interest and activity within local churches. Of course, engaging churchgoers on an issue that has traditionally fallen well outside the evangelical agenda is not a simple proposition, particularly given the diversity and diffusion of the conservative Christian community. Climate care faces difficult trends among laity that intersect with the backlash of Beisner and the old guard, but other challenges are marked by their own particularities, as well as unique opportunities.

5

Engaging People in the Pews

RAYMOND RANDALL IS a resident of Winter Park, Florida. A fan of Sean Hannity and Rush Limbaugh, he works as a business infrastructure consultant and worships at Northland, Joel Hunter's megachurch network outside Orlando.[1] Though a devout believer, Randall had never considered creation care to be part of his Christian responsibility. Instead, he thought of capitalism and environmentalism as antithetical and saw environmental issues as entangled in thorny scientific and political debates. Surely, concern for the environment would require that he "forsake my chosen political party; abandon my affinity for capitalism; scoff at the cable news channel and AM radio talk show hosts I've enjoyed for years; [and] endure the ridicule of my Christian friends who think I've gone off the deep end."[2] That was before God nudged him to recognize his neglected duty. According to Randall, in 2005 and 2006, he was divinely urged to become a steward of creation.

After engaging sustainability issues in his corporate consulting work and attending a viewing of *The Great Warming* documentary at Northland, in which Richard Cizik features prominently, he found himself with new perspectives and enjoying the transformation.[3] Randall now sees creation care as "another way I can love my neighbors," a means to "initiate dialogues and relationships with people" who might not share an evangelical orientation, and "a responsibility for all Christians" rather than "an option or something for fanatics."[4] He heads Northland's Creation Care Task Force, overseeing a comprehensive environmental audit of the church's vast campus, a creation care expo attended by some 2,500 members of the congregation, and C3, a creation care conference cosponsored by the NAE and the Environmental Protection Agency, among other initiatives.[5] Under Randall's once unlikely leadership, the Task Force is weaving creation care into the fabric of Northland's megachurch community.

Those concerned with issues of sustainability may find this story hope-ful, speaking to the possibility of hearing God's call to care for creation and changing minds and hearts in the process. Yet the question begs: How rep-resentative is Raymond Randall of his fellow churchgoers? Are leaders like Joel Hunter reaching the evangelical public with any success? Is climate care garnering a following among this large body of believers? The answers shed light on the life of climate care beyond leaders' engagement and the dynamics involved in building grassroots support.

Polls tell one part of the story.[6] They suggest evangelical public opinion on climate change echoes that of all Americans—high awareness of the issue but low concern—yet also indicate that evangelicals' belief that climate change is real, human caused, and problematic lags behind that of the public at large. Despite higher rates of skepticism, lay evangelicals are not homogenous in their perspectives, nor definitively opposed. Polls only go so far, however. They sketch an outline, while the details and causes of the opinions they record remain veiled.

To understand lay perspectives more fully, I took the Evangelical Climate Initiative's "Call to Action" and used it as the basis for small group discus-sions in evangelical churches. In a variety of congregations in the southeastern United States, I went directly to people in the pews to discover if leaders' emphasis on climate care resonates with the evangelical public or if a dis-sonance between leadership and laity persists.[7] For most churchgoers, these discussions were their first exposure to the idea of evangelical climate care, prompting a variety of responses that echo the community's diversity. At the same time, clear trends emerged, reflecting certain shared sentiments, per-spectives, and worldviews. These areas of consensus and sources of contention illuminate the evangelical public's engagement with climate change, or lack thereof.

Sharing the Good News?

Called to Care: "The Whole Assembly Agreed"
(1 Chronicles 13:4)

The congregants I spoke to generally agreed with the theological emphases of the "Call to Action"—creation care and neighbor care. They widely con-sented to and frequently endorsed the notion of a biblical call to care for the Earth. At Harvest Ministries, an urban, nondenominational church, Heather, a congregant, told me: "It's a stewardship issue—the idea of taking care of the world that God's created and entrusted us with."[8] This outgoing young woman, like most other churchgoers I met, viewed the Earth as God's creation, in line with general evangelical adherence to orthodox beliefs on the matter. For them, God is "creator and master of the world." Often employing this term *steward-ship* in conjunction with such a view, participants described a resulting responsibility not merely as something implicit in the notion of "God's world" but as something bequeathed by God himself to human beings.[9] Candace, a middle-aged, no-nonsense member of Eastgate, a large Southern Baptist church, put it simply: "God did give us a responsibility to care for the Earth." As outlined in the Genesis creation accounts, God constructed a relationship of trust and duty with his human creations, and the churchgoers I met expressed their own role within the creation as an outgrowth of this biblical narrative.

Genesis 1:28 was clearly on the minds of many: "God blessed them and said to them, 'Be fruitful and increase in number; fill the Earth and subdue it. Rule over the fish in the sea and the birds in the sky and over every living creature that moves on the ground.'" Some, like gray-haired Glenn at Highland Methodist, an evangelical mainline church, even referenced the text directly. "Genesis makes it clear that God made creation and gave us mastery over it and gave us responsibility for it," he said. "So I think we're in partnership with God. And this is based on a reading of Genesis." For Glenn and others, "mastery" does not imply freedom to exploit creation willfully but the opposite. This special role for human beings requires respect and reverential behavior, for damaging God's creation means "insulting God as the artist."

Adding texture to this understanding, at times churchgoers' comments evoked the garden imagery that runs through Genesis 2. "I think as Christians we're looking to tend and to keep what God gave us," Paul remarked during the conversation at Canaan Baptist, an independent fundamentalist church in the suburbs. "We need to be the stewards," this talkative professional continued. "We need to tend to this as we would a garden." The emphasis in this and related comments was on "tending" and "keeping" something precious, for as Genesis 2:15 states: "The Lord God took the man and put him in the Garden of Eden to work it and take care of it." Thus, the notion of God's created world, and of human beings' particular place in it, mediates lay evangelicals' conceptions of human-environment—or human-creation—relations, and for them the meaning of that relationship is explicitly biblically grounded.

Similarly, the congregants I met accepted the theological stipulation to care for the poor, expressed in the "Call to Action" as a bedrock principle of climate care. The biblical call to "love our neighbors" was a widespread notion they shared. Sam, a contemplative member of the nondenominational

Grace Fellowship, said, "The call to care for the least of these—the poor, the orphan, the wounded, and on and on and on—are very much foundational to most people's understanding of what it means to be a Christian." Referencing Matthew 25:40—"Truly I tell you, whatever you did for one of the least of these brothers and sisters of mine, you did for me"—Sam emphasized the necessity of looking after the most vulnerable as a benchmark for Christian behavior.

People regularly cited their own actions in response to this call, such as contributing time and money to "Christian organizations." "Most of my Christian life has been lived in response to the first part of it, trying to help the poor and work with the downtrodden," explained Ed, an elderly gentleman at Woodland Church of the Nazarene, in reference to the "Call to Action." As with stewardship, churchgoers recognized and even embraced these God-given commands.

Climate Gap: "A Great Chasm Has Been Set in Place" (Luke 16:26)

Despite accepting these theological precepts, few parishioners perceived that they in any way oblige Christians in regard to climate care. For the majority, a gulf remained between concepts of creation care and neighbor care, on the one hand, and a willingness to accept climate change as an issue demanding action, on the other. Some churchgoers actively rejected a link between the two.

Also a member of Woodland, Darrell told me frankly: "As Christians, we're supposed to be stewards of what God's given us. I agree completely with that. But I see climate change as a different thing." Brooke, a middle-aged woman at Hamilton Vineyard, expressed a similar sentiment about the "Call to Action":

> I feel like it was a valid argument, if you accept the first [scientific] claim. But I'm of the same thinking as Travis that I'm not sure I accept claim one. But at the same time I do think that part of claim three—that Christian moral convictions demand our response—I feel very strongly about that. I agree with that. And I agree with, you know, stewardship of the creation that's in the scripture passages.

Darrell, Brooke, and others did not dispute the biblical call to care for creation. They did, however, construct a division between it and the ECI's claim that such a call renders action on climate change a Christian responsibility. This perceived disconnect between stewardship and climate change produced a generally conflicted response to the idea of climate care.

Similarly, congregants frequently saw love of neighbor as distinct from climate change and were unwilling to apply that precept to the issue. Some saw climate care as a distraction from aiding the poor, arguing other activities could be "more meaningful and helpful." Bob, an outspoken member of True Community, a suburban Evangelical Free church, articulated this distinction vehemently:

> Does the church have a responsibility to the poor? Certainly, there's no question about that. But because of our concern for the poor should we focus more on global climate change? No! We should be focused on the poor, caring for the poor. The poor are the poor whether the earth's temperature is rising a degree or not rising a degree over the last thirty years, or if it rises another degree over the next thirty years. To speculate about hurricanes and tornado activity and tidal waves and all these things and say we've got to stop these things from hurting the poor—no, we've got to go help the poor.

As with stewardship, while neighbor care is indisputable, Bob and others resisted its application to and constructed clear distinctions between that duty and climate change.

This theology-climate gap was so strong even those few who did connect the two remained fully conscious of the gulf. On one hand, churchgoers who supported climate care hoped the link with neighbor care could be convincing. For instance, in response to the notion that the issue is not serious, Warren, another young parishioner at Harvest Ministries, rejoined:

> Well, the second page here says, no, no, it *will* be the end of the world for certain people in certain areas that live with arable farmland, that live with certain dependencies on the environment that could, in fact, shift. Maybe the land won't be covered up by an ocean, but it doesn't matter. They're still going to suffer mass consequences from it. I think that's the right way to get people to care about it more.

During our discussion at True Community, Russell commented similarly, "What I appreciate about the claim is that it moves evangelicals, as they're reading through this, from [climate change] just being an issue of light bulbs. It sort of brings you into a larger sense of a global community." For these churchgoers, climate change should be seen as a "justice issue" and given a "human face." Because concern for the poor is already a widely held, widely engaged evangelical concern, they hope it can provide a foundation to approach climate change.

On the other hand, those with a keen interest in promoting creation care were not as sure, often bemoaning the link between the "fundamental message" of stewardship and the issue of climate change. "Global warming particularly is such a politicized issue," explained Sam at Grace Fellowship. "I'm a little bit concerned that if this is the starting-off point to getting Christians engaged more broadly in environmental issues, it might turn off a lot right away because it's associated with politics and Al Gore and various other things." Aware that many of their fellow evangelicals are skeptical of the issue and that political baggage accompanies it, Sam and others saw climate change as deleterious to efforts to engender stewardship more broadly. Creation care resonates among evangelicals but has not taken hold to the same degree as neighbor care, making the link riskier.

In Absentia: "You Will Look for Me, but You Will Not Find Me" (John 7:34)

Absent from group discussions, I was surprised to find, were theological issues perceived in years past to underpin Christian "antienvironmentalism." Beginning with Lynn White in 1967, numerous scholars and practitioners have pointed to traditional readings of Genesis as a justification for environmentally damaging behavior.[10] Echoing Genesis 1:28, White argued that the biblical doctrine of human dominion over nature established the cultural context for modern-day environmental degradation. But dominion interpretations of Genesis, typically based on Genesis 1:28, did not arise in church-based discussions. None of the lay evangelicals I met referenced the text to condone environmental exploitation or to argue that human beings have a God-given right to use the Earth at will. Rather, as detailed above, they read Genesis as a call to stewardship and to care for a divinely created world.

Over the years many experts have also cited associations of environmentalism with paganism as conventional grounds for evangelical pause.[11] Conceiving of creation as made by God, evangelical theology expressly rejects any notion that creation itself is divine. Thus, in the past, conservative Christians may have perceived a number of reasons for apprehension or aversion. First, the pantheism or "nature worship" of some ecospiritual perspectives can be disconcerting. Second, the implicit reference to Greek mythology in James Lovelock's "Gaia Hypothesis" points to polytheistic underpinnings of this well-known environmental view.[12] Third, the "biospheric egalitarianism" or moral equivalency of Arne Naess's deep ecology conflicts with a Christian perspective that perceives human beings to be unique among creatures. Fourth, connections between mystical new age movements and environmentalism indicate the green movement is tied to an alternative spirituality. Once again, however, these topics did not come up during group discussions. Paganism no longer appears to be the driving concern it once was.

In addition to dominion beliefs and apprehension of paganism, a number of commentators have blamed end times theology drawn from the book of Revelation for undermining environmental concern. Premillennial dispensationalism is a particular brand of evangelical eschatology. It suggests that, in the final phase of the present historical era, worldly apocalypse will hasten a secret rapture of saved Christians from the Earth, before a seven-year tribulation and Christ's subsequent Second Coming.

Considering this theology, journalist Bill Moyers asks, "Why care about the Earth when the droughts, floods, famine, and pestilence brought on by ecological collapse are signs of the apocalypse foretold in the Bible? Why care about global climate change when you and yours will be rescued in the rapture?"[13] Fellow journalist Glenn Scherer makes a related argument:

Many Christian fundamentalists feel that concern for the future of our planet is irrelevant, because it *has* no future. They believe we are living in the End Time, when the son of God will return, the righteous will enter heaven, and sinners will be condemned to eternal hellfire. They may also believe, along with millions of other Christian fundamentalists, that environmental destruction is not only to be disregarded but actually welcomed—even hastened—as a sign of the coming Apocalypse.[14]

Scherer and Moyers, like many critics, cite dispensationalism as an obstacle, but they overstate public support for that eschatology and lack subtlety in their assessments of its effects. As John Green argues, "the notion that an imminent Judgment Day absolves people of environmental responsibility is now a 'fringe' belief."[15]

In line with Green and contradicting criticisms, the group discussions I facilitated did not turn explicitly to questions of eschatology—the end times, an impending rapture, or Christ's Second Coming. No one offered eschatological rationale as a basis for rejecting environmental concern. The only time a congregant brought up related theological issues was at Canaan Baptist, the most fundamentalist of the churches I visited, and he did so for the purpose of refuting such notions of environmental apathy. A middle-aged professional, Paul countered the suggestion that "we don't need to worry about [environmental degradation] because in the end God's going to wipe the slate clean anyway." He argued, instead, that such a view is "totally contrary to scripture and taking a few verses grossly out of context."

Scientific Skepticism

Climate Science: "Sharp Dispute and Debate" (Acts 15:2)

While the theology behind climate care was not contentious, the science of climate change proved a major focus of debate among the parishioners with whom I spoke. At least one participant in every group discussion accepted the mainstream scientific consensus on the issue. The majority, however, expressed a measure of dissent.

"I think it's important to think about [climate change] and act upon it," said Jeff, a newlywed at Harvest Ministries. Like most who concurred with the science of climate change, sharing a sense that climate change is "real" and necessitates action, he expressed his support somewhat tepidly, unprepared to defend against dissenters. Only a small handful were emphatic about climate care. "We're talking about thousands and thousands of cubic miles [of ice] disappearing," stated Ed at Woodland Nazarene. "OK, this is huge. And that's what makes it urgent." A less convinced but comparatively open-minded subset of people expressed the need to "study more" before coming to any definite conclusions.

Uncertainty and skepticism about climate change, on the other hand, often produced quite virulent responses. "A lot of us don't feel that the science is very founded," Chris explained simply during my visit to True Community. Like this recent college graduate, those highly doubtful or categorically dismissive of climate science tended to be disproportionately outspoken in the group discussions, frequently referencing climate skeptics to bolster their arguments. "I'll say it," Cody said to begin the conversation at Hamilton Vineyard. "I disagreed with the pamphlet. I have not been convinced of global warming." He explained to the group that he had "seen scientific data that stated the climate has not changed the way that they predicted it. The amount of ice that was supposed to have melted at the poles, they actually measured more than they thought was going to be there. I have not been convinced of the scientific data."[16]

Concerning causation specifically, parishioners disputed the notion that human actions, such as fossil fuel combustion and deforestation, have brought about climate change. Christy, a middle-aged woman at Highland Methodist, said, "I'm not sure that it's humans, that it's our nature that's causing all this." Rejecting anthropogenic climate change, many argued instead that longer-term "natural cycles" are responsible. "This is just an era in which we're moving toward a warmer climate," declared Clyde, an elderly member of Eastgate Baptist. "But we will go back into the ice age."

Some of the hottest disputes arose around the existence of scientific consensus on the issue of climate change and even the notion of scientific consensus itself. During our discussion at suburban Highland Methodist, Ray critiqued the "Call to Action" by saying:

> It says, "Since 1995 there's been general agreement among the scientist community most engaged with the issue that climate change is happening." An agreement by scientists—you know, scientists deal with the facts. They deal with evidence. They paint the facts. When I hear the term "an agreement" or "a consensus" with scientists, I have a hard time.

Ray and others articulated a sense that debates continue to rage with a large, even equal number of dissenters from the IPCC's consensus claims, and some cited past scientific assertions about "global cooling" to discredit present reports of warming trends.

Messengers: "Men Who Fear God, Trustworthy Men" (Exodus 18:21)

Tied to scientific skepticism, churchgoers frequently expressed a distrust of information sources. Some suggested scientists are pressured into "accepting" climate change, lest they risk excommunication from the scientific community. They questioned the financial motivation driving researchers in the quest to keep their jobs and bring in funding. "I always try to follow the money," said Dwight at Highland Methodist. "Who are the scientists? Where do they get their money? And, you know, if everything's fine, then they don't get their grant money anymore." Echoing a similar distrust to that of elite scientists, a number of people said they could not look to the "secular," "liberal," "mainstream" media for "real facts." "I think this [idea of climate change] is largely generated by the media," explained Jerry, a retiree at Canaan Baptist. He and others worry about the "bias" and "agenda" that may be at work.

Driven by a distrust of scientists and the media and a sense of uncertainty about climate change, many churchgoers desire trustworthy information imparted by trustworthy messengers. "There seem to be opposing views on everything, so I don't know who to trust," lamented James, a recent college graduate, during my visit to Eastgate Baptist. Some called for messengers of climate change in whom evangelicals specifically can have confidence. Evan, an outspoken member of Hamilton Vineyard, put it this way:

> You know, I'd like to slam dunk what [was] said earlier about trust because I think so much of this boils down to that. Out of this room very few of us have gained our opinions because we've looked at hard data. And even if we've looked at hard data, only a small percentage have learned how to interpret that hard data. And so really, you know, most of us like me are left [wondering], Who are we going to listen to? Who do we trust? And I think we go back to people who share our worldview and people who share our values.

In other words, the "hard data" of scientific information may mean something quite different when conveyed and interpreted by a fellow evangelical Christian than it would by an admitted atheist. "Facts" are not value neutral.

Not surprisingly, then, many parishioners responded positively to the list of ECI signatories as intellectually, culturally, and religiously reputable. They were swayed by climate care leaders' evangelical and scholarly credentials. Also during the conversation at Hamilton Vineyard, Chet, a talkative middle-aged man, explained:

> When I look at the people that are on this list—you've got the presidents of all these Christian colleges—*evangelical* Christian colleges. These guys aren't slouches. They're not mental midgets. They're presidents of universities. They're *committed* evangelical Christian leaders. Now while I haven't done probably the necessary research that I should, if I'm going to put my trust in some guys, you know, what they have to say is going to have a huge impact.

For Chet and others, evangelical college and university presidents were particularly convincing signatories, as were such well-known pastors as Bill Hybels of Willow Creek Community Church outside Chicago.

Nonetheless, the presence of signatories' names did not impact people unfamiliar with them or those who found them to be unqualified or too liberal—too distant from their own worldviews. At Woodland Nazarene, Pam said, "Because I'm not familiar with these individuals, that's not going to sway me." Similarly, Gerald explained to the True Community group, "They have authority, but in the realm in which they function—not in this realm." By no means did the names of climate care leaders sway skeptics, who found ways to dismiss them. For those most distrusting of climate science, the "Call to Action" read as a piece of "propaganda" or an attempt to "brainwash" readers with "fear" and "hype." Calling it "too emotional," "alarmist," "unbalanced," and "manipulative," these churchgoers perceived the text to have little to no factual credence, given its grounding in what they saw as the false science of climate change.

Evolution-Creation Debates: "Falsehood Rather Than...Truth" (Psalms 52:3)

Two underlying causes seem to drive churchgoers' doubt. First, with roots in the evolution-creation debate, a general culture of scientific skepticism exists in many evangelical circles, one culture that hangs heavy over evangelical discussions of climate change. Distrust of scientists and what David Gushee calls a "populist anti-science sentiment" transfer easily from the former issue to the latter.[17] Or, as author Andy Crouch puts it, "Thanks to the creation-evolution debate, mistrust between scientists and conservative Christians runs deep."[18]

American evangelicals debated the concept of evolution and its compatibility with the scriptural authority of Genesis throughout the twentieth century. At its outset, some evangelical thinkers reconciled the two with "theistic evolution"—God created the process of evolution as part of creation—while more theologically conservative individuals campaigned against the "godless" theory. Meanwhile, the struggle for control of American Protestantism that was occurring between fundamentalists and liberals supportive of Darwin's theory came to a head in 1925 with the famous Scopes Trial.

Though the trial's outcome was technically a victory for antievolutionists, its media coverage and public reception convinced many fundamentalists of

deep American antipathy toward them. Combined with the reactions of liberal Protestant leaders and institutions, evidencing their defection from "true"
Christian faith, the experience led fundamentalists to withdraw from mainline Protestantism, as well as segments of evangelicalism willing to accom-
modate modern science. They founded separate fundamentalist institutions
and ultimately a distinct subculture. From then on, antievolutionism was an
entrenched fundamentalist stance.

Despite some leaders' attempts to diminish it, the controversy has continued within more moderate evangelicalism, specifically around teaching
the "alternative theory" of intelligent design in public schools. Evangelicals
today hold a range of opinions on the issue, from reading the Genesis creation accounts as literary interpretations of historical events to taking them
as entirely literal.[19] These faith-science tensions grounded in the creation-
evolution debate generate a general distrust of mainstream science: The elite,
atheist scientists who support evolution are the same ones promoting the
issue of climate change. In the view of some, if they get the former so wrong,
why should evangelicals trust them on the latter? The scientific methods, processes, and institutions meant to engender reliability have "failed" on the issue
of evolution; surely they can do no better on climate change. Though the people I met did not directly make this connection, the culture of scientific skepticism shaped by these longstanding debates infused the group discussions.

Climate's Non-Problematicity: "Why Do You Worry about the Rest?" (Luke 12:26)

The second driver of scientific skepticism is less theological and more political.
Given evangelicals' tendency to identify as conservative and the historical link
between conservative theology and conservative politics in the United States,
the conservative movement's effort to construct what sociologist William
Freudenburg calls the "non-problematicity" of climate change has lingering
effect.[20] During the 1990s, key conservative actors of the antienvironmental
countermovement, particularly right-wing think tanks, mobilized to challenge the legitimacy of climate change as a social problem and redefine it as
nonproblematic.[21] A central prong of this effort was to argue that the evidence
for climate change is flimsy, even fallacious, to manufacture uncertainty.

In 2002, conservative strategist Frank Luntz sent a watershed memo to the
Republican Party that bolstered efforts to undermine the science of climate
change. Addressing the key to "winning the global warming debate," Luntz
cites voter opinion that a scientific consensus on the issue does not exist.[22] He

urges, "Should the public come to believe that the scientific issues are settled, their views about global warming will change accordingly. Therefore, *you need to continue to make the lack of scientific certainty a primary issue.*"[23] The Bush administration and Republican policymakers took up Luntz's suggestions, while conservative television and talk radio pundits echoed similar messages, helping to maintain public doubt. These efforts have contributed to division in American public perception of climate change that runs starkly along partisan lines.[24]

Leaders of climate care's opposition have partnered with a number of the actors and think tanks leading climate denialism in the United States, as well as the contrarian scientists, whose work they fund to provide a "research" foundation for their efforts. Given those connections and historical ties between conservative countermovement actors, the Republican Party, and American evangelicals, perhaps a widespread trend of scientific uncertainty among churchgoers is to be expected. Manifesting palpably in group discussions, climate skepticism reveals a central dissonance between climate care leaders and the evangelical public.

Competing Interests

Other Priorities: "Which Is the Most Important?" (Mark 12:28)

A number of congregants I met made cases for the relative importance of other "evangelical" issues or for focusing on concerns other than climate care. Occasionally, they advocated more traditional priorities such as abortion. "I don't think we as Christians are unconcerned," explained Mark, an older member of Canaan Baptist. "I just [wonder], Where are we on abortion? Where are we on some of the other major issues?" Comments like Mark's were common, reflecting widespread and relatively longstanding evangelical support for "pro life" issues, a moral and political rallying cry for the community.

At times, such concerns sparked conversation about expanding "the evangelical agenda." Some churchgoers seemed distressed that evangelicals might neglect existing responsibilities. As Suzanne posed plainly at Hamilton Vineyard, "What's more important than abortion? I mean, that's murder." Others, however, advocated for a broader issue suite. Janice voiced an alternative opinion within Hamilton's congregation: "One of the things you tend to hear evangelicals talking about is gay marriage and abortion, as if that's the only two issues that matter to Christians. But there are so many more things—you know, fair trade and environmental issues and human trafficking." As with evangelical leaders, what concerns "count"—or do not—is an active and often intergenerational debate in many churches, shaping evangelical consideration of climate change.

A number of congregants also urged evangelicals to focus on the central Christian mission to spread the "good news" and save unredeemed souls. "The greater mission is to communicate the gospel," Tim reasoned at Canaan Baptist. "That's where I think this situation misses the point." Four decades younger than Tim, James made a similar comment at Eastgate: "From an evangelical point of view, I think it would be more important to care about your evangelism." Blanche, an elderly woman, reiterated, "Our first responsibility, as Pastor Nelson pointed out this morning, is to tell [the poor] about Jesus and the salvation of their souls."

Evangelicals believe fiercely in their call to evangelism—proclaiming the gospel of Jesus Christ to facilitate conversions to Christianity. To their mind, contemporary Christians share the Great Commission given by Jesus to the disciples:

> Then Jesus came to them and said, "All authority in heaven and on Earth has been given to me. Therefore go and make disciples of all nations, baptizing them in the name of the Father and of the Son and of the Holy Spirit, and teaching them to obey everything I have commanded you. And surely I am with you always, to the very end of the age."
>
> (Matt. 28:18–20)

Thus, for some, the ultimate cosmological consequences at play render a focus on climate change, seemingly at the expense of evangelism, simply illogical.

At Canaan Baptist, Richard underlined that eternity is at risk:

> So when I was looking at the Christian moral convictions [of the "Call to Action"], I said, OK, let's say that these folks are correct and we reduce global warming. For someone in Africa or in a poorer nation, so what? We feel good, but how does that impact them? And if they don't accept Christ, they still go to hell. It's just not as warm. That makes no sense to me.

Comments like Richard's reflect a sarcophobic sensibility or spirit-flesh dualism that privileges the spiritual and otherworldly at the expense of the physical world.[25] Beneath such comments, dispensationalism may have formed a tacit undercurrent, as that eschatological persuasion suggests Christians should be singularly focused on conversion, given limited time before the rapture and tribulation.

As with other evangelical concerns, debate about the theology behind and proper methods of evangelism exists, but all evangelicals believe that converting people to Jesus Christ is an essential aspect of their Christian responsibility. Whether deeming climate change less important than other concerns or seeing it as a distraction to saving souls, parishioners who expressed these views considered the issue to be less significant than climate care leaders suggest. Climate change must compete for evangelical attention and engagement against other, far more established religious concerns.

Disengagement: "But He Wanted to Justify Himself" (Luke 10:29)

At one point or another, conversation would turn to the reasons for individuals' or society's inaction. Many churchgoers expressed uncertainty about what steps one should take to combat the problem. "It's kind of like diet books," Justin analogized at Grace Fellowship. "How do you lose weight? Well, today you do this, and then next week, you know. Red wine, yes; red wine, no. Carbs good; carbs bad. Every day there's a new story about what works and what doesn't. So it's hard to choose. You know, it's hard to judge." Hence, even when people felt "called to action" on climate care, they often espoused confusion about "the most pressing course of action."

A recurring image or symbol of this uncertainty was the compact fluorescent light bulb, with mercury risks representing the inevitably ambiguous nature of measures to reduce greenhouse gas emissions. "I think it can be frustrating," lamented Mary Anne, an older woman, also at Grace Fellowship. "One thing I'm being told would be helpful would be to change light bulbs. But then, if you don't dispose of those bulbs, there's mercury in them and that could poison." She went on, "That can get frustrating too because for everything you hear you might be able to do, you hear, well, here's this negative. And then that can make you just be pessimistic." The difficulty of knowing what to do is real, as is the demotivating nature of not knowing. Believing that proposed solutions might not really be solutions at all, Mary Anne and others were paralyzed by the complexity of the climate problem. In light of uncertainty and feeling helpless, they opt for inaction.

Other congregants resisted action on climate change because it would demand undesirable lifestyle changes or "sacrifices." "All of us are going to have to live like the poor," lamented Hal, a retiree at Highland Methodist. "They don't have SUVs; we need to get rid of them. You need to sacrifice like they have to sacrifice. And if you live like the poor, it may not be a problem. It's not causing the poor any inconvenience because they're not jumping on jet airplanes." Like Hal, some people perceived that mitigation of climate change implies antimodernity or antiproductivity that is seen as an environmentalist pipedream.

Some such comments were marked by a deep sense of fatalism. "You know," said Robert at suburban Cannon Cove Church of Christ, "you're never going to convince people in Western civilization to give up what it's going to take to go back to the horse and buggy days, to get rid of the consumption of oil. It's just not going to happen." For some, current patterns of consumption and the comforts they afford are simply too ingrained to alter. Churchgoers frequently invoked this image of horse and buggy, again echoing worries about reversing "progress."

In addition to uncertainty or concern about sacrifice, I repeatedly heard a core justification for inaction: People do not have the power to cause or to rectify climate change. Ken, a middle-aged member of Highland Methodist, noted, "It's almost arrogant to think that, well, I have more power than God almighty, that we collectively can change the climate." Travis expressed a parallel sentiment at Hamilton Vineyard: "It's almost hubris to assume that we can do a whole lot about it." For Ken, Travis, and others, affecting God's creation in such a profound way is simply beyond the bounds of human capacity, and belief in climate change implies a misplaced confidence in the power of human beings.

Instead, some lay evangelicals I met externalized responsibility for responding to climate change, displacing it as divine concern. "Let God worry about the climate," Bob said bluntly at True Community. Perhaps grounded in Calvinist theology that understands divine sovereignty to be absolute, such perspectives suggest climate change is "that which only God can do." Because God ordains all, human beings are simply relieved of any measure of accountability.

Political Divides

Agents of Change: "As Each Part Does Its Work"
(Ephesians 4:16)

As with the science of climate change, strategies to ameliorate the problem also generated a great deal of debate. Outspoken enthusiasm for the solutions proposed in the "Call to Action" was generally slim, but people's positive responses often supported the notion of different responsibilities for different actors: governments, businesses, churches, and individuals. Donald, a retiree at Cannon Cove, explained that climate change demands this variety of responses: "The government has a role to play to make this work, just like you have a role to play. Everybody's got a role to play. And we have to keep coming at it from every side." A college student at Woodland Nazarene, Tiffany supported the ECI's "call for different levels of responsibility with different levels of power." She continued, "I think that's appropriate. People who have more power have more responsibility. And that's why Americans are particularly called to this because we have so many of the resources."

A few people suggested government should have a part in climate mitigation, their responses largely grounded in a sense that individual actions are merely "a drop in the bucket," when much more significant change is required. "Is putting one light bulb in one light going to really to do that much and have that much of an effect?" Jeff wondered during our discussion at Harvest Ministries. "Maybe, but I feel like there has to be some type of governmental laws or regulation of big business to really make the change." In other words, to some extent climate change is a collective problem requiring a collective response.

Far more prominent was support for individual action as the solution. Alterations in "lifestyle," "individual initiatives," and "individual contributions" can "make a difference," people claimed. Jerry, an elderly gentleman at Canaan Baptist, spoke evocatively on the topic: "As far as an individual responsibility, you can kind of equate it to a candlelight service, where it's dark and they light one candle and that lights two. And it goes on, and finally the whole area gets lighted up. If the individual would do his part, you know, we could make a difference—a large difference." As Jerry and others expressed, individuals have enormous capacity to effect change, particularly as a "body of believers." "I think we forget that a group of people smaller than what's sitting here right now changed the course of history because of Jesus," said Courtney, a young professional at Hamilton Vineyard. With Christian history as a source of inspiration and guidance, she felt, "we should be able to make a difference."

Churchgoers sympathetic to climate care affirmed evangelical leaders' engagement with the issue, feeling "encouraged," "inspired," "excited," and "hopeful." "I think it's good that the religious leaders of the United States have come together to do this," Donald said approvingly at Cannon Cove. Some even shared a sense of pride in these leaders and personal empowerment that this evangelical voice on climate change has emerged in the public sphere—if at too late a date. A young mother at Cannon Cove, Beth "was just pleased to read a document put together by Christians that basically feel the same way I do about climate change." Janice expressed this sentiment more forcefully at Hamilton: "It's about time. A lot of times the church is kind of at the forefront of a lot of different social issues—civil rights and things like that. But you really haven't seen that so much with environmental issues, global warming in particular. And so it's good that they're focusing on just that." These parishioners were heartened to see that not only "Greenpeace people" but Christian leaders are spreading the message of climate care, and they felt the "Call to Action" "strengthened [their] convictions" and "edified [their] passion" to care about and act on climate change. For a few, then, responding to the problem *is* a responsibility of evangelicals, both in leadership positions and in church pews.

Regulation Resistance: "So If the Son Sets You Free, You Will Be Free Indeed" (John 8:36)

As with negative reactions to climate science, negative responses to proposed solutions were particularly aggressive. Congregants who expressed such perspectives generally disputed the centrality of federal policy or articulated a deep distrust of government. Greg, a young father at Cannon Cove, critiqued the "Call to Action" from this point of view:

> Right from the get-go, they talk about it: wanting as a group of evangelical Christians to shape public policy, rather than going and doing this amongst ourselves and being an example like Christ is—you know, using the Christian model of being an example to the world of power. They want to put all their energy into changing and shaping public policy to change what's here in the United States. So how did I feel about this? It's the right message and wrong conclusion.

Greg and others expressed that government is impotent at best and, in its ineptitude, regularly worsens problems it tries to address. "To ask our super inefficient government to try to come up with policies that can change something right now is a bit ridiculous," Hunter bemoaned at Hamilton Vineyard. In other words, looking to legislation and regulation for solutions is folly.

The libertarian, free market ideology that all regulation is interference and damaging to American economic interests was prevalent. As such, some churchgoers argued against climate policy of any kind, often referencing the Kyoto Protocol to make their case. Concern about the United Nations as an intrusive international organization and about China's and India's refusal to take on emissions targets and timetables further entrenched this opposition. "The cost of Kyoto is like ten trillion US dollars," Paul argued at Canaan Baptist. "All that's going to do is to reduce the parts per million of CO_2 from 655 predicted down to 602, whereas today they're in the 450 range. So you're going to do ten trillion dollars' worth of effort to reduce an imperceptible degree of greenhouse gases. Is that worth it?" He thought not. "The cost-benefit analysis doesn't take a Ph.D., a masters. I think our fourth-grade kids in school could probably come up with the answer to that. Four trillion dollars could go for a lot of other more important things."

In addition to making average Americans suffer an economic hit, some churchgoers argued, climate legislation would also negatively impact the world's poor by diverting current resources and undermining their availability in the future. Josh, a young man at True Community, told me:

> The best thing we can do for the poor given geography and everything else is to have money available for them, which is why I think it's so ironic that so much of the environmental movement seems concerned with sapping the strength from business, which is what, after all, keeps the economy strong and allows us to make the kind of money that we do and be the most prosperous nation and help the poor when they're in trouble. Most of these initiatives are taking away our ability to help the poor by sapping industry.

If climate change is indeed a problem, some advised, "technological fixes" such as nuclear power—pursued within free market structures—would be the best approach to mitigation.

A Politicized Climate: "Kingdom Divided Against Itself" (Matthew 12:25)

Skepticism about the role of government in climate mitigation and potential economic impacts again echoes the "non-problematicity" arguments of the conservative antienvironmental countermovement. In addition to undercutting the science of climate change, actors involved in this countereffort have consistently claimed that climate change policies would do more harm than good.[26] According to environmental sociologists Aaron McCright and Riley Dunlap, the conservative countermovement sees depictions of climate change as a significant problem and proposals for an international treaty to address it as "direct threats to sustained economic growth, the free market, national sovereignty, and the continued abolition of governmental regulations."[27]

Some of the same individuals and organizations that have influenced the climate debate on Capitol Hill and long blocked passage of substantive climate policy also maintain outright ties to climate care's detractors. In opposition to moderate evangelical leaders, the evangelical Right has developed what David Gushee calls an "offensive defensive," partnering with conservative think tanks and policymakers and propagating the message via conservative Christian talk radio that climate change is a liberal hoax. Though cloaked in overtly religious language, the core views of climate denialism emerge in the Cornwall arguments and others. Again, the historical connection between conservative politics and conservative Christianity and the influence of the echo chamber of conservative media were evident in group discussions, as churchgoers echoed these discourses.

Lay evangelicals' concerns about proposed solutions were further heightened by disproportionately Democratic support for mitigating climate change, to their mind suggesting it is a distinctively nonevangelical concern. During the Ronald Reagan administration (1981–1989), the years following the 1994 Republican Revolution in Congress, led by former speaker of the House Newt Gingrich, and the George W. Bush administration (2001–2009), the Republican Party's antienvironmental orientations entrenched an environmental partisan divide. As Dunlap and McCright have argued, "Nowhere is the partisan gap on environmental issues more apparent than on climate change."[28] Though polarization is particularly elite-driven, it extends to the American public, and parishioners seemed highly aware of the divide.[29]

Given this Republican-Democratic split, many of the churchgoers I met described attending to climate change as "political" and raised uncertainty about the agenda behind efforts to promote ameliorative action. At times, such suspicion went so far as to tie climate mitigation to communism or socialism. During the Hamilton Vineyard discussion, Rhonda said, "I find it honestly appalling that this issue has been co-opted by those who would use it to advance what's nothing more than a socialist agenda."

A sense of climate change as a leftist issue manifested most palpably in relation to former vice president and Nobel laureate Al Gore. Congregants often cited Gore as a negative voice, someone pushing a particular political ideology via climate change, whose personal lifestyle choices fail to reflect his proclaimed interest in the issue. At Cannon Cove, Greg expanded on this perspective in regard to environmental concerns: "I find the issues to be linked to the American infatuation with consumerism, and unfortunately Al Gore is not a good spokesperson when it comes to that. His opulence is ridiculous."

Others perceived Gore's interest in the issue as purely a moneymaking scheme, often invoking a comparison between indulgences and carbon offsets. "Part of this latest craze is that we have the idea that people are supposed to buy carbon offsets from the company that Al Gore is trying to get started," Josh said at True Community. "So it's a similar system [to Kyoto] on a domestic level in which people would pay for their sins." Pushing big government and seeking to gain financially, Gore seemed to epitomize the link between liberal politics and climate change, and perceived failures of individual behavior made him all the more worthy of criticism. His image functioned as the ultimate liberal other and a foil against which people could reject the progressive cultural trappings of environmentalism.

Constricting Scale and Structure

Locality: "Hold Me Personally Responsible"
(Genesis 43:9)

Ultimately, most churchgoers' perspectives were shaded by questions of scale, an issue woven throughout many of their comments. Congregants did not articulate structural barriers to engagement with climate change, such as inadequate public transportation or product unavailability; they focused on their own and others' personal actions, such as recycling; and they resisted systemic approaches to mitigating climate change, such as federal policy. The majority of people I met did not conceive of climate change in structural terms, and they expressed different attitudes toward both problems and solutions that are direct, immediate, small scale, or individualized and those that are indirect, distant, large scale, or structural.

This trend evidenced itself in churchgoers' emphasis on immediate issues that "clearly" require our attention (e.g., pollution), as opposed to the more remote issue of climate change. During the conversation at True Community, Chris, a college student, put it this way:

> Instead of dealing with global warming, if you dealt with strictly pollution, then you'd have something much more measurable. You can walk

into an area, you can inhale, and you can cough your lungs out and know something is wrong here. I think if it had been written such that they say, We think it's wrong, the kind of conditions people have to live in and here are ways that air quality could be improved, then you're talking about something that should have a fairly immediate effect on people.

For Chris and many others, though the "Call to Action" attends to the temporally and spatially distant issue of climate change, local and tangible environmental problems merit focus. They thought combating such indisputable environmental issues as smog should be the focus of Christian stewardship, as these problems are more amenable to individual action, and would find an emphasis on "real down, concrete, life-affecting issues" more convincing.

Similarly, churchgoers stressed "direct" actions rather than more indirect, structural ones. As their comments on neighbor care show, some urged evangelicals to help the poor directly, for instance by feeding the hungry, and described the idea that combating climate change could impact poverty issues as absurdity. "I don't buy in that I have a moral conviction [on climate change]," Rhonda explained to me at Hamilton Vineyard, "because it's a side issue from actually helping people. The conviction that I have as a Christian is to directly be involved in people's lives and basic needs of what goes on and what they do." She saw her focus on the poor as something entirely separate. "My conviction is to help people as a Christian," she said, "not based on the premise that using a different light bulb or something is going to make a difference in the Third World, but because my obligation is actually to help them *directly*." Rhonda and others emphasized intimate, interpersonal interaction with those in need as a particularly Christian approach and duty.

Connected to these notions, some parishioners expressed skepticism that individual actions could make an impact at a larger scale or in a more systemic way. Sandra, a middle-aged woman at True Community, responded to the "Call to Action" by saying:

First you're making me assume that, you know, climate change is something that can be reversed or cured, which it can't. If it's going to happen, it's going to happen. Now, do I do energy-cutting things? Yes. Am I trading in my gas guzzling van for something a little more fuel-efficient? Yes. But I can't see that doing that really has any impact on the poor. It's just my part of the puzzle in trying to be a little more responsible with the stewardship I've been given.

Again and again, I encountered this kind of preference for the individualized and small scale as opposed to the structural and large scale. For Rhonda, Sandra, and so many others, "individual responsibility" is the key but not often conceived of systemically.

Religious Toolkit: "We Live by Faith, Not by Sight" (2 Corinthians 5:7)

These perspectives on scale suggest that more embedded theological notions—though seemingly less connected with climate change than stewardship—pose challenges for climate care. Christian Smith and his colleague Michael Emerson explore evangelical perspectives on race in their book *Divided by Faith* (2000). They argue that the conceptual schemes of most white evangelicals prevent them from recognizing the structural aspects of racism in the United States, seeing it instead as a problem "of individuals and individuals only."[30] Drawing on sociologist Ann Swidler's concept of the cultural toolkit, Emerson and Smith claim that evangelicals "use their religio-cultural tools not only in directly religious contexts, but in helping them make sense of issues like race relations."[31] The resistance to systemic thinking they document is grounded in three such tools.

First, drawn from a theological understanding of free will and rooted in a tradition that stretches back almost to the Reformation, *accountable free will individualism* suggests that individuals act independently of structures and institutions with personal accountability for their own actions. Though evangelicals have hotly debated the relationship between God's sovereignty and human free will, most strongly affirm the latter. This is American individualism in the extreme, strengthened by understandings that the individual is the central site of religious experience and that individuals exercise agency over their own prospects for salvation.

Second, *relationalism* emphasizes the core importance of interpersonal relationships to evangelicalism. This tool is rooted theologically in the centrality of having an individual relationship with Jesus Christ. This intimate connection between God and believer is epitomized in the personal reception of Jesus during conversion or the process of being born again. Moreover, in this framework, sin is limited to individuals, with emphasis on how the Christian acts in his or her relationships with others.

Third, *antistructuralism* is the "inability to perceive or unwillingness to accept social structural influences."[32] To many evangelicals, such explanations are not only unhelpful but also downright wrong. This disinclination to acknowledge the role and importance of structures links directly with accountable free will individualism, which suggests structural arguments are merely an attempt to shift blame away from oneself. In addition, institutions are perceived as harmful, using "their power to undermine individualism."[33] A general acceptance of free market principles magnifies the hindrances of this cultural toolkit, so, with these factors working in concert, the evangelical subculture "tends toward high-energy but simplistic and unidimensional solutions to complex problems."[34]

Just as this influence extends beyond the bounds of religion to shape evangelicals' conceptions of race, church-based discussions suggested that it also works against a systemic understanding of the complex causes of and possible solutions to climate change. We simply cannot grasp the problem and potential strategies for its amelioration, while simultaneously rejecting structural thinking and emphasizing the individual as the sole locus of change. This focus engenders a presumption that unilevel solutions can somehow solve multilevel problems, but given its immensely structural nature, climate change cannot be solved by the behaviors of individual actors alone. Refusing to see how certain structures produce the issue of climate change, structural solutions seem counterintuitive, and that blind spot allows people to continue inadvertently participating in them.[35]

The Elusive Grass Roots

While creation care and neighbor care resonated with the churchgoers I met, they were far from the only perspectives at work. Scientific uncertainty undermined engagement with climate change, while political ideologies were strong determinants for positions on the issue. In concert with the added challenge of individualism and antistructuralism, these embedded orientations competed with the theological precepts of climate care, limiting the persuasiveness of its message.

While communicating climate care via evangelical messengers and with evocative Christian language had some success, particularly among people whose opinions on addressing climate change were favorable or moderate rather than stringently opposed, it is not a silver bullet. Given the highly charged nature of the issue, religious story lines of creation care and neighbor care could only carry people so far before being derailed by competing ones—often those of organized climate change denial, perpetuated by conservative media. Moreover, the "Call to Action" provided an impetus for people to express preformed ideas but did not create any conversion moments. Even the best messages and messengers struggle to overcome preexisting perceptions and biases.

Among laity, then, interest in climate change is nascent at best. Leaders face an uphill battle to overcome many people's skepticism or downright opposition, and a widespread climate care movement remains relatively elusive. To create such broad change within the evangelical subculture, leaders must demonstrate more clearly that engaging climate change does not mean embracing a larger progressive political platform and that evangelical theology and ethics, including creation care, are bigger than any political party. Confronting the more embedded theological challenges of individualism and antistructuralism may be more difficult, as they are far more rooted in the evangelical worldview.[36]

Nonetheless, group discussions pointed to some fertile ground. While high-level leaders have little capacity for engaging churchgoers directly, organizations on the ground do. Some parishioners spoke of church-based environmental initiatives already taking place: an "environmental stewardship ministry," a series of Wednesday evening talks titled "God Is Green," and an environmental club at a local evangelical university. These efforts suggest a beginning. Discussions also indicated that climate care has a few grassroots supporters. "If there's even the slightest chance that we might somehow have some kind of cause in this," Chet urged his fellow congregants at Hamilton Vineyard, "it's important to err to the side of grace, to err to the side of better safe than sorry."

Ultimately, climate care faces difficulty because it attempts to resonate with lay evangelicals' existing values and beliefs while simultaneously trying to change them. Striking a balance between accommodating and altering may be difficult to achieve on climate change as opposed to stewardship more generally—particularly when the issue runs up against fundamentally oppositional political ideology and theology. Given the challenges faced within the community, focusing on the issue of climate change may be strategically problematic. Even Raymond Randall, Northland's creation care guru, has said he avoids the topic "at all costs," for fear of scaring off fellow believers.[37] Because evangelicals start with scripture and then apply it to specific social or cultural issues, bolstering the biblical foundation of general creation care may need to precede specific climate advocacy.

The pressing nature of climate change might frustrate the timeline for the development of such a robust public theology, but its existence would likely strengthen any support for climate care and, in turn, prospects for a long-term movement. A wide creation care following would comprise a constituency currently lacking and without which evangelical leaders' claims may ring hollow. These strategic questions have become central concerns for climate care leaders. The emerging debates and varying approaches to tackling these challenges will shape the future of their advocacy definitively.

6

Sowing Seeds of a Movement

SCOTT SABIN CONSIDERS himself an unlikely environmentalist.[1] He developed an interest in social justice during a Spanish immersion program in Guatemala, which exposed him to Christians "living their faith on the edge" in the face of conditions he had never known. Upon returning to his hometown of San Diego, California, inspiration in tow, Sabin sought out faith-based organizations involved with poverty issues and discovered Floresta (now called Plant with Purpose), an NGO that integrates justice concerns with creation care. For the rural poor in developing countries, deforestation and poverty are often interlocked in a downward spiral—precisely what Plant with Purpose seeks to reverse through its efforts to weave together environmental restoration, economic empowerment, and spiritual inspiration. Since 1984, the group and its partners have planted more than four million trees from the coasts of Haiti to the foothills of Mount Kilimanjaro. Where does climate change fit into this focus on deforestation? Though he recognizes an important connection and is personally a signatory to the ECI, in his current role as executive director of the organization, Sabin has "fairly studiously avoided the climate conversation because that closes doors." When reaching out to potential donors, supporters, and volunteers within the evangelical community, he finds that the hot-button issue of climate change can be quite problematic.

Scott Sabin is not alone in this sentiment. In interviews, many leaders explained that climate change can be an impasse in their efforts to engage the evangelical public, as my discussions with churchgoers also showed. Because the issue often keeps those with ears from hearing, Matthew Sleeth tries to "find common ground," which opens up possibilities for dialogue between creation care advocates like himself and the uninitiated or incredulous.[2] Similarly, Dan Boone finds it easier to talk to fellow evangelicals about general environmental concern from a Christian perspective.[3] By start-ing with creation care rather than climate change, he can create spaces of agreement and consensus. "I get a whole lot further down the road before the quills go up," he said. In these leaders' experiences, the issue of climate change impedes productive dialogue and keeps people from engaging with creation care, whereas they can reach people's "hearts" with scripture and stories that resonate rather than alienate. Hence, appropriate treatment of climate change becomes a strategic challenge, and leaders' responses to it have everything to do with the future of a climate care movement.

These leaders have a grand goal: to weave creation care into the fabric of American evangelical life. In order to accomplish it, they must trans-form a primarily grasstops phenomenon into a grassroots movement. As churchgoers' opinions suggest, though creation care resonates theo-logically, it has not become a significant action item for them and often remains disconnected from a willingness to accept or address climate change. Sabin and his compatriots recognize these issues have not taken root among the evangelical public the way they have at the leadership level—at least among the evangelical Left and Center. In particular, they see local churches as crucial hubs for reaching the grass roots and are acutely attuned to challenges faced in those communities, not least of which is the divisive nature of climate change. So while they feel strongly about the importance of this issue, they also worry that pursuing it directly among the public could hinder their effectiveness as creation care advocates sowing the seeds of a movement.

But among their other target audience, American policymakers, the climate change discussion has never been more necessary, as both domestic legislation and an international treaty to succeed the Kyoto Protocol hang in the balance. In this political realm, challenges also persist. Exhibiting a signifi-cant shift from Bush era stagnation on climate policy, President Obama has voiced strong support for reducing greenhouse gas emissions and increasing renewable energy capacity and production. During his 2008 campaign, he identified energy and climate as a pressing, critical priority to tackle upon tak-ing office. To the disappointment of the environmental community, however, economic stimulus, health care, and financial reform superseded legislation to reduce America's greenhouse gas emissions, squandering much of Obama's political capital in the process.

On Capitol Hill, the House of Representatives passed the American Clean Energy and Security Act (ACES)—also known as Waxman-Markey—on June 26, 2009. It was a historic political success and a promising sign of prospects for federal climate policy. Still, only 219 representatives voted for the bill—a diluted version of the original—while 212 voted against it, many because they continue to reject the need to reduce greenhouse gas emissions. Legislative negotiating ultimately delivered the victory, as even Democrats were internally divided about ACES.[4]

Many anticipated that when the Senate took up its version of the bill, dilution would be even more extensive and deliberations even more tempestuous. Still, some held out hope. But despite bipartisan cooperation between Democrat John Kerry of Massachusetts, Independent Joe Lieberman of Connecticut, and Republican Lindsay Graham of South Carolina and despite concessions to appease Republicans and industry and interest groups, the Senate effort failed. Lacking synchronization between the senators championing the legislation, the White House, and Senate majority leader Harry Reid, when the Kerry-Lieberman bill finally came to the floor, a path to sixty votes—once tenuous at best—was unachievable.[5] When he had the opportunity, Obama did not broker passage of the kind of robust policy he advocated during his campaign. With the GOP gaining six Senate seats and sixty-four House seats and majority during the 2010 midterm elections, Capitol Hill appears unlikely to provide fertile ground for climate legislation any time soon.

Among the international community, negotiations are also strained. In December 2009, negotiators, ministers, and heads of state gathered in Copenhagen, Denmark, with a substantial objective: a new climate agreement to replace the Kyoto Protocol when it expires in 2012. By most accounts, the talks were a debacle and barely achieved the Copenhagen Accord, which countries "took note of" but did not adopt. The accord garnered a good deal of opposition from governments and civil society. It recognizes the scientific case for keeping global temperature rise below 2°C—higher than some would like—but does not delineate emissions reductions necessary to do so. Moreover, as a nonbinding agreement, it lacks legal teeth. At Copenhagen, many hopes were dashed, and the road to a treaty that commits countries to action on climate change now seems even thornier and more interminable.

Debates within the United States and negotiations among the international community reveal that the tremendously politically charged nature of climate change persists. Given these circumstances, the voices of evangelical climate advocates may never have been more important. They have a growing capacity to speak across party lines—to both liberal and conservative policymakers—and perhaps to contribute to greater bipartisan support for climate legislation, or, at the very least, to reduced opposition to it. The call to action in the policy arena is exigent. Faced with these dual challenges of engendering political will and engaging the evangelical public, climate care leaders must grapple with a difficult question: Can they do both simultaneously?

Growing Fissures

Understandably, these leaders are wrestling with the tension between what must happen at the national and international policy level to address climate change and what needs to be done among evangelical churchgoers to stimulate public engagement, particularly given the links between the two. This tension has prompted a leadership fissure to materialize. In the interest of engendering a culture of creation care in the evangelical community, one group has broken away from the ECI, arguing that the volatile issue of climate change must be set aside and a more general, palatable stewardship advocated. They respond to ongoing church goer opposition not just by emphasizing creation care and minimizing discussion of climate change but by turning away from the divisive issue completely. The remaining ECI organizers dispute this approach due to the urgency of the climate problem and the need for systemic regulatory solutions to it.

Based outside Atlanta, Georgia, Jim Jewell and Rusty Pritchard had been part of the joint advocacy team of the ECI and the EEN. Jewell handled the ECI's public relations and served as its spokesperson, while Pritchard directed national outreach for the EEN with a focus on climate change. In 2008, the two decided to split from the group and cofound a new creation care organization called Flourish, hoping to help "churches, families, and individuals... live out authentic, Christ-centered lives with a faithfulness to our stewardship mandate."[6] Jewell came to serve as the ministry's CEO and Pritchard as its president, in pursuit of the following mission: "Flourish inspires and equips churches to better love God by reviving human lives and the landscapes on which they depend."[7]

Without naming it concretely, the two had alluded to this new organization when I interviewed them in their former roles.[8] At the time, Jewell cited the need to "step back from the climate change issue and rush headlong into the church with good, strong creation care initiatives... to re-educate in ways that don't throw up barriers." Similarly, Pritchard emphasized the need for intensive "handmaiden work" that does not have a high profile but diligently cultivates "support from within evangelical churches." They were looking to amend the same issues that emerged in my discussions with churchgoers.

Finding an Ally: "My Partner and Co-Worker" (2 Corinthians 8:23)

To launch their new organization, Jewell and Pritchard partnered with a young, outgoing faith and culture writer, also based in the Atlanta area, Jonathan Merritt. Son of former Southern Baptist Convention president James Merritt, he had experienced a profound awakening to environmental consciousness a few years prior.[9] Merritt spent his undergraduate years at Liberty University, a fundamentalist Baptist institution in Lynchburg, Virginia, founded by the late Jerry Falwell. Merritt describes himself as "an enemy of the environment" during that time. "I actually took pride in exerting my freedom to destroy God's creation," he recalled candidly.

While pursuing a master's degree at Southeastern Baptist Theological Seminary in Wake Forest, North Carolina, he had a conversion experience. In class one day, Professor John Hammett's words triggered a shift: "When we destroy God's creation, which is God's revelation, it is similar to ripping a page out of the Bible." "It broke me," Merritt said, "because I remember thinking, I would never do that. *I would never tear a page out of the Bible.* I've always had such a reverence for God's word—I'm a Southern Baptist for Pete's sake." This eye-opening moment set Merritt on a path to personal lifestyle changes and subsequently to creation care advocacy in the church.

After switching to energy-saving light bulbs, forgoing bottled water, and purchasing a low-emissions vehicle, Merritt sensed a further divine calling: "I really felt like God was sort of nudging me and saying, 'What can you do in your circle of influence to make a bigger impact?'" That circle of influence was significant. Merritt drew on his "pristine evangelical lineage" and personal connections in the SBC to develop the Southern Baptist Environment and Climate Initiative (SBECI) and "A Southern Baptist Declaration on the Environment and Climate Change"—a creation care statement that includes a section on climate care.[10] (See Appendix H.) Launched on March 10, 2008, the SBECI declaration includes in its list of signatories the SBC president at that time, Johnny Hunt, and three former executives of the largest Protestant denomination in the United States–Jack Graham, Frank Page, and Merritt's father, James.[11]

Though Merritt garnered support from high-profile SBC leaders, he also experienced a great deal of resistance from what he called "the Southern Baptist machine" or the SBC's "company men." Richard Land, president of the SBC's Ethics and Religious Liberty Commission, had gotten wind of Merritt's initiative and plans to launch it at the National Press Club in Washington, DC. Merritt poignantly remembers a phone call he received from a research fellow at the politically conservative ERLC, delivering a message from Land that intended, in no uncertain terms, to stop him. "If I were to go forward," Merritt recounted, "[Land] would release the full power of the arsenal of his email contact list, sending out an email to every Southern Baptist, to everyone on his list, questioning my character and some of my professional affiliations, and force me to cancel this meeting."[12] Despite this alarming opposition, Merritt moved forward with his advocacy work, but the evangelical Right had, again, made clear its hostility to creation care efforts, particularly those incorporating climate change.

Although he included climate care in the SBECI declaration, Merritt's perspectives make him a fitting ally for Jewell and Pritchard. He, too, expressed a strong passion for engaging the evangelical public in creation care. "I don't believe real change happens at the government level," he said. You have to "change hearts and minds." Merritt also sees the local church as the key place to engender a movement, where a grass roots can be cultivated. With these shared advocacy objectives, the three embarked on a new program to realize their vision of "reviving lives and landscapes."

Flourish Conference: "And the Assembly Gathered" (Leviticus 8:4)

In May 2009, Flourish had what Merritt called its "coming out party," held at Cross Pointe Church in Duluth, Georgia.[13] Perched on 70 acres of land outside Atlanta, the church is housed in a former Boeing missile manufacturing facility, and Merritt's father serves as its senior pastor. Set within the mainstream evangelical context of a *southern* Southern Baptist church, the conference's lineup of speakers included Andy Crouch, Joel Hunter, Jo Anne Lyon, Tri Robinson, Scott Sabin, and Matthew Sleeth, among other creation care leaders. Jim Ball and Alexei Laushkin of the EEN were key attendees. So, too, were Calvin Beisner and Barrett Duke, representing the evangelical Right's opposition to climate care.

Pritchard's keynote set the event's tone and plainly captured an alternative vision to the one promoted by the ECI.[14] He began by expressing his discomfort with the label "environmentalist," given its associations with "judgmentalism, self-righteousness, finger-wagging, legalism...gloom and doom, and apocalyptic vision." Most importantly, he rejected an association with politics. "Our engagement on environmental issues doesn't need to start with politics," Pritchard insisted. "That is the thesis of this conference. That's the thesis of our new organization." To his mind, a political approach has left the church divided on environmental issues, and that division impedes efforts to spread creation care. Then Pritchard honed in on his key critique: The movement must "start somewhere other than climate politics," he said bluntly. "Nothing is more divisive."

Instead, Pritchard made a case for finding "common ground" and opening dialogue among people who may disagree on politics. His alternative vision is for Christians to discover their unique contribution to the environmental conversation, not simply to "adopt and baptize the ideological perspectives that are out in the modern world." He seeks a faith-based stewardship distinct from conventional environmentalism, a line he feels the ECI has not drawn clearly enough.

Two subsequent blog posts further clarify Pritchard's stance and, by proxy, that of Flourish. In the first, he notes, "A funny thing happened on the way to the conference."[15] As attendees filled the main room, Pritchard was struck by the audience's composition. People "from across the political spectrum" were gathering—people "who in the past tended to see each other as opponents because they hold different perspectives on global warming." This diverse, unlikely composition stirred him to confess having "fallen into the trap of thinking about environmental issues primarily through the lens of politics." While he was coordinating climate outreach for the EEN, this perspective dominated his thinking. Though Prichard does not reject climate change as an important issue now, he sees the need for unity, conversation, and spaces of agreement. With this "stronger center of gravity," his post suggests, "we'll find agreement on politics further downstream."

In a second blog entry, Pritchard boldly claims, "I'm no environmental-ist."[16] Wary of being labeled with the term, he finds it too narrow, inadequate for representing his point of view. "It smacks of single issue activism," he writes. "In truth, I care about social justice, healthy families, strong neighborhoods, walkable streets, flavorful food, sustainable ecosystems, well-treated livestock, and good theology. We need a bigger vision of what we're doing, and 'environmentalism' just doesn't cut it." For him, creation care means something much broader.

In advance of the Flourish conference, Jewell expressed similar sentiments in an email to David Neff, subsequently cited on the *Christianity Today* website.[17] "This is a conference about church ministries and personal faithfulness," Jewell wrote, "not political action and global warming." He went on to explain that Flourish would not take a public stand on climate change "because the heated rhetoric about global warming and disagreements on the role of government have paralyzed the church's consideration of deeper responsibilities to care for God's creation as a matter of Christian discipleship." His point is clear: Climate change produces deadlock. In a blog post of his own, Jewell also takes up the issue of language.[18] Like Pritchard, he dislikes the term *environmentalist,* preferring "deep green Christian" and "advocate for Christian environmental stewardship" instead. Paired with Pritchard's keynote, their comments are unambiguous: Flourish is pursuing an alternative direction.

Three key themes define this alternative path. First, Jewell and Pritchard aim to delineate between the language of conventional environmentalism and creation care. In this sense, Flourish's strategy is, at its heart, discursive. The organizers work to develop a unique lexicon and compelling story lines and to deploy them to their organization's ends. In doing so, they hope to overcome some of the challenges evident in focus group discussions and in surveys of evangelical opinion on climate change.

Second, and complementary, they aim to demarcate an advocacy approach focused on church ministries and personal faithfulness from one that emphasizes politics and policy. Jewell and Pritchard retreat from a structural approach and focus instead on cultivating individual engagement. They view such a track as essential for developing a grassroots creation care movement.

Third, and again interrelated, they see climate change as the quintessential topic of conventional environmental discourse and the archetypal issue for environmental advocacy with a primarily political thrust. It represents the exact language and approach Flourish rejects. Overall, it is abundantly clear that Jewell and Pritchard are trying to frame their advocacy and the broader creation care movement differently—and in distinction to the ECI.

Not surprisingly, when offered a brief and evidently unplanned opportunity to address the audience of the Flourish conference, Ball and Lauskin publicly defended their work. Ball described the ECI as a group of senior evangelical leaders who have resolved "to be active on the issue of climate change."[19] "We're very proud of the work we do," he stated decisively and made no apologies for their approach. Lauskin amended Ball's comments, suggesting divine justification: "Some of us are called to the policy realm."[20] Faced with tension at the conference, the ECI and EEN representatives asserted unwavering commitment, rectitude, and religious legitimation for their advocacy on climate change.

These words were supplemented by Larry Schweiger of the National Wildlife Federation—the only speaker from a secular environmental organization at the Flourish gathering. En route with Ball to one of Al Gore's advocacy trainings, he used his presentation time to make a case for the urgency of acting on climate change, rejecting the notion that it is a "liberal idea," as "those who would have us not work on this issue" have framed it. Instead, Schweiger urged that Christians must become involved in politics at this decisive moment "to get climate policy right." They ought not leave these crucial debates to others. Here, again, alignment between the ECI and conventional environmental approaches to addressing climate change was clear—as, implicitly, was Flourish's distance.

Issues Versus Ethics: "They Disagreed among Themselves" (Acts 28:25)

Clearly, then, a fissure has emerged, but how precisely can it be characterized? Recent research on US-based religious-environmental organizations draws out a helpful distinction: issues-based versus ethics-based advocacy approaches. According to researchers Angela Smith and Simone Pulver, the first tends to focus on a specific topic, placing secondary emphasis on effecting a change in values. As such, it echoes what they call "mainstream environmentalism's penchant for technocratic, legal, scientific, and policy-oriented solutions to specific issues," while neglecting the longer-term program of fomenting a public environmental ethic.[21] The second approach, on the other hand, holds that such an ethic is the necessary starting point to guide perceptions of responsibility to others and the environment and the consequent actions that need to be taken. It calls for broad changes in thought and action and views specific issues as important but ancillary concerns. This issues-based versus ethics-based distinction illuminates the fissure between the ECI and Flourish, specifically, and within strategic approaches for the evangelical creation care movement more generally.

Their public statements and interview comments clearly indicate that the leaders of both Flourish and the ECI share a sense of the theological significance of creation care. At the conference, Pritchard publicly acknowledged the influence Ball's mentorship and Christology—"that Jesus, in his death on the cross, was reconciling all things to himself"—has had on his thinking.[22]

Their words also suggest that both sides recognize the reality and importance of climate change. In his interview, Jewell noted, "time is short" and "there's a lot of urgency" on the issue.[23] Merritt included climate change in his SBECI declaration. But despite this theological and scientific agreement, these leaders deeply disagree on their advocacy approach.

The notion of Sabbath helps illuminate this disagreement. The cover of the Flourish conference program—also the inaugural issue of *Flourish* magazine—depicts a mountain scene with a pair of crossed legs, adorned in hiking attire. Just above the craggy peaks in the distance, the heading reads: "Practicing Sabbath." An article inside expands on the topic, as did Sleeth in his conference address.[24]

The Fourth Commandment entreats:

> Remember the Sabbath day by keeping it holy. Six days you shall labor and do all your work, but the seventh day is a Sabbath to the Lord your God. On it you shall not do any work, neither you, nor your son or daughter, nor your manservant or maidservant, nor your animals, nor the alien within your gates. For in six days the Lord made the heavens and the Earth, the sea, and all that is in them, but he rested on the seventh day. Therefore the Lord blessed the Sabbath day and made it holy. (Exod. 20:8–11)

In *Creation Care* magazine, Sleeth writes that this commandment— "Remember the Sabbath day by keeping it holy"—means "Don't be a run-on sentence. Don't go 24/7."[25] Or, as he put it in his Flourish talk, simply stop. In particular, Sleeth calls Christians to forgo consumerism as a Sabbath practice.

For this former emergency room doctor, contemporary reinvigoration of the Fourth Commandment has a twofold rationale: The way we live has destructive consequences for ourselves and for our planet. Embracing a day of rest, of idleness, would benefit the entirety of creation—both human and non-human. For Christians, Sabbath could be a day to tread lightly on the planet, to be better stewards, to cultivate reverence for God's world, and to appreciate the goodness of creation. The notion integrates religious practice and environmental practice, casting them as one in the same and the positive effects of embracing Sabbath as inherently multidimensional. It offers practical application of Flourish's goal to revive lives *and* landscapes, in the interest of loving and honoring God. Thus, the idea establishes a threefold interconnection of God, human beings, and the natural world, suggesting mutual betterment.

Similarly instructive is an emphasis on using creation care to grow and bring vitality to churches and to evangelize those outside the community—a topic that was prominent at the Flourish conference and addressed in the first issue of *Flourish* magazine. Describing the work of Rand Clark and the Genesis Church in Castle Rock, Colorado, Merritt writes that though it is not "a means to an evangelistic end…creation care can become a natural connecting point for believers and non-believers."[26] Likewise, Robinson spoke about the environmental stewardship ministry at his church.[27] "It has given us a voice among the unchurched in a way I could never have dreamed would be possible," he said. Because creation care allows evangelicals to cross lines, especially among younger generations, Robinson sees it as one of the "most powerful means of evangelism on [E]arth today." So in addition to showing pastors that creation care is "biblically right," the leaders of the movement also need to demonstrate that engaging the issue benefits local churches. These comments suggest that the aim of evangelical creation care, particularly as Flourish is taking it up, goes far beyond specific environmental concerns and clearly beyond an interest in climate policy. Its ultimate focus is more sweeping and more poignantly religious.

The ECI's specific focus on climate change and the central role for structural change achieved legislatively clearly contrasts Flourish's focus on broader notions of creation care and the role for individual believers, families, and churches to play. Thus, the cleft between the two is rooted in their issues-based versus ethics-based approaches and can be characterized as follows:

Table 6.1 highlights the distinctions between the ECI and Flourish, but it is not meant to overdetermine them. Certainly, overlap exists, and

Table 6.1

	ECI (issues-based)	Flourish (ethics-based)
Primary focus	Climate change	Creation care
Approach	Politically engaged	Apolitical
Primary locus of change	Structural	Individual
	Policy, systems	Hearts, minds
Key agents	Policymakers	Churchgoers
	Grass tops	Grass roots
Key institutions	Decision making, regulatory bodies	Local churches, families, neighbourhoods
Aim	Secure federal climate legislation	Embed creation care within evangelicalism
Time horizons	Primarily near-term	Primarily long-term

evangelical creation care efforts range across a full spectrum, from one pole to the other, along which organizers move as well. For example, before taking a more specialized position as executive vice president for policy and climate change, Ball previously served as president of the EEN, which has a broad creation care mission. Nonetheless, these characterizations remain useful for understanding the organizations' differences and the root causes of the fissure in leadership.

Promise or Peril?

Paired with the conditions outlined at the beginning of the chapter, this fissure also contributes to the dynamic moment currently faced by evangelical climate care—not just because Flourish is still in its infancy. In some ways, these recent events point to the movement's maturation; a growing diversity of voices and organizations mirrors the historical progression toward the diverse landscape of secular environmentalism in the United States today. But whether the changes will be a boon or a bane and to what degree the leaders will coordinate or collaborate remains as yet unclear.

Synergy or Divergence?

Evangelical leaders alone cannot a creation care movement make. Without an engaged grass roots, they are simply a group of advocates whose voices are less influential because they do not speak on behalf of constituents. A grassroots following is necessary both to shore up evangelical leaders' impact on climate politics and to exert direct influence as citizens on elected officials. But the climate challenges faced among churchgoers evidence the difficulties of speaking to and seeking to sway the evangelical public and policymakers simultaneously. In this sense, different efforts aimed at engaging the evangelical grass roots and prevailing on decision makers might be synergistic. Indeed, Angela Smith and Simone Pulver's research suggests issues-based and ethics-based approaches are ultimately complementary and essential to effecting change.[28]

While advocacy bipolarity, hinging on the fulcrum of climate change, might be strategically necessary, it also runs the risk of becoming fractured and could weaken the movement's efforts. While Flourish's approach may offer additional, currently lacking on-ramps to creation care, the movement might also lose its capacity to speak as a single voice when necessary, for instance at critical decision-making moments. That, as some experts argue, is the dynamic that has hampered the secular environmental movement.[29]

Moreover, Flourish evinces a more definitive break from conventional environmentalism than the ECI does. The paradox in its approach is that Flourish takes both a less radical stance on issues and a more radical stance in terms of fundamental social change. It also exhibits a more distinctively evangelical flavor. Given these characteristics, the organization's opportunities for partnership outside the evangelical community may be restricted. These potential impediments to collaboration within the creation care movement and without could lead to injurious divergence rather than advantageous synergy.

Present or Future?

The urgency of addressing climate change brings the issue of time horizons to the fore. Ball articulated a profound sense that humanity is "late."[30] Ameliorative efforts are far overdue. Similarly, Scott Sabin bemoaned constraints on talking about climate change in the present, suggesting that evangelical leaders will inevitably look back in coming decades and wish they had engaged more robustly.[31] As in the blog posts previously cited, Rusty Pritchard addressed this issue in his interview:

> I can assure you the next generation or just a few years down the road, [evangelical churchgoers] are going to be right there with us....I can preach on the one hand the urgency [of climate change]—and I think we have to do what we can—but I'm also pretty convinced that we're not going to get this generation of churches if we don't take a different tack as well.[32]

These leaders are trapped in a temporal quagmire pitting climate policy aims against grassroots movement goals—a conflict between immediate impact and deeper, but more distant, shifts. Climate change is an urgent issue requiring action without delay, and public support must help generate the political will to implement extensive measures in response. At the same time and paradoxically, generating necessary engagement among evangelical churchgoers could be impossible while maintaining an emphasis on climate change and regulatory solutions. Consequently, pursuing an immediate impact on policy and generating deeper but longer-term shifts conflict. For these leaders, their human agency is coming up against both biophysical and sociocultural reality, challenging what they can feasibly achieve.

Individual or Structural?

While Flourish's approach is more likely to resonate among evangelical churchgoers at present, it also risks playing into the theological individualism and antistructuralism that impede understanding of and support for action on more systemic environmental issues such as climate change. If Flourish caters to this individualism to engage churchgoers, its leaders may struggle to leverage that engagement to more structural ends in the future. An expert on social movements, sociologist David Meyer strongly criticizes such an approach: "To adopt a model that suggests that changes in individual consciousness, from the bottom up, will ultimately manage global warming by spreading word person to person is not only naïve, but ultimately counterproductive." Moreover, he argues, "Allowing the notion that individual consumer choices can substitute for substantial policy change would not only be a misdirection of resources, but also a way to produce frustration and failure."[33]

An individual approach—or one modestly extended to church communities and neighborhoods—would do little to address the current theological challenges faced among the evangelical public and might constrain the movement's long-term prospects. Flourish's tack may be able to sidestep the challenges of science, economics, and politics. To transform creation care from simply "personal responsibility"—which risks being little more than "feel-good" environmentalism—to something more widely effective, however, these leaders have to overcome the individualism and antistructuralism revealed in churchgoers' group discussions. If they lay their organizational foundations by playing into individualism, the trend may be difficult to challenge in the future; and building a "feel-good" consensus on creation care may simply mean deferring inevitable encounters—potentially clashes—with science, economics, and politics down the road. Given the importance of US climate action, denying the significance of structural, policy-based change seems disingenuous.

Aiding the Opposition?

Flourish's approach raises another key issue: Are they conceding ground to the evangelical Right's resistance to address climate change, especially through government regulation? Ken Wilson spoke to this worry, noting the strategy's inherent risk.[34] "It's a real treacherous path strategically," he explained, "because in a sense it's exactly following the path being carved out by the serious climate skeptics, like James Dobson and company. So it's kind of a yielding to this idea [that] climate change is almost off-limits."

To probe these concerns, another moment at the Flourish conference proved illuminating. An attendee of the gathering, Barrett Duke, like Ball and Laushkin, was also granted a brief opportunity to make an impromptu address. "I really like what the folks at Flourish are doing here," he said, "because they're finding common ground."[35] He noted that, regardless of audience members' stances on climate change, the group could agree on the need to care for creation. In particular, he welcomed eschewing policy questions.

Despite these comments, Duke's colleagues have not laid down their climate arms. Instead, they have continued to lobby against climate legislation, particularly Calvin Beisner, who also attended the Flourish conference, and Richard Land, the leader of Duke's own organization. During debates about the Waxman-Markey legislation, Beisner critiqued it as "a tax on the poor," while Land suggested it will put the United States "at a competitive disadvantage" globally.[36] While Duke proclaimed to embrace Flourish's apolitical approach that silences calls to ameliorate climate change, his associates have continued their overtly political course that aims to subvert mitigation efforts. This inconsistency of word and deed suggests that those opposed to evangelical climate care are happy to see part of its former leadership turn away from policy advocacy and toward the local church. For Beisner and company, the shift may mean their opposition is less formidable; by "finding common ground" Flourish may unintentionally be aiding anticlimate care efforts.

Spaces of Agreement

The leaders of the ECI, Flourish, and other evangelical creation care organizations are likely to continue working out these alternative visions and strategies for some time to come. Whether this process will result in conflict or collaboration is unclear, yet fertile ground for agreement is also evident. The issue of climate adaptation and other efforts that maintain climate change within broader creation care are possible pathways to solidarity.

Climate Adaptation: "Be Openhanded Toward Your . . . Poor and Needy" (Deuteronomy 5:11)

Evangelical attention to climate adaptation is growing. A number of evangelical leaders spoke passionately on the subject, citing it as a core concern tied intimately to neighbor care. They also suggest the idea of adaptation might productively engage other leaders and evangelical churchgoers, moving past skepticism about the anthropogenic nature of climate change and uncertainty about strategies for mitigation, while resonating with evangelicals' more established history of engagement in relief and development work.

Tri Robinson explained that, regardless of cause, the evidence that the climate is changing is compelling, and "it is killing people."[37] Noting the efforts of his church's environmental ministry to relieve victims of natural disasters in Iowa, Louisiana, and Texas, he stated plainly, "Let's not just talk about it; let's go help. And if people are going to be under water in Bangladesh, you can either deny there's a problem or you can get over there on the frontlines and do something about it. I don't care what caused it; people are getting hurt." In the face of the suffering wrought by climate impacts, Robinson believes the key question is simple: "What are we going to do about it?"

Ken Wilson similarly explained that "those evangelicals who are convinced about the science can go for the mitigation stuff," but he would like to see all evangelicals challenged to engage in adaptation.[38] He thinks a "breakthrough" could be achieved "if we actually got evangelicals to stop and say, Wait a minute. The climate is changing. It's hurting people and we're in a position to help." As he put it, this approach would be strategically savvy: "I think once you get people even acknowledging that it's a problem, that it's causing harm to people, [and] you actually live with that reality long enough and see what the problems are, then you actually *hope* that it's caused by human activity—because if it's not, we're screwed." Adaptation might be a roundabout path to accepting climate science and mitigation measures and to more extensive evangelical engagement with climate change.

Robinson and Wilson have incorporated their shared perspective into a seven-year plan of action on climate change for Vineyard churches and American evangelicalism. In November 2009, they traveled to England to launch it, alongside leaders from the world's different faith traditions. Collected in the resulting publication *Many Heavens, One Earth*, Robinson and Wilson's plan includes nine proposed initiatives.[39] (See Appendix I.) One initiative aims "to develop a strategy" in collaboration with the NAE's creation care advisory group, "to bridge the cultural divide between evangelicals who support action to mitigate human-caused climate change and evangelicals who are skeptical about climate change science." The two pastors hope they can "move beyond the partisan rhetoric surrounding climate change in order to focus American evangelicals on the fact of climate change (irrespective of cause)." In doing so, they expect "evangelicals skeptical of anthropogenic climate change could thus be mobilized to aid in adaptation efforts, especially through global missions, where evangelicals are already helping populations vulnerable to the dangers of a warming climate."[40] Robinson and Wilson use adaptation to move beyond paralyzing scientific and political disagreements about climate change to beneficial action in response.

As their seven-year plan suggests, adaptation also resonates with evangelicals' more established history of engagement in relief and development work, a tradition that continues to expand. Founded in 1978, the Association of Evangelical Relief and Development Organizations is a network of more than sixty groups working in this field that seeks "to enable its membership to effectively support the church in serving the poor and needy."[41] Two of the most influential AERDO members are World Relief, which was founded in 1944 as a relief effort of the NAE and pursues the mission of "[e]mpowering the local Church to serve the most vulnerable"; and World Vision, which was founded in 1950 and works "with the poor and oppressed to promote human transformation, seek justice, and bear witness to the good news of the Kingdom of God."[42] Like many evangelical aid organizations, these groups have an interest in both spiritual and social transformation. Sharing their holistic perspective, megachurches are increasingly engaging in this work, and individual believers experience such efforts through short-term mission trips. Relief and development helps encourage a broader "world vision" among evangelicals and represents innocuous territory within the evangelical landscape.

Emerging out of this existing network, Ball noted the recent creation of the Evangelical Collaboration for Climate Adaptation (ECCA), a coalition of relief and development groups and a direct outgrowth of the ECI.[43] The partner organizations include the Christian Reformed World Relief Committee, Floresta (now Plant with Purpose), Food for the Hungry, MAP International, World Hope, World Relief, and World Vision. Despite its relatively limited treatment in the ECI's "Call to Action," funding for adaptation assistance has been a key policy issue for the initiative and a space where many leaders indicated evangelicals can make a unique contribution.[44]

In addition to supporting the ECI's calls for mitigating greenhouse gas emissions, particularly through a cap and trade program, the ECCA lays out its "requests" for US adaptation policy, explaining:

[H]elping the poor in poor countries with adaptation is an investment in prevention that will reap huge financial, social, and security

dividends in the future. Helping with adaptation is also our responsibility, given that the poor have done the least to help cause the problem
and the US is the largest contributor to the problem, based on past and
present emissions.[45]

As with the ECI, although the ECCA frames its work with a biblical call—to
care for "the least of these" (Matt. 25:40)—it draws on mainstream science
and policy solutions in making its case. Unlike the individual signatory process used for the "Call to Action," however, entire organizations are signing on
as participants in this collaborative effort, so the institutional weight behind
it has significant potential.

All of this points to rich resources as well as burgeoning efforts for creation care leaders and other relief and development advocates to further the
cause of adaptation. Utilized effectively, adaptation as a feature of evangelical
relief and development might prove to be fertile ground for taking proactive
measures, despite the absence of an evangelical consensus on anthropogenic
climate change, and for building greater agreement around the issue. It might
prove to be a linchpin of solidarity for the movement.

Caring for Creation and Climate: "Standing Firm"
(1 Thessalonians 3:8)

The joint efforts of evangelical leaders and secular scientists also indicate
possible middle roads for moving forward. In their work with Evangelicals
and Scientists United to Protect Creation and the Friendship Collaborative,
Richard Cizik, Joel Hunter, and Ken Wilson insist on keeping climate
change as part of the creation care conversation. Speaking about both efforts,
Wilson explained, "We're committed to...raising the climate issue: putting
the science out there, countering the counterclaims and whatnot, but doing
it in a respectful, brotherly way."[46] In other words, he and his fellow leaders will stand firm on the issue but do so with civility and cordiality. They
will be steadfast in their message and advocacy but avoid inflaming their
opposition.

ESUPC's introduction to creation care for "busy pastors" includes a
three-page section on climate change. Again, it cites mainstream scientific
bodies, including the Intergovernmental Panel on Climate Change and the
Environmental Protection Agency, and highlights Sir John role as an evangelical messenger of climate science. To assuage readers' potential concerns,
the booklet notes former president George W. Bush's acknowledgment that

climate change is "a serious challenge" and reports corporate support for taking action. It also takes the time to address detractors:

> Virtually everyone agrees the Earth is warming. Those who dispute the scientific consensus tend to disagree about the degree to which human activity contributes to the warming. Because the science is complex, and the probability that human activity is the cause has been esti-mated at 90 percent, it is understandable that some in the scientific community would interpret the scientific data differently. Prudence, however, suggests that we not ignore the widespread consensus that does exist.[47]

ESUPC also adds that fossil fuel impacts on national security and public health, especially on "the most vulnerable among us, including the poor and the unborn," provide additional reasons to reduce their use. Placed in the cen-ter of the document, this treatment of climate change displays a firm com-mitment by these leaders not to shy away from the issue but to pursue it with respectful yet resolved perseverance.

Like the ESUPC booklet, the Friendship Collaborative workshops inter-weave presentations on science and theology, building dialogue between scientists and evangelicals. As these conversations develop, climate change is frequently integrated as a topic, not eschewed as too thorny an issue. Participants publicly model productive conversation about climate change—a shared concern that crosses the religion-science binary many audience mem-bers may perceive. In addition, the initiative's website includes the popular guide to the IPCC's reports, *Climate in Peril*, in its list of recommended resources.[48] The Friendship Collaborative displays an evident interest in pub-lic education on climate change.

As the work of these groups exemplifies, Cizik, Hunter, Wilson, and oth-ers are not willing to abandon the issue of climate change in order to advance creation care more generally, yet their simultaneous commitment to engaging churches is clear. They recognize the difficulties the issue may present but also realize that turning away from it would be to succumb to their opponents and to climate contrarians. Maintaining this steady but moderate pitch alongside their scientist colleagues, they hope to win over evangelical pastors and their congregants on climate change. Robinson and Wilson made a further com-mitment to this approach in their seven-year action plan for *Many Heavens, One Earth*. Their inclusion of climate change is unambiguous. They envision engagement with the issue as a core facet of the creation care movement in the coming years—a key element of its expansion beyond a group of senior leaders to become embedded in American evangelical life.

Lingering Questions

Exploring these recent debates and evolving approaches ultimately leaves us with more questions than answers. How will the fissure between ECI and Flourish leadership play out? Will an issues-based, policymakers' approach and an ethics-based, grassroots approach be beneficially synergistic or detrimentally divisive? Will middle-ground tacks that maintain climate change on the creation care agenda resonate—or not—among evangelical pastors and parishioners? Can adaptation bridge the divide? All these questions stem from the real difficulty these leaders face: To move their efforts forward they must bring the evangelical public and its pastoral leadership on board.

This dynamic moment and the questions it raises also reveal challenges that go beyond ideological debate. Church-based discussions uncovered limitations to the claims of evangelical climate care, but the issues raised here provide evidence that obstacles and conflicts go beyond ideology and communication. Evangelical climate advocates have heard the poignant questions of values and ethics posed by climate change and have successfully reframed the issue with inescapable moral and theological dimensions. Yet this communication effort has not been sufficient to build a robust movement, and for evangelical creation care at present, issues of advocacy appear to be most testing.

The ECI-Flourish fissure suggests that, though these leaders have reframed climate change with a uniquely evangelical lens, using distinctly evangelical language, they have yet to fully resolve how to pursue the issue in their own particular way. They have defined a moral framework for understanding it but continue to negotiate how that understanding translates into approaches, strategies, and tactics—the details of action. The ECI applies a lens and language different from conventional environmentalism but largely relies on the same solutions and strategies as its secular counterparts. Flourish, on the other hand, wants to change the latter as well, focusing on churches and recasting evangelical practices, while refraining from policy issues and political engagement. The discursive divergence between these two groups reflects larger fractures in their advocacy approach and ultimately in the creation care movement.

The split also raises a further question: With its issue-based approach, has the ECI fallen prey to some of the same shortcomings of secular environmentalism? Although its treatment of the ethical and theological dimensions of climate change may be compelling, the group also forwards the kind of professionalized, policy-based approaches that tend not to engender public engagement. The ECI's funding comes largely from secular foundations that support conventional environmental advocacy, a fact that is particularly pertinent here. In an extensive study of the American environmental movement, environmental sociologist Robert Brulle discovered that foundation funding often co-opts environmental groups. To receive this support, organizations professionalize their staffs, shape projects, moderate their political aims, and use conventional political tactics, all in keeping with foundations' desires. Though some of these shifts may serve groups well, the "locus of control" lies with the "financial patrons" rather than grassroots constituents, precluding more organic engagement.[49] Though the ECI's language is often uniquely evangelical, its advocacy reveals this influence, which may well detract from the initiative's ability to convey an inspiring vision and foment a thriving creation care movement among the churchgoing public.

Clearly, the ECI and Flourish leaders hold many beliefs and conceptions of the world in common. Their most fundamental theological notions—creation care, stewardship, neighbor care, and eschatology—are largely shared. Nonetheless, their approaches to interacting with and being advocates in that world differ. One would assume that these shared ideas connect to shared advocacy, so how can differences in action be accounted for? In the case of faith-based efforts, intervening, complicating, potentially conflicting ideas— secular environmentalism but also politics and economics—offer some explanation. Multiple perspectives compete and merge with one another in the realm of faith-based environmental advocacy. For example, the story line of creation care can become challenged by divergent story lines of government regulation, generating a split like that between Flourish and the ECI. Ultimately, these recent events within the creation care movement demonstrate the limitations of religion to create a unified environmental vision and course of action. As with all conversations about climate change, those rooted in religion tend to become more and more complex and fractured in the process of exchange and debate.

As in 2006, when the ECI launched its "Call to Action," today the evolution of evangelical climate advocacy and the broader creation care movement faces another key moment. Though commanding less of the media limelight, it is equally significant. New directions have emerged, but the firmness of their trajectories, much less their impacts, remains unknown. Even so, as movement leaders distill their own approaches to environmental and social change, recent debates remind observers that viewing these efforts as fundamentally concerned with addressing climate change or pursuing sustainability is a misreading. For creation care advocates, the ultimate goal is being faithful to and serving God. That connection imbues creation care with its deep significance. Outsiders to the community would be remiss to neglect this *sine qua non*, especially because it may generate tension between approaching climate change as a matter of faith and climate change as a matter of public life. In the end, as Alexei Laushkin noted, "There's still a lot left in the air, but we're definitely in a new harvest time and probably planting more seeds to grow."

Conclusion

God took the man and put him in the Garden of Eden to
work it and take care of it.

GENESIS 2:15

CLIMATE CHANGE REMAINS one of the most pressing issues facing the
global community today. Though ameliorative efforts have transpired in
fits and starts, to truly address it would require collective action on a scale
never seen before. In order to achieve that kind of extended, coordinated
engagement, we have to think of creative ways to build dynamic partnerships,
generate concerted action at individual and organizational levels, and create extensive governmental and policy change. From my perch within secular environmentalism, I began this project seeking alternative levers to shift
American political will and public engagement on climate change. The promise of evangelical climate care as one such lever is undeniable. Given American
evangelicalism's size, dominance, cultural position, moral resources, and powerful mechanisms of communication, the emerging movement has real power
to unlock solutions by bridging God and green.

This book explores that promise and charts the many ways in which
American evangelicals are engaging with climate change as a matter of both
private faith and public life. Part of the contemporary mosaic of American
evangelicalism, climate care emerged from a multifaceted historical context. Shifting trends of general evangelical engagement in the public sphere
gave way to emerging engagement with environmental issues in particular,
first through the development of ecotheology and subsequently in advocacy
efforts. Moderating events then further tapered that engagement toward climate change. In a concurrent, synergistic process, creation care inched inward
from the periphery of the evangelical agenda, while the movement's leaders
became increasingly attuned to climate change, paving the way for the ECI,
the most substantive example of climate care advocacy to date.

The gravitational core of the ECI is its "Call to Action," a manifesto that weaves typically mainstream and uniquely evangelical story lines to construct its response to the issue of climate change. It illustrates a new mode of communicating the topic, grounded in a theological and uniquely evangelical ethic. Aimed at both policymakers and the churchgoing public, the document's singular contribution lies in the way it endows that material phenomenon with meaning, rooted in biblical texts. By locating climate change within the narrative of creation and its care, originating in Genesis, the text casts evangelical Christians as agents in an unfolding drama and heightens the significance of their engagement by giving it transcendent dimensions. Herein lies climate care's most potent call to action.

The clout and credibility of the "Call to Action" stem from its list of signatories, most senior leaders from the growing evangelical Center, who speak with a significant public voice and translate the word of climate care into deed. Interpersonal witnessing and conversion experiences have been key to building a network of evangelical climate champions, attracting leaders from higher education, media and entertainment, relief and development, denominational and parachurch organizations, and churches. Though individual levels of involvement vary, leaders focus their advocacy effort across these spheres of influence and on various nodes of change, particularly evangelical colleges and universities and local pastors. In addition to a shared commitment to a particular issue, climate care advocates are united by their faith, theology, and religious identity, factors that distinguish their efforts from conventional environmentalism. At the same time, though, they demonstrate a clear willingness to engage with secular efforts and the scientific community.

Their advocacy has not gone without challenge, of course. Climate care has roused pointed opposition from the evangelical Right, making it a trenchant fault line in contemporary evangelicalism. This opposition is about more than just climate change, however. Climate care leaders embrace a new evangelical politics, with its global outlook, broader agenda, openness to collaboration, and partisan flexibility, all of which diverge from and in various ways threaten the evangelical Right—particularly the possible destabilization of its alliance with the Republican Party. These leaders also embrace a social ethics that simultaneously harkens back to key moments in evangelical history and develops a fresh vision, reorienting from a focus on the self to a focus on the other and insisting on the relevance of *this* world while maintaining hope about what is to come. Climate change reveals tensions broader than the issue itself and brings to a head deeper battles with American evangelicalism centering on economics, the role of government, and individual versus social theology and ethics. It forces a reckoning with political alliances, public-private divides, and fundamental philosophies.

This backlash has dented climate care efforts to some extent, diverting energy from other critical efforts, for the movement's real challenge is how it engages the community's grass roots. All the theological, political, and ethical elements that unite leaders and undergird their advocacy also place them out in front of their constituents—the evangelical public. While the theology of creation care and neighbor care generally resonates, on the specific matter of climate change, a gulf remains between many churchgoers and leaders engaged with climate care. Scientific skepticism, conservative political ideology, and theological individualism and antistructuralism make the issue a site of discursive struggle. Among laity, climate change is beleaguered by ongoing uncertainty, partisan political baggage, and lack of systemic thinking. Hence, leaders face significant challenges in bringing the evangelical public on board and integrating climate care into the fabric of American evangelical life.

These challenges to engaging churchgoers, along with rising exigency of action to combat climate change, confront climate care advocates with difficult questions and create tension within their ranks. While some want to maintain a focus on climate and policy, others are moving toward a strategy of avoiding that issue altogether, focusing instead on the church and more general creation care. Still others find themselves somewhere between the extremes of this divide. The climate fault line raises tensions between the near-term urgency of addressing climate change, though advocacy may be hemmed in by constituents' lack of support, and the longer-term aim to build a robust movement, which demands grassroots engagement. Therefore, the leaders face a paradox: Climate change and churchgoers may be incompatible foci, yet they both remain essential.

Ultimately, while a remarkable sea change among leaders of the Left and Center has taken place, the vigor and impact of its wake are somewhat uncertain, not least because engagement among churchgoing constituents lags and advocacy approaches remain under development. With so much hanging in the balance, this is a dynamic moment for evangelical climate care. Its lasting influence remains unsettled. What, then, is the meaning of climate care—for the issue of climate change and for American evangelicalism?

How we speak about climate change is critical, and many disparate voices contribute to the conversation. We cannot understand the discursive landscape around climate change without attending to the contributions made by religion and, in the United States, evangelicals in particular. Ignoring them leads, at best, to incomplete understanding of the dynamics at work; at worst, it furthers misconceptions of what Gregory Hitzhusen calls the erroneous "specter of biblical anti-environmentalism."[1]

Exploring the particularities of climate care—how it constructs and communicates the issue of climate change—adds texture to religion's role in these debates, illuminating its strengths and shortcomings, successes and struggles. Through the language and discourse of climate care, evangelical leaders bring their personal beliefs and values to bear on the public sphere. In particular, this faith-based communication has both pragmatic and constitutive dimensions, as language is used strategically but also, less deliberately, creates meaning for those who speak and hear it. Evangelical climate advocacy involves both rational and visceral elements.

The case of climate care also helps us account for the possibilities and limitations of religion to ameliorate climate change or to contribute to environmental sustainability more generally. As these advocates and their opponents from the evangelical Right demonstrate, religious language has progressive and conservative force. It can contribute to how the status quo is changed or how it is maintained. As Christian Smith argues, "Religion *can* help to keep everything in its place. But it can *also* turn the world upside-down."[2] Yet exploring the phenomenon of climate care reminds us that faith-based discourses do not exist in silos. Other potentially conflicting story lines may intervene; they must contend with those—both secular and religious—that may limit and thwart them. Moreover, this discursive activity is crucial to the dynamic between religious leaders and their constituents, for no one-to-one relationship exists between the two. Though they are connected, the evangelical public has its own unique stories to tell, some of which are captured here.

While the example of evangelical climate care suggests religion can produce effective communication of climate change, its contributions to our conversations on the topic go beyond that. Science helps us understand the nuts and bolts of the issue: sources of emissions, the warming they will produce, attendant climatic shifts, and impacts on the world's social and environmental systems. Yet climate change presents us with many questions that go far beyond the scope of physics and biology. What are our responsibilities to those who live outside our national borders? How should we balance the needs and wants of present and future generations? Does ecosystem health trump economic growth or vice versa? Who should bear the brunt of mitigation and adaptation costs? The policies designed to mitigate greenhouse gas emissions are also insufficient. Though they offer tools for improving energy efficiency and producing cleaner energy, they leave us struggling to build a fruitful consensus out of thorny politics, largely because these bigger questions of values and beliefs persist, simmering below the surface.

A potent ethical resource in the United States, religion can connect the *what* of climate science and policy to the *so what* of values and beliefs. It can help answer these critical questions about human life on an earth whose climate is changing—profound questions of ultimate meaning, the bread and butter of faith traditions. Bringing religion into conversation with science, economics, and policy may morph gridlocked debate into productive dialogue and effective action. I have also shown, however, that climate care extends beyond the realm of words. In particular, much of its evolution has hinged on extradiscursive factors, such as the fortuitous inclusion of Rick Warren's signature on the "Call to Action" or the institutional alliances of Richard Cizik. There are other complementary and contravening forces, bringing complexity to this phenomenon.

When considering the intersection of religion and the environment, emphasis is often placed on how religion mediates human-environment relations, functioning as a lens or matrix. When I began this research, I focused on the influence that faith and the faithful might have on climate change and the public and political will to tackle it; and throughout this book, I have shown the deeper theological issues at work, shaping the ebbs and flows of the movement and its impact. Yet environmental issues shape religion and the religious as well. Evangelicals are having an impact on climate change, but climate change is also influencing American evangelicalism, contributing to changes in its leadership, theology, ethics, alliances, and engagement in the public sphere. Thinking about religion as an agent of environmental change is too myopic. The phenomenon of climate care invites us to revisit the connections among human beings, their faith traditions, and the environments in which they live. The interactions at this nexus of believers, their systems of belief, and the material world are multidirectional and conjointly interactive.

Climate care also highlights the key role of language and discourse at this interface. While many elements of religion—beliefs, cosmologies, symbols, rituals, ethics, stories, practices, norms, structures, and institutions—shape human-environment relations, discursive aspects are particularly significant. In the case of climate care, communication plays a core role in mediating the mutual engagement of evangelicals and climate change. Leaders bring strategic and meaning-making discourses to bear on the issue, while climate change challenges, bolsters, and shifts various discourses within the community.

Because of this reciprocal relationship, exploring the language of climate care—and its detractors—offers insight not only into how evangelicals are reshaping the meaning of climate change and the politics that surround it; doing so also more broadly sheds light on the diverse, at times fractious patchwork of American evangelicalism.[3] Mike Hulme calls climate change "an idea circulating with potency" in the realm of religion.[4] By probing the meanings, beliefs, ideologies, and ethics functioning beneath the story lines of climate care, we can learn something about the evangelical actors, contexts, and vantage points producing them. Indeed, climate care leaders are using the issue—and the narratives constructed about it—to engender changes over and above greenhouse gas mitigation. Understanding their deployment of the idea illuminates those other ends. As such, secular practitioners and scientists, especially those looking to coordinate or collaborate with evangelical creation care efforts, would benefit from understanding this unique and increasingly influential perspective and area of advocacy, where alliances are feasible and where significant disagreements persist.

The centrality of meaning to climate care also invites nonevangelicals— especially climate advocates—to reconsider their own applications of meaning to the issue, the values and beliefs that undergird the ways they talk about and act on it. Though many may not see climate change as a problem with religious dimensions, the ethical questions it poses are inescapable. The increasing attention religion pays to them and its insistence on nonenvironmental dimensions of climate change serve as a reminder: We would be remiss not to do the same, lest we overlook underlying ideological drivers or conceive of climate change in a detrimentally simplistic way. The stories we tell about climate change serve "as mirrors that reveal important truths about the human condition," but we must probe those stories—including our own—to make such discoveries.[5]

Ultimately, evangelical climate advocacy challenges existing binaries in thought and action related to environmental concerns. Pervasive dichotomous thinking restricts us to such categories as liberal/conservative, secular/religious, human/environment, and material/spiritual, which limit the way we conceive of issues and our possible responses to them. But, clearly, religion and environment are not inimical, nor are scientists and evangelicals or political liberals and theological conservatives on definitively opposing sides. Synergies between them are apparent and increasingly intersect on the issue of climate change. In their advocacy, evangelical leaders are actively transgressing such boundaries, many of which limit thought and action on environmental issues. The existence of climate care invites their reconsideration, lest they limit us to half truths and half solutions.

At the outset of President Obama's tenure, the issue of climate change appeared to be gaining traction in Washington, DC—perhaps even enough traction to pass federal climate policy of some kind. I was in the thick of my research and assumed evangelicals would be one critical piece of that legislative achievement. But today, despite passage of the Waxman-Markey legislation in the House of Representatives, no regulation is in place, and the climate denial machine continues to perpetuate uncertainty. Denying climate change has emerged as a key tenet of the Tea Party platform, frequently echoed by such conservative leaders as Rush Limbaugh, Sarah Palin, and Sean Hannity. A disavowal of science is already dominating Republican discourse ahead of the 2012 elections. At the same time, many of the issue's former champions on Capitol Hill have backed away from it—most notably Lindsay Graham, Republican senator from South Carolina, who retreated from his leadership role on Senate climate legislation in late April 2010.

The claims of climate skeptics and a "bifurcated flow of conflicting information on global warming" have further politicized the issue and deepened a partisan divide over that time, among both the decision-making elite and the electorate.[6] Attacks on mainstream climate science and scientists, notably "Climategate," and the hacked emails of University of East Anglia climate researchers—appear linked to declines in public opinion about the reality and significance of climate change.[7] Traction gained seems to have slipped.

Allying with conservative efforts, climate care's opposition also persists in its endeavors to discredit climate change and faith-based efforts to address it. Intersections of the two continue to emerge periodically: Calvin Beisner appeared on Glenn Beck's Fox News program to discuss Resisting the Green Dragon; Tea Party supporters have marshaled religious language in their opposition to climate legislation and those who support it; policymakers have cited the Bible to convey their climate skepticism.[8] Efforts like Resisting the Green Dragon play directly into the partisan divide and provide another tool to chip away at public concern.

When the ECI was launched in 2006, it faced the enormous challenge of Bush administration hostility to climate science and regulation. Though no longer from the same source, that hostility remains today, testing in its diffuseness across corporations, conservative foundations, think tanks, front groups, politicians, and pundits. These many different actors, however, share a fundamental resistance. Climate change implicitly points to flaws in our current economic and political system—a system that has served them well. Climate change denialists resist acknowledging the issue and the structural problems it posits, presumably for fear they would have something to lose in addressing it.

With interests entrenched, the partisan divide deeper, and opposition redoubling, climate care's challenges are as substantial as ever, suggesting the movement continues to face a long road ahead. At the same time, these changes have increased the importance of climate care's role, for it persists as a critical lever for motivating political will and public engagement. Simultaneously, concomitant issues, notably the 2010 Deepwater Horizon oil spill and Mountain Top Removal coal mining in Appalachia, have drawn additional advocates into the creation care coalition, broadening and strengthening it.[9] Though not directly focused on climate change, their efforts generate valuable ancillary momentum. Moreover, as secular groups and other faith-based initiatives wrestle with the difficult dynamics of partisanship and skepticism, while seeking to engage disparate audiences within the American public, climate care remains an essential part of the constellation of efforts and collaboration across them vital.

Mark 11:15 portrays a scene at the Temple Mount in Jerusalem, in which Jesus arrived and, apparently outraged, began to expel the merchants engaging in commercial pursuits: "Jesus entered the temple area and began driving out those who were buying and selling there. He overturned the tables of the money changers and the benches of those selling doves." Jesus challenged what had become business as usual—politicization and commercialization of this sacred space, which benefited the privileged and preyed on the poor. His act of overturning the tables was bold, symbolically suggesting the complete rejection of this corrupt system. He sought, it appears, to reinvigorate what his religion should have been concerned with, how the faithful should have been engaging. Similarly, climate care challenges entrenched perspectives and practices perceived to be economically, morally, politically, and theologically corrupt, with the hope of installing more authentic ones in their place.

But its leaders cannot simply upend business as usual. Though the shifts they seek to precipitate may be just as bold as Jesus's in Mark 11:15, the challenges with which they contend are far more complex. Change will not be achieved in one daring move but may be made possible through a resolute, extended series of many such acts. Some will generate headlines, such as launching the "Call to Action"; most will pass unnoticed. Despite the long road ahead, climate care leaders evidence clear commitment to the cause, perseverance in their advocacy, and resolutely hopeful visions. They are dedicated to shaping American evangelicalism into the kind of faith community that would enshrine care of creation and its human community as essential concerns and obligate believers to engage threats to them, perhaps none more patent than climate change. As Joel Hunter put it, "right now…we're kind of wandering in the wilderness, but we're making it toward the Promised Land."

"On the Care of Creation: An Evangelical Declaration on the Care of Creation" (1994)

"The earth is the Lord's, and the fullness thereof"

PSALM 24:1

As followers of Jesus Christ, committed to the full authority of the Scriptures and aware of the ways we have degraded creation, we believe that biblical faith is essential to the solution of our ecological problems.

Because we worship and honor the Creator, we seek to cherish and care for the creation.

Because we have sinned, we have failed in our stewardship of creation. Therefore we repent of the way we have polluted, distorted, or destroyed so much of the Creator's work.

Because in Christ God has healed our alienation from God and extended to us the first fruits of the reconciliation of all things, we commit ourselves to working in the power of the Holy Spirit to share the Good News of Christ in word and deed, to work for the reconciliation of all people in Christ, and to extend Christ's healing to suffering creation.

Because we await the time when even the groaning creation will be restored to wholeness, we commit ourselves to work vigorously to protect and heal that creation for the honor and glory of the Creator—whom we know dimly through creation but meet fully through Scripture and in Christ. We and our children face a growing crisis in the health of the creation in which we are embedded, and through which, by God's grace, we are sustained. Yet we continue to degrade that creation.

These degradations of creation can be summed up as (1) land degradation; (2) deforestation; (3) species extinction; (4) water degradation; (5) global toxification; (6) the alteration of atmosphere; (7) human and cultural degradation.

Many of these degradations are signs that we are pressing against the finite limits God has set for creation. With continued population growth, these degradations will become more severe. Our responsibility is not only to bear and nurture children but to nurture their home on earth. We respect the institution of marriage as the way God has given to insure thoughtful procreation of children and their nurture to the glory of God.

We recognize that human poverty is both a cause and a consequence of environmental degradation.

Many concerned people, convinced that environmental problems are more spiritual than technological, are exploring the world's ideologies and religions in search of non-Christian spiritual resources for the healing of the earth. As followers of Jesus Christ, we believe that the Bible calls us to respond in four ways:

First, God calls us to confess and repent of attitudes which devalue creation, and which twist or ignore biblical revelation to support our misuse of it. Forgetting that "the Earth is the Lord's," we have often simply used creation and forgotten our responsibility to care for it.

Second, our actions and attitudes toward the Earth need to proceed from the center of our faith and be rooted in the fullness of God's revelation in Christ and the Scriptures. We resist both ideologies which would presume the Gospel has nothing to do with the care of nonhuman creation and also ideologies which would reduce the Gospel to nothing more than the care of that creation.

Third, we seek carefully to learn all that the Bible tells us about the Creator, creation, and the human task. In our life and words we declare that full good news for all creation which is still waiting "with eager longing for the revealing of the children of God" (Romans 8:19).

Fourth, we seek to understand what creation reveals about God's divinity, sustaining presence, and everlasting power, and what creation teaches us of its God-given order and the principles by which it works.

Thus we call on all those who are committed to the truth of the Gospel of Jesus Christ to affirm the following principles of biblical faith and to seek ways of living out these principles in our personal lives, our churches, and society.

The cosmos, in all its beauty, wildness, and life-giving bounty, is the work of our personal and loving Creator.

Our creating God is prior to and other than creation, yet intimately involved with it, upholding each thing in its freedom and all things in relationships of intricate complexity. God is transcendent, while lovingly sustaining each creature; and immanent, while wholly other than creation and not to be confused with it.

God the Creator is relational in very nature, revealed as three persons in One. Likewise, the creation which God intended is a symphony of individual creatures in harmonious relationship.

The Creator's concern is for all creatures. God declares all creation "good" (Genesis 1:31); promises care in a covenant with all creatures (Genesis 9:9–17); delights in creatures which have no human apparent usefulness (Job 39–41); and wills, in Christ, "to reconcile all things to himself" (Colossians 1:20).

Men, women, and children, have a unique responsibility to the Creator; at the same time we are creatures, shaped by the same processes and embedded in the same systems of physical, chemical, and biological interconnections which sustain other creatures.

Men, women, and children, created in God's image, also have a unique responsibility for creation. Our actions should both sustain creation's fruitfulness and preserve creation's powerful testimony to its Creator.

Our God-given, stewardly talents have often been warped from their intended purpose: that we know, name, keep, and delight in God's creatures; that we nourish civilization in love, creativity, and obedience to God; and that we offer creation and civilization back in praise to the Creator. We have ignored our creaturely limits and have used the earth with greed, rather than care.

The earthly result of human sin has been a perverted stewardship, a patchwork of garden and wasteland in which the waste is increasing. "There is no faithfulness, no love, no acknowledgment of God in the land....Because of this the land mourns, and all who live in it waste away" (Hosea 4:1, 3). Thus, one consequence of our misuse of the Earth is an unjust denial of God's created bounty to other human beings, both now and in the future.

God's purpose in Christ is to heal and bring to wholeness not only persons but the entire created order. "For God was pleased to have all his fullness dwell in him, and through him to reconcile to himself all things, whether things on earth or things in heaven, by making peace through his blood shed on the cross" (Colossians 1:19–20).

In Jesus Christ, believers are forgiven, transformed, and brought into God's kingdom. "If anyone is in Christ, there is a new creation" (2 Corinthians 5:17). The presence of the kingdom of God is marked not only by renewed fellowship with God, but also by renewed harmony and justice between people and by renewed harmony and justice between people and the rest of the created world. "You will go out in joy and be led forth in peace; the mountains and the hills will burst into song before you, and all the trees of the field will clap their hands" (Isaiah 55:12).

We believe that in Christ there is hope, not only for men, women, and children, but also for the rest of creation which is suffering from the consequences of human sin.

Therefore we call upon all Christians to reaffirm that all creation is God's; that God created it good; and that God is renewing it in Christ.

We encourage deeper reflection on the substantial biblical and theological teaching which speaks of God's work of redemption in terms of the renewal and completion of God's purpose in creation.

We seek a deeper reflection on the wonders of God's creation and the principles by which creation works. We also urge a careful consideration of how our corporate and individual actions respect and comply with God's ordinances for creation.

We encourage Christians to incorporate the extravagant creativity of God into their lives by increasing the nurturing role of beauty and the arts in their personal, ecclesiastical, and social patterns.

We urge individual Christians and churches to be centers of creation's care and renewal, both delighting in creation as God's gift and enjoying it as God's provision, in ways which sustain and heal the damaged fabric of the creation which God has entrusted to us.

We recall Jesus's words that our lives do not consist in the abundance of our possessions, and therefore we urge followers of Jesus to resist the allure of wastefulness and overconsumption by making personal lifestyle choices that express humility, forbearance, self-restraint, and frugality.

We call on all Christians to work for godly, just, and sustainable economies which reflect God's sovereign economy and enable men, women, and children to flourish along with all the diversity of creation. We recognize that poverty forces people to degrade creation in order to survive; therefore, we support the development of just, free economies which empower the poor and create abundance without diminishing creation's bounty.

We commit ourselves to work for responsible public policies which embody the principles of biblical stewardship of creation.

We invite Christians—individuals, congregations, and organizations—to join with us in this evangelical declaration on the environment, becoming a covenant people in an ever-widening circle of biblical care for creation.

We call upon Christians to listen to and work with all those who are concerned about the healing of creation, with an eagerness both to learn from them and also to share with them our conviction that the God whom all people sense in creation (Acts 17:27) is known fully only in the Word made flesh in Christ the living God who made and sustains all things.

We make this declaration knowing that until Christ returns to reconcile all things, we are called to be faithful stewards of God's good garden, our earthly home.

"Oxford Declaration on Global Warming" (2002)

More than seventy leading climate scientists, policymakers, and Christian leaders from across six continents gathered for "Climate Forum 2002" in Oxford, England, to address the growing crisis of human-induced climate change. The forum recognizes the reality and the urgency of the problem, which particularly affects the world's poorest peoples and the very fabric of the biosphere. The forum also recognizes that the Christian community has a special obligation to provide moral leadership and an example of caring service to people and to all God's creation. To that end, the forum offers the following statement to church, business, and governmental leaders.

Human-induced climate change is a moral, ethical and religious issue.

- God created the Earth and continues to sustain it. Made in God's image, human beings are to care for people and all creation as God cares for them. The call to "love the Lord your God and love your neighbor" (Matthew 22:37–39) takes on new implications in the face of present and projected climate change. God has demonstrated his commitment to creation in the incarnation and resurrection of Jesus Christ. Christ who "reconciles all things" (Colossians 1:20) calls his followers to the "ministry of reconciliation" (2 Corinthians 5:18–19).
- Human-induced climate change poses a great threat to the common good, especially to the poor, the vulnerable, and future generations.
- By reducing the Earth's biological diversity, human-induced climate change diminishes God's creation.

Human-induced climate change, therefore, is a matter of urgent and profound concern.

The Earth's climate is changing, with adverse effects on people, communities, and ecosystems.

- There is now high confidence in the scientific evidence of human influence on climate as detailed by the Intergovernmental Panel on Climate Change (IPCC) and endorsed by eighteen of the world's leading academies of science.
- Human activities, especially the burning of coal, oil, and natural gas (fossil fuels) are rapidly increasing the concentrations of greenhouse gases (especially carbon dioxide) in the global atmosphere. As a result the global climate is warming, with rising sea levels, changes in rainfall patterns, more floods and droughts, and more intense storms. These have serious social, economic, and ecological consequences.
- The harmful effects of climate change far outweigh the beneficial ones:
  - In many arid and semiarid areas, the quantity and the quality of fresh water will continue to decrease.
  - Although agricultural productivity may increase in temperate northern latitudes, it will decrease throughout the Tropics and sub-Tropics.
  - A greater incidence of diseases, such as malaria, dengue fever, and cholera, is expected.
  - Sea-level rise and increased flooding is already displacing people and will eventually affect tens of millions, especially in low-income countries. Some island states are likely to disappear altogether.
  - Important ecosystems, such as coral reefs and forests, will be destroyed or drastically altered, undermining the very foundation of a sustainable world.

Action is needed now, both to arrest climate change and to adapt to its effects.

- We must take immediate steps to stabilize the climate. This means reducing global emissions of carbon dioxide (the most important greenhouse gas) to below 1990 levels well before the middle of the twenty-first century.
- While industrialized nations have largely caused the problem, its most severe effects fall upon the peoples of developing countries. Industrialized countries need therefore to make much greater reductions in emissions in order to allow for economic growth in developing countries.
- We urge industrialized nations to take the lead in reducing their emissions. They have the technical, financial, and institutional ability to do so now.
- We urge industrialized countries to assist developing countries in gaining access to cleaner and renewable forms of energy.
- We urge that actions be taken to increase energy efficiency, in transportation, buildings, and industry. Many actions can produce savings or be taken at little or no net cost. Examples were presented to the forum of such actions by thirty-eight major multinational companies.
- We urge greater use and development of renewable sources of energy.

- We urge increased financial investment and that banking initiatives be grasped to enable the necessary changes.
- The cost of inaction will be greater than the cost of appropriate action.
- Adapting to the impacts of climate change (e.g., droughts and flooding) is not an alternative to mitigation but is essential given that the climate is already changing and further change is inevitable.

Christian denominations, churches, and organizations need to take action to:

- Increase awareness of the facts of global climate change and its moral implications;
- Set an example through individual and collective actions that reduce greenhouse gas emissions;
- Increase demand for technologies and products that produce less emissions of carbon dioxide;
- Urge immediate and responsible action by national governments, in cooperation with other governments under the Framework Convention on Climate Change. This should be, first, to ensure the successful operation of the Kyoto Protocol (which some countries, including the United States, Canada, and Australia, have not yet ratified) and, second, to establish an effective program of emissions reductions in the period immediately following that covered by that Protocol.

We, the forum participants, recognize the urgency for addressing human induced climate change, repent of our inaction, and commit ourselves to work diligently and creatively to adopt solutions in our own lives and in the communities we influence. We call upon leaders in churches, business, and government to join us in recognizing human induced climate change as a moral and religious issue and to take necessary action to maintain the climate system as a remarkable provision in creation for sustaining all life on Earth.

"Sandy Cove Covenant and Invitation" (2004)

We are a gathering of evangelical Christians who provide institutional, pastoral, and intellectual leadership in a wide variety of life settings. We have come together at Sandy Cove, Maryland, in order to pray, reflect, and learn together about our role as stewards of God's creation. We are convinced that God has moved among us in our time together over these three days.

We represent a variety of perspectives and varying levels of expertise about environmental issues. Some of us have given our entire lives to caring for all of God's creation, while for others the issue is a new one. For all of us, this meeting has resulted in a deepening of our concern about God's creation, a joyful sense of community, and a desire to work together on these issues in days ahead.

In reflecting on Scripture and on the pressing environmental problems that beset our world, we are persuaded that we must not evade our responsibility to care for God's creation. We recognize that there is much more we need to learn, and much more praying we need to do, but that we know enough to know that there is no turning back from engaging the threats to God's creation.

We feel called of God to covenant together to move the work of creation care ahead in a variety of ways. Therefore:

- We covenant together to make creation care a permanent dimension of our Christian discipleship and to deepen our theological and biblical understanding of the issues involved.
- We covenant together to draw upon the very best and most trustworthy resources that can help us understand the particular environmental challenges we face today, as well as promising solutions, as fully and accurately as possible.

- We covenant together to share our growing knowledge and concern about these issues with other members of our constituencies.
- We invite our brothers and sisters in Christ to engage with us the most pressing environmental questions of our day, such as health threats to families and the unborn, the negative effects of environmental degradation on the poor, God's endangered creatures, and the important current debate about human-induced climate change. We covenant together to engage the evangelical community in a discussion about the question of climate change with the goal of reaching a consensus statement on the subject in twelve months.

Our continuing goal is to motivate the evangelical community to fully engage environmental issues in a biblically faithful and humble manner, collaborating with those who share these concerns, that we might take our appropriate place in the healing of God's creation and thus the advance of God's reign.

An Excerpt from "For the Health of the Nation: An Evangelical Call to Civic Responsibility" (2004)

We Labor to Protect God's Creation

As we embrace our responsibility to care for God's Earth, we reaffirm the important truth that we worship only the Creator and not the creation. God gave the care of his Earth and its species to our first parents. That responsibility has passed into our hands. We affirm that God-given dominion is a sacred responsibility to steward the Earth and not a license to abuse the creation of which we are a part. We are not the owners of creation, but its stewards, summoned by God to "watch over and care for it" (Genesis 2:15). This implies the principle of sustainability: Our uses of the earth must be designed to conserve and renew the Earth rather than to deplete or destroy it.

The Bible teaches us that God is not only redeeming his people but is also restoring the whole creation (Romans 8:18–23). Just as we show our love for the Savior by reaching out to the lost, we believe that we show our love for the Creator by caring for his creation.

Because clean air, pure water, and adequate resources are crucial to public health and civic order, government has an obligation to protect its citizens from the effects of environmental degradation. This involves both the urgent need to relieve human suffering caused by bad environmental practice. Because natural systems are extremely complex, human actions can have unexpected side effects.

We must therefore approach our stewardship of creation with humility and caution.

Human beings have responsibility for creation in a variety of ways. We urge Christians to shape their personal lives in creation-friendly ways: practicing effective recycling, conserving resources, and experiencing the joy of contact with nature. We urge government to encourage fuel efficiency, reduce pollution, encourage sustainable use of natural resources, and provide for the proper care of wildlife and their natural habitats.

"Climate Change: An Evangelical Call to Action" (2006)

As American evangelical Christian leaders, we recognize both our opportunity and our responsibility to offer a biblically based moral witness that can help shape public policy in the most powerful nation on Earth and therefore contribute to the well-being of the entire world.[1] *Whether* we will enter the public square and offer our witness there is no longer an open question. We are in that square, and we will not withdraw.

We are proud of the evangelical community's long-standing commitment to the sanctity of human life. But we also offer moral witness in many venues and on many issues. Sometimes the issues that we have taken on, such as sex trafficking, genocide in the Sudan, and the AIDS epidemic in Africa, have surprised outside observers. While individuals and organizations can be called to concentrate on certain issues, we are not a single-issue movement. We seek to be true to our calling as Christian leaders, and above all faithful to Jesus Christ our Lord. Our attention, therefore, goes to whatever issues our faith requires us to address.

Over the last several years many of us have engaged in study, reflection, and prayer related to the issue of climate change (often called "global warming"). For most of us, until recently this has not been treated as a pressing issue or major priority. Indeed, many of us have required considerable convincing before becoming persuaded that climate change is a real problem and that it ought to matter to us as Christians. But now we have seen and heard enough to offer the following moral argument related to the matter of human-induced climate change. *We commend the four simple but urgent claims offered in this document to all who will listen, beginning with our brothers and sisters in the Christian community, and urge all to take the appropriate actions that follow from them.*

CLAIM 1: HUMAN-INDUCED CLIMATE CHANGE IS REAL

Since 1995 there has been general agreement among those in the scientific community most seriously engaged with this issue that climate change is happening and is being caused mainly by human activities, especially the burning of fossil fuels. Evidence gathered since 1995 has only strengthened this conclusion.

Because all religious/moral claims about climate change are relevant only if climate change is real and is mainly human-induced, everything hinges on the scientific data. As evangelicals we have hesitated to speak on this issue until we could be more certain of the science of climate change, but the signatories now believe that the evidence demands action:

- The Intergovernmental Panel on Climate Change (IPCC), the world's most authoritative body of scientists and policy experts on the issue of global warming, has been studying this issue since the late 1980s. (From 1988–2002, the IPCC's assessment of the climate science was chaired by Sir John Houghton, a devout evangelical Christian.) It has documented the steady rise in global temperatures over the last fifty years, projects that the average global temperature will continue to rise in the coming decades, and attributes "most of the warming" to human activities.
- The US National Academy of Sciences, as well as all other G8 country scientific academies (Great Britain, France, Germany, Japan, Canada, Italy, and Russia), has concurred with these judgments.
- In a 2004 report and at the 2005 G8 summit, the Bush administration has also acknowledged the reality of climate change and the likelihood that human activity is the cause of at least some of it.[2]

In the face of the breadth and depth of this scientific and governmental concern, only a small percentage of which is noted here, we are convinced that evangelicals must engage this issue without any further lingering over the basic reality of the problem or humanity's responsibility to address it.

CLAIM 2: THE CONSEQUENCES OF CLIMATE CHANGE WILL BE SIGNIFICANT, AND WILL HIT THE POOR THE HARDEST

The earth's natural systems are resilient but not infinitely so, and human civilizations are remarkably dependent on ecological stability and well-being. It is easy to forget this until that stability and well-being are threatened.

Even small rises in global temperatures will have such likely impacts as: sea level rise; more frequent heat waves, droughts, and extreme weather events such as torrential rains and floods; increased tropical diseases in now-temperate regions; and hurricanes that are more intense. It could lead to significant reduction in agricultural output, especially in poor countries. Low-lying regions, indeed entire islands, could find themselves under water. (This is not to mention the various negative impacts climate change could have on God's other creatures.)

Each of these impacts increases the likelihood of refugees from flooding or famine, violent conflicts, and international instability, which could lead to more security threats to our nation.

Poor nations and poor individuals have fewer resources available to cope with major challenges and threats. The consequences of global warming will therefore hit the poor the hardest, in part because those areas likely to be significantly affected first are in the poorest regions of the world. *Millions of people could die in this century because of climate change, most of them our poorest global neighbors.*

Jesus said: "Love your neighbor as yourself."
Mark 12:31

CLAIM 3: CHRISTIAN MORAL CONVICTIONS DEMAND OUR RESPONSE TO THE CLIMATE CHANGE PROBLEM

While we cannot here review the full range of relevant biblical convictions related to care of the creation, we emphasize the following points:

- Christians must care about climate change because we love God the Creator and Jesus our Lord, through whom and for whom the creation was made. This is God's world, and any damage that we do to God's world is an offense against God himself (Genesis 1; Psalms 24; Colossians 1:16).
- *Christians must care about climate change because we are called to love our neighbors,* to do unto others as we would have them do unto us, and to protect and care for the least of these as though each was Jesus Christ himself (Matthew 22:34–40; Matthew 7:12; Matthew 25:31–46).
- Christians, noting the fact that most of the climate change problem is human-induced, are reminded that when God made humanity he commissioned us to exercise stewardship over the earth and its creatures. Climate change is the latest evidence of our failure to exercise proper stewardship and constitutes a critical opportunity for us to do better (Genesis 1:26–28).

Love of God, love of neighbor, and the demands of stewardship are more than enough reason for evangelical Christians to respond to the climate change problem with moral passion and concrete action.

CLAIM 4: THE NEED TO ACT NOW IS URGENT.
GOVERNMENTS, BUSINESSES, CHURCHES, AND INDIVIDUALS
ALL HAVE A ROLE TO PLAY IN ADDRESSING CLIMATE
CHANGE—STARTING NOW

The basic task for all of the world's inhabitants is to find ways now to begin to reduce the carbon dioxide emissions from the burning of fossil fuels that are the primary cause of human-induced climate change.

There are several reasons for urgency. First, deadly impacts are being experienced now. Second, the oceans only warm slowly, creating a lag in experiencing the consequences. Much of the climate change to which we are already committed will not be realized for several decades. The consequences of the pollution we create now will be visited upon our children and grandchildren. Third, as individuals and as a society we are making long-term decisions today that will determine how much carbon dioxide we will emit in the future, such as whether to purchase energy efficient vehicles and appliances that will last for ten to twenty years or whether to build more coal-burning power plants that last for fifty years rather than investing more in energy efficiency and renewable energy.

In the United States, the most important immediate step that can be taken at the federal level is to pass and implement national legislation requiring sufficient economy-wide reductions in carbon dioxide emissions through cost-effective, market-based mechanisms such as a cap-and-trade program. On June 22, 2005 the Senate passed the Domenici-Bingaman resolution affirming this approach, and a number of major energy companies now acknowledge that this method is best both for the environment and for business.

We commend the senators who have taken this stand and encourage them to fulfill their pledge. We also applaud the steps taken by such companies as BP, Shell, General Electric, Cinergy, Duke Energy, and DuPont, all of which have moved ahead of the pace of government action through innovative measures implemented within their companies in the U.S. and around the world. In so doing they have offered timely leadership.

Numerous positive actions to prevent and mitigate climate change are being implemented across our society by state and local governments, churches, smaller businesses, and individuals. These commendable efforts focus on such matters as energy efficiency, the use of renewable energy, low CO_2 emitting technologies, and the purchase of hybrid vehicles. These efforts can easily be shown to save money, save energy, reduce global warming pollution as well as air pollution that harm human health, and eventually pay for themselves. There is much more to be done, but these pioneers are already helping to show the way forward.

Finally, while we must reduce our global warming pollution to help mitigate the impacts of climate change, as a society and as individuals we must also help the poor adapt to the significant harm that global warming will cause.

CONCLUSION

We the undersigned pledge to act on the basis of the claims made in this document. We will not only teach the truths communicated here but also seek ways to implement the actions that follow from them. In the name of Jesus Christ our Lord, we urge all who read this declaration to join us in this effort.

"For by Him (Christ) all things were created: things in heaven and on earth."

Colossians 1:16

APPENDIX E

1. Cf. "For the Health of the Nation: An Evangelical Call to Civic Responsibility," approved by National Association of Evangelicals, October 8, 2004.

2. Intergovernmental Panel on Climate Change 2001, Summary for Policymakers; http://www.grida.no/climate/ipcc_tar/wg1/007.htm. (See also the main IPCC website, www.ipcc.ch.) For the confirmation of the IPCC's findings from the US National Academy of Sciences, see, *Climate Change Science: An Analysis of Some Key Questions* (2001); http://books.nap.edu/html/climatechange/ summary.html. For the statement by the G8 Academies (plus those of Brazil, India, and China) see *Joint Science Academies Statement: Global Response to Climate Change*, (June 2005): http://nationalacademies.org/ onpi/06072005.pdf. Another major international report that confirms the IPCC's conclusions comes from the Arctic Climate Impact Assessment. See their *Impacts of a Warming Climate*, Cambridge University Press, November 2004, p. 2; http://amap.no/acia/. Another important statement is from the American Geophysical Union, "Human Impacts on Climate," December 2003....For the Bush Administration's perspective, see *Our Changing Planet: The U.S. Climate Change Science Program for Fiscal Years 2004 and 2005*, p. 47; http://www.usgcrp.gov/usgcrp/Library/ocp2004–5/default.htm. For the 2005 G8 statement, see http:// www.number-10.gov.uk/output/Page7881.asp.

"An Urgent Call to Action: Scientists and Evangelicals Unite to Protect Creation" (2007)

SUMMARY

Scientific and evangelical leaders recently met to search for common ground in the protection of the creation. We happily discovered far more concordance than any of us had expected, quickly moving beyond dialogue to a shared sense of moral purpose. Important initiatives were already underway on both sides, and when compared they were found to be broadly overlapping. We clearly share a moral passion and sense of vocation to save the imperiled living world before our damages to it remake it as another kind of planet. We agree not only that reckless human activity has imperiled the Earth—especially the unsustainable and short-sighted lifestyles and public policies of our own nation—but also that we share a profound moral obligation to work together to call our nation, and other nations, to the kind of dramatic change urgently required in our day. We pledge our joint commitment to this effort in the unique moment now upon us.

BACKGROUND

This meeting was convened by the Center for Health and the Global Environment at Harvard Medical School and the National Association of Evangelicals. It was envisioned as a first exploratory conference, based on a shared concern for the creation, to be held among people who were in some ways quite different in their worldviews. It now seems to us to be the beginning point of a major shared effort among scientists and evangelicals to protect life on Earth and the fragile life support systems that sustain it, drawing on the unique intellectual, spiritual, and moral contributions that each community can bring.

OUR SHARED CONCERN

We agree that our home, the Earth, which comes to us as that inexpressibly beautiful and mysterious gift that sustains our very lives, is seriously imperiled by human behavior. The harm is seen throughout the natural world, including a cascading set of problems such as climate change, habitat destruction, pollution, and species extinctions, as well as the spread of human infectious diseases, and other accelerating threats to the health of people and the well-being of societies. Each particular problem could be enumerated, but here it is enough to say that we are gradually destroying the sustaining community of life on which all living things on Earth depend. The costs of this destruction are already manifesting themselves around the world in profound and painful ways. The cost to humanity is already significant and may soon become incalculable. Being irreversible, many of these changes would affect all generations to come.

We believe that the protection of life on Earth is a profound moral imperative. It addresses without discrimination the interests of all humanity as well as the value of the nonhuman world. It requires a new moral awakening to a compelling demand, clearly articulated in Scripture and supported by science, that we must steward the natural world in order to preserve for ourselves and future generations a beautiful, rich, and healthful environment. For many of us, this is a religious obligation, rooted in our sense of gratitude for Creation and reverence for its Creator.

One fundamental motivation that we share is concern for the poorest of the poor, well over a billion people, who have little chance to improve their lives in devastated and often war-ravaged environments. At the same time, the natural environments in which they live, and where so much of Earth's biodiversity barely hangs on, cannot survive the press of destitute people without other resources and with nowhere else to go.

We declare that every sector of our nation's leadership—religious, scientific, business, political, and educational—must act now to work toward the fundamental change in values, lifestyles, and public policies required to address these worsening problems before it is too late. There is no excuse for further delays. Business as usual cannot continue yet one more day. We pledge to work together at every level to lead our nation toward a responsible care for creation, and we call with one voice to our scientific and evangelical colleagues, and to all others, to join us in these efforts.

"Principles for Federal Policy on Climate Change" (2007)

The following principles are provided by the Evangelical Climate Initiative (ECI), which represents more than 100 evangelical leaders—including college presidents, megachurch pastors, international aid executives, and denominational heads. Because of their commitment to Jesus Christ, these leaders are compelled to seek ways to help our country solve the global warming problem. As spelled out more fully in the ECI statement, *Climate Change: An Evangelical Call to Action*, ECI leaders believe that love of God, love of neighbor, and the demands of stewardship are more than enough reason for us to respond with moral passion and concrete action. The values and principles found in the Bible—such as prudence, care for the poor, and stewardship of God's provision—compel us to seek sound and just policies in keeping with classic Christian thought. As such, ECI leaders contend that the following principles should guide government officials as they establish policies at the federal level to begin to solve global warming.

1. The problem is real, the objective clear

We believe that human-induced global warming is real and, based on nearly universal agreement in the scientific community, we encourage policymakers to accept this fact and to take action to slow, stop, and reverse the trend of increasing US greenhouse gas emissions. Discussions in the policy arena should now concentrate on solutions.

We agree with the objective of the Framework Convention on Climate Change (FCCC), a treaty that President George H. W. Bush signed and that was ratified by the Senate. The FCCC's objective is "to achieve stabilization of greenhouse gas concentrations in the atmosphere at a low enough level to prevent dangerous anthropogenic interference with the climate system." The federal government should honor this treaty.

Based on the findings of the Intergovernmental Panel on Climate Change (IPCC), the world's most authoritative body on the subject, in the US reductions from the year 2000 levels on the order of 80 percent by 2050 will be necessary to prevent such dangerous human-induced interference with the climate system.

2. *Maximize freedom in solving the problem*

We believe human beings are free moral agents whom God enables to choose to do what is right; they should be free to live the lives he intends for them. Thus, governments should expand and protect freedom to allow individuals to do his will. Freedom flourishes when the rule of law prevents chaos. In the case of global warming, a proper policy framework will establish the "rules of the road" and what businesses call "regulatory certainty." This can enhance freedom by allowing us to begin to solve a problem whose impacts will severely limit that freedom in the future if not addressed.

To protect freedom, unnecessary government regulations must be avoided. Government policies should be structured to allow the free market to solve the problem to the greatest extent possible. We should use the least amount of government power necessary to achieve the objective.

3. *Maximize protection from harm from generation to generation*

A primary function of government is to protect all of its citizens from undue harm, be it from foreign invaders, criminals, or pollution that impacts human health. Such protection helps to create the conditions for citizens, families, and communities to flourish. The harm from global warming is likely to be widespread, diverse, and deadly—heat waves, floods, droughts, intensification of hurricanes, the spread of infectious diseases, and refugee crises. The impact will be worse for our children, our grandchildren, and their children if we fail to act today. Strong and decisive government leadership is required now to address this threat and to promote life, liberty, and the pursuit of happiness, and a policy that will be truly family-friendly for generations to come.

4. *Take special care to protect the most vulnerable*

Jesus calls His followers to protect the poor, and as citizens in a democracy we want our government to do the same. The most important way that federal government policy can protect the poor here and around the world from the impacts of global warming is to begin to solve the problem by reducing CO_2 emissions 80 percent by 2050.

In addition, we recommend the following policies to protect the poor from both the impacts of climate change as well as any possible adverse impacts from climate legislation itself:

- consumer protection/assistance (e.g., LIHEAP) and weatherization assistance for low-income families;
- transition assistance for dislocated workers and communities;

- adaptation and mitigation assistance to least-developed countries, and;
- research into adaptation and mitigation measures for low-income households in the US and the poor in least-developed countries.

With all of these policies, we favor an approach whereby faith communities can work in partnership with governments to deliver such services and assistance.

5. Enhance national and energy security, international religious freedom, and rural economic development

The massive impacts of climate change around the world will have serious national security implications, creating a less stable world. American reliance on foreign oil also undermines our national security and makes us dependent on undemocratic, despotic foreign regimes that restrict the religious liberty of their peoples, threaten the stability of democratic allies such as Israel, and constrain our ability to occupy the moral high ground in foreign policy on human rights and religious freedom. Thus, we are in favor of climate policies that reduce our dependence on foreign oil (e.g., increasing fuel economy) and thereby enhance energy security and our advocacy of religious liberty and human rights.

In addition, a robust climate policy that increases our use of renewable sources like solar, wind, and biofuels will be a lifeline for struggling rural economies and will stabilize the economic outlook for family farms.

6. Disburse decision-making authority to the lowest possible level

We believe that in general the flourishing of freedom occurs when the power to make decisions resides at the lowest possible organizational level. A robust response to the threat of global warming will involve individuals, families, churches, businesses, and governments at multiple levels. In particular, we believe in states' rights and responsibilities as the laboratories of democracy. Strong action on climate by states, businesses, families, and individuals should be encouraged and not weakened by action at the federal level.

Given that the problem is global, and that nation-states are primary seats of government authority, important decisions must be made at the national level and between nations at the international level. While state actions and voluntary initiatives have resulted in positive benefits in the US, national emissions have continued to rise at a level inconsistent with long-term climate protection. In addition, businesses are now facing an inefficient patchwork of regulations. Thus, an economy-wide federal policy with mandatory targets and timetables for major sources of emissions is needed to achieve an 80 percent reduction by 2050. However, this policy should allow for maximum freedom for businesses and the states.

7. Solve the problem through the free market and protection of property rights

Harnessing the power of the market will allow innovation, ingenuity, and entrepreneurship to generate climate solutions, and will ensure that US businesses can compete internationally in clean technologies. To help ensure competitiveness, climate policy should provide: (1) a stable, long-term, substantial research and development program; (2) long-term regulatory certainty; and (3) a robust price signal that reflects the true social cost of greenhouse gas pollution.

We feel it is important to recognize that global warming pollution invades the property rights of all its victims, and restricts their freedom by forcing them to bear costs they should not have to pay because of the actions of others—in either the quality of the air they breathe, the geography they hold dear, the insurance costs they bear, or the future environment of the children they love. Climate policy should ensure that the costs of global warming pollution are reflected in the price of goods and services that produce greenhouse gases. When prices are right, the free market can do its job.

We believe that the preferable market-based mechanisms will be the ones that are politically achievable in the near term. The US now has extensive experience in managing a successful cap-and-trade program for sulfur dioxide (SO_2), and there is growing political support for a cap-and-trade system. This could also allow us access to a global trading system, providing further efficiencies. We support a cap-and-trade approach, by itself or in combination with a revenue-neutral global warming pollution tax whereby those who act to reduce global warming pollution receive a tax cut.

8. Start now and solve the problem in the most cost-effective, least disruptive way possible

Significant reductions in global warming pollution should start sooner rather than later in order to minimize disruption to the economy and to avoid the necessity of drastic, steep reductions in the future. Shifting swiftly to a course that includes emissions reductions will minimize economic damage from climate change and will create a smooth transition to a new energy future.

9. Lead by example

Regardless of whether all nations agree to be part of the solution, America must do the right thing. America is committed to democracy, human rights, and the rule of law regardless of the actions of other nations, and the same must be true of our response to global warming. We do not have to wait for China and India to act before we do. We have contributed by far the most CO_2 to the atmosphere. We should lead by example and create the technologies everyone will need to help solve the problem.

10. Learn from the future

Our understanding will continue to grow, and we may find that we must accelerate steps that address climate change. Climate policies must be flexible to account for what we will learn in the future. In addition, we must avoid making decisions now that constrain our ability to control greenhouse gas emissions in the future. Specifically, we must encourage innovation and prevent energy infrastructure developments that lock us into old, inefficient technologies for years to come.

"A Southern Baptist Declaration on the Environment and Climate Change" (2008)

PREAMBLE

Southern Baptists have always been a confessional people, giving testimony to our beliefs, which are based upon the doctrines found in God's inerrant word—the Holy Bible. As the dawning of new ages has produced substantial challenges requiring a special word, Southern Baptist churches, associations, and general bodies have often found it necessary to make declarations in order to define, express, and defend beliefs. Though we do not regard this as a complete declaration on these issues, we believe this initiative finds itself consistent with our most cherished distinctives and rooted in historical precedent.

The preamble to the *Baptist Faith and Message 2000* (BFM 2000) declares: "Each generation of Christians bears the responsibility of guarding the treasury of truth that has been entrusted to us (2 Timothy 1:14). Facing a new century, Southern Baptists must meet the demands and duties of the present hour. New challenges to faith appear in every age."

We recognize that God's great blessings on our denomination bestow upon us a great responsibility to offer a biblically-based, moral witness that can help shape individual behavior, private sector behavior, and public policy. Conversations like this one demand our voice in order to fulfill our calling to engage the culture as a relevant body of believers. Southern Baptists have always championed faith's challenges, and we now perpetuate our heritage through this initiative.

We are proud of our deep and lasting commitments to moral issues like the sanctity of human life and biblical definitions of marriage. We will never compromise our convictions nor attenuate our advocacy on these matters, which constitute the most pressing moral issues of our day. However, we are not a single-issue body. We also offer moral witness in other venues and on many issues. We seek to be true to our calling as Christian leaders, but above all, faithful to Jesus Christ our Lord. Therefore, our attention goes to whatever issues our faith requires us to address.

We have recently engaged in study, reflection, and prayer related to the challenges presented by environmental and climate change issues. These things have not always been treated with pressing concern as major issues. Indeed, some of us have required considerable convincing before becoming persuaded that these are real problems that deserve our attention. But now we have seen and heard enough to be persuaded that these issues are among the current era's challenges that require a unified moral voice.

We believe our current denominational engagement with these issues has often been too timid, failing to produce a unified moral voice. Our cautious response to these issues in the face of mounting evidence may be seen by the world as uncaring, reckless, and ill-informed. We can do better. To abandon these issues to the secular world is to shirk from our responsibility to be salt and light. The time for timidity regarding God's creation is no more.

Therefore, we offer these four statements for consideration, beginning with our fellow Southern Baptists, and urge all to follow by taking appropriate actions. May we find ourselves united as we contend for the faith that was delivered to the saints once for all. *Laus Deo!*

Statement 1: Humans must care for creation and take responsibility for our contributions to environmental degradation.

There is undeniable evidence that the Earth—wildlife, water, land, and air—can be damaged by human activity, and that people suffer as a result. When this happens, it is especially egregious because creation serves as revelation of God's presence, majesty, and provision. Though not every person will physically hear God's revelation found in Scripture, all people have access to God's cosmic revelation: the heavens, the waters, natural order, the beauty of nature (Psalms 19; Romans 1). We believe that human activity is mixed in its impact on creation—sometimes productive and caring, but often reckless, preventable, and sinful.

God's command to tend and keep the Earth (Genesis 2) did not pass away with the fall of man; we are still responsible. Lack of concern and failure to act prudently on the part of Christ-followers reflects poorly to the rest of the world. Therefore, we humbly take responsibility for the damage that we have done to God's cosmic revelation and pledge to take an unwavering stand to preserve and protect the creation over which we have been given responsibility by Almighty God Himself.

Statement 2: It is prudent to address global climate change.

We recognize that we do not have any special revelation to guide us about whether global warming is occurring and, if it is occurring, whether people are causing it. We are looking at the same evidence unfolding over time that other people are seeing.

We recognize that we do not have special training as scientists to allow us to assess the validity of climate science. We understand that all human enterprises are fraught with pride, bias, ignorance, and uncertainty.

We recognize that if consensus means unanimity, there is not a consensus regarding the anthropogenic nature of climate change or the severity of the problem. There is general agreement among those engaged with this issue in the scientific community. A minority of sincere and respected scientists offer alternate causes for global climate change other than deforestation and the burning of fossil fuels.

We recognize that Christians are not united around either the scientific explanations for global warming or policies designed to slow it down. Unlike abortion and respect for the biblical definition of marriage, this is an issue where Christians may find themselves in justified disagreement about both the problem and its solutions.

Yet, even in the absence of perfect knowledge or unanimity, we have to make informed decisions about the future. This will mean we have to take a position of prudence based partly on science that is inevitably changing. We do not believe unanimity is necessary for prudent action. We can make wise decisions even in the absence of infallible evidence.

Though the claims of science are neither infallible nor unanimous, they are substantial and cannot be dismissed out of hand on either scientific or theological grounds. Therefore, in the face of intense concern and guided by the biblical principle of creation stewardship, we resolve to engage this issue without any further lingering over the basic reality of the problem or our responsibility to address it. Humans must be proactive and take responsibility for our contributions to climate change—however great or small.

Statement 3: Christian moral convictions and our Southern Baptist doctrines demand our environmental stewardship.

While we cannot here review the full range of relevant Christian convictions and Baptist doctrines related to care of the creation, we emphasize the following points:

- We must care about environmental and climate issues because of our love for God— "the Creator, Redeemer, Preserver and Ruler of the Universe" (BFM 2000)— through whom and for whom the creation was made.[1] This is not our world, it is God's. Therefore, any damage we do to this world is an offense against God Himself (Genesis 1; Psalms 24; Colossians 1:16). We share God's concern for the abuse of His creation.
- We must care about environmental issues because of our commitment to God's Holy and inerrant Word, which is "the supreme standard by which all human conduct, creeds, and religious opinions should be tried" (BFM 2000). Within these Scriptures we are reminded that when God made mankind, He commissioned us to exercise stewardship over the Earth and its creatures (Genesis 1:26–28). *Therefore, our motivation for facing failures to exercise proper stewardship is not primarily political, social, or economic—it is primarily biblical.*

- We must care about environmental and climate issues because we are called to love our neighbors, to do unto others as we would have them do unto us, and to protect and care for the "least of these" (Matthew 22:34–40; Matthew 7:12; Matthew 25:31–46). The consequences of these problems will most likely hit the poor the hardest, in part because those areas likely to be significantly affected are in the world's poorest regions. Poor nations and individuals have fewer resources available to cope with major challenges and threats. Therefore, "we should work to provide for the orphaned, the needy…[and] the helpless" (BFM 2000) through proper stewardship.
- Love of God, love of neighbor, and Scripture's stewardship demands provide enough reason for Southern Baptists and Christians everywhere to respond to these problems with moral passion and concrete action.

Statement 4: It is time for individuals, churches, communities, and governments to act.

We affirm that "every Christian should seek to bring industry, government, and society as a whole under the sway of the principles of righteousness, truth, and brotherly love" (BFM 2000).

We realize that we cannot support some environmental issues as we offer a distinctively Christian voice in these arenas. For instance, we realize that what some call population control leads to evils like abortion. We now call on these environmentalists to reject these evils and accept the sanctity of every human person, both born and unborn.

We realize that simply affirming our God-given responsibility to care for the Earth will likely produce no tangible or effective results. Therefore, we pledge to find ways to curb ecological degradation through promoting biblical stewardship habits and increasing awareness in our homes, businesses where we find influence, relationships with others, and in our local churches. Many of our churches do not actively preach, promote, or practice biblical creation care. We urge churches to begin doing so.

We realize that the primary impetus for prudent action must come from the will of the people, families, and those in the private sector. Held to this standard of common good, action by government is often needed to assure the health and well-being of all people. We pledge, therefore, to give serious consideration to responsible policies that acceptably address the conditions set forth in this declaration.

CONCLUSION

We the undersigned, in accordance with our Christian moral convictions and Southern Baptist doctrines, pledge to act on the basis of the claims made in this document. We will not only teach the truths communicated here but also seek ways to implement the actions that follow from them. In the name of Jesus Christ our Lord, we urge all who read this declaration to join us in this effort. *Laus Deo!*

"Vineyard Churches: Seven-Year Plan for American Evangelicalism" (2009)

SUMMARY OF THE PLAN'S INITIATIVES

- Facilitate an annual Creation Care Leadership Summit to gather evangelical leaders in the field of creation care for prayer, planning, and co-ordination of efforts. *Purpose*: to network established and emerging leaders in creation care; to learn from each other and coordinate efforts for optimal impact on the wider American Evangelical Community.
- Facilitate a high level event to inspire, equip, and empower the most influential evangelical pastors to actively support creation care in the evangelical church community. *Purpose*: to expand the number of influential evangelical pastors committed to promoting environmental stewardship.
- Support a Creation Care Churches Clearing House to identify American evangelical church congregations committed to creation care. *Purpose*: to promote best creation care practices among evangelical churches and establish the most accurate data regarding churches committed to creation care.
- Support Best Church Practices for creation care congregations. *Purpose*: to develop environmental quality standards for model congregations to set the pace for growth in environmental stewardship among American evangelical churches.
- Seek to establish a Church Network Task Force to promote creation care within each of three influential American evangelical church networks: Willow Creek Association, Saddleback Resources, and Vineyard: A Community of Churches. *Purpose*: to develop a model for promoting creation within the three most influential "postdenominational" church networks in American Evangelicalism.
- Promote Creation Care among younger generations of American evangelicals through a partnership with Renewal (an evangelical, student-led creation care

movement on Christian college campuses) and Intervarsity Christian Fellowship (an evangelical, student-led organization on secular college campuses). *Purpose*: to inspire, equip, and empower a new generation of evangelical leadership committed to integrating faith and environmental stewardship.

- Work with the NAE Creation Care Advisory Group to develop a strategy to bridge the cultural divide between evangelicals who support action to mitigate human-caused climate change and evangelicals who are skeptical about climate change science. *Purpose*: to move beyond the partisan rhetoric surrounding climate change in order to focus American evangelicals on the fact of climate change (irrespective of cause); evangelicals skeptical of anthropogenic climate change could thus be mobilized to aid in adaptation efforts, especially through global missions, where evangelicals are already helping populations vulnerable to the dangers of a warming climate.
- Promote a new partnership between evangelical global missions leaders and creation care leaders. *Purpose*: to mobilize the vast network of evangelical missionaries working among vulnerable populations to assist in improving environmental conditions affecting those populations.
- Integrate evangelical concern for creation care with the much broader movement of growing evangelical concern for other justice issues. *Purpose*: to frame environmental concern within the biblical concern for justice, which is an increasing concern of the American evangelical community.

Key Figures and Affiliations

Name	Affiliation	Signatories		
		ECI	Cornwall	ESUPC
Leith Anderson	President, National Association of Evangelicals; Senior Pastor, Wooddale Church	✓		
Robert Andringa	Former President, Council for Christian Colleges and Universities	✓		
Jim Ball	Executive Vice President for Policy and Climate Campaign, Former President, Evangelical Environmental Network	✓		✓
Calvin Beisner	National Spokesperson, Cornwall Alliance		✓	
Dan Boone	President, Trevecca Nazarene University	✓		
Eric Chivian	Director, Center for Health and the Global Environment, Harvard Medical School; Executive Committee Member, Creation Care for Pastors			✓
Richard Cizik	Former Vice President for Governmental Affairs, National Association of Evangelicals; Founder and President, New Evangelical Partnership for the Common Good	✓		✓

(*continued*)

Name	Affiliation	Signatories		
		ECI	Cornwall	ESUPC
Chuck Colson	Founder, Prison Fellowship		✓	
Paul Corts	President, Council for Christian Colleges and Universities	✓		
Andy Crouch	Author, Editor, and Producer; Special Assistant to the President, Christianity Today International	✓		
Calvin DeWitt	Professor of Environmental Studies, University of Wisconsin, Madison; Former Director, Au Sable Institute for Environmental Studies			✓
James Dobson	Founder, Focus on the Family		✓	
Barrett Duke	Vice President for Public Policy and Research, Ethics and Religious Liberty Commission of the Southern Baptist Convention		✓	
Paul Gorman	Founder and Former Executive Director, National Religious Partnership for the Environment			
David Gushee	Professor of Christian Ethics, Mercer University; Founder, New Evangelical Partnership for the Common Good	✓		✓
Ted Haggard	Former President, National Association of Evangelicals; Former Pastor, New Life Church			
John Houghton	Former Chair, Scientific Assessment Working Group of the Intergovernmental Panel on Climate Change; Chairman, John Ray Initiative			
Joel Hunter	Senior Pastor, Northland, A Church Distributed; Executive Committee Member, Creation Care for Pastors	✓		✓

Name	Affiliation	Signatories		
		ECI	Cornwall	ESUPC
Jim Jewell	Chairman of the Board and Founder, Flourish; Former Campaign Director, Evangelical Climate Initiative; Former Chief Operating Officer, Evangelical Environmental Network			
D. James Kennedy	(1930–2007); Televangelist; Founder, Coral Ridge Ministries		✓	
Richard Land	President, Ethics and Religious Liberty Commission of the Southern Baptist Convention		✓	
Alexei Laushkin	Senior Director of Communications, Evangelical Environmental Network			
Stan LeQuire	Former Director, Evangelical Environmental Network			
Duane Litfin	Former President, Wheaton College	✓		
Larry Lloyd	Former President, Crichton College	✓		
Jo Anne Lyon	Founder and Former CEO, World Hope; General Superintendent, Wesleyan Church	✓		
Brian McLaren	Author and Theologian; Founding Pastor, Cedar Ridge Community Church	✓		
James Merritt	Senior Pastor, Cross Pointe Church; Former President, Southern Baptist Convention			
Jonathan Merritt	Founder and Spokesperson, Southern Baptist Environment and Climate Initiative; Manager of Church Programs, Flourish			
David Neff	Editor n Chief, *Christianity Today*	✓		
Michael Nyenhuis	President and CEO, MAP International	✓		
Tony Perkins	President, Family Research Council		✓	
John Phelan	Former President, North Park Theological Seminary	✓		

(*continued*)

Name	Affiliation	Signatories		
		ECI	Cornwall	ESUPC
Rusty Pritchard	Founder and President, Flourish; Former National Outreach Director, Evangelical Environmental Network			
Pat Robertson	Host, *700 Club*; Founder, Christian Coalition			
Tri Robinson	Senior Pastor, Vineyard Boise	✓		
Scott Sabin	Executive Director, Plant with Purpose	✓		
Carl Safina	Marine Ecologist; President, Blue Ocean Institute; Founder, The Friendship Collaborative			✓
Larry Schweiger	President and CEO, National Wildlife Federation			
Ron Sider	Professor of Theology, Eastern University; Founder and Director, Evangelicals for Social Action; Founder, Evangelical Environmental Network	✓		
Matthew Sleeth	Author; Executive Director, Blessed Earth	✓		
Nancy Sleeth	Program Director, Blessed Earth			
Gus Speth	Professor, Vermont Law School; Former Dean, Yale School of Forestry and Environmental Studies			✓
Richard Stearns	President, World Vision	✓		
John Stott	(1921–2011); Theologian, Author, and Speaker; Former Rector, All Souls Church, Langham Place			
Steve Timmermans	President, Trinity Christian College	✓		
Rick Warren	Author; Founder and Senior Pastor, Saddleback Church	✓		
Loren Wilkinson	Professor of Interdisciplinary Studies and Philosophy, Regent College			✓
Ken Wilson	Senior Pastor, Ann Arbor Vineyard; Executive Committee Member, Creation Care for Pastors; Founder, The Friendship Collaborative	✓		✓

Notes

PREFACE

1. Like many efforts within American evangelicalism, climate care is led vastly by white men. Women hold few positions of leadership in the community generally and, likewise, in this movement in particular. Moreover, although many black Protestants identify as evangelical—by embracing the label directly or by adhering to evangelical belief and practice—significant differences between white and black evangelicals necessitate separate treatment in research. The same applies to Latino evangelicals. While religious beliefs and practices may cut across lines of race within American evangelicalism, the histories and experiences of those communities are vastly different and cannot be treated under an umbrella approach. Hence, this book focuses on the predominantly white evangelical community and congregations therein and the largely male leadership at the helm of climate care. For more on race and gender in American evangelicalism, see Conrad Hackett and D. Michael Lindsay, "Measuring Evangelicalism: Consequences of Different Operationalization Strategies," *Journal for the Scientific Study of Religion* 47, no. 3 (2008): 499–514; D. Michael Lindsay, *Faith in the Halls of Power: How Evangelicals Joined the American Elite* (New York: Oxford University Press, 2007), 8–10, 223–226.

2. Drawn from the work of Maarten Hajer, story lines are defined as generative narratives through which people can make complex, fractured issues or phenomena coherent and imbue them with meaning. He explains: "Story lines...not only help to construct a problem; they also play an important role in the creation of a social and moral order in a given domain. Story lines are devices through which actors are positioned, and through which specific ideas of 'blame' and 'responsibility' and of 'urgency' and 'responsible behavior' are attributed." See Maarten A. Hajer, *The Politics of Environmental Discourse: Ecological Modernization and the Policy Process* (Oxford, UK: Oxford University Press, 1995), 64–65.

3. For two excellent treatments of the key ethical issues related to climate change, see Stephen M. Gardiner, "Ethics and Global Climate Change," *Ethics* 114, no.

3 (2004): 555–600; James Garvey, *The Ethics of Climate Change: Right and Wrong in a Warming World* (London: Continuum, 2008).

4. R. Marie Griffith, *God's Daughters: Evangelical Women and the Power of Submission* (Berkeley: University of California Press, 1997); Lindsay, *Faith in the Halls of Power*.

5. Lynn White, "The Historical Roots of Our Ecologic Crisis," *Science* 155, no. 3767 (1967): 1,203–1,207.

6. Wendell Berry, "Christianity and the Survival of Creation," in *Sex, Economy, Freedom, and Community* (New York: Pantheon, 1993), 93–116.

INTRODUCTION

1. All Bible passages are taken from the *New International Version* (*NIV*). Prepared by more than 100 evangelical scholars, the *NIV* is widely used in academia and frequently favored among conservative Protestants.

2. The Celebration of Faiths and the Environment took place in Windsor, UK, November 2–4, 2009, and was jointly organized by the Alliance of Religions and Conservation and the United Nations Development Program. For text of the action plans, see Mary Colwell, Victoria Finlay, Alison Hilliard, and Susie Weldon, eds., *Many Heavens, One Earth: Faith Commitments to Protect the Living Planet* (Bath, UK: Alliance of Religions and Conservation, 2009).

3. Ban Ki-moon, speech given at the Celebration of Faiths and the Environment, Windsor, UK, November 3, 2009. For a transcript, see http://www.windsor2009.org/ARC-UNDPWindsor2009-SpeechBanKi-moon.pdf (accessed June 1, 2011).

4. For other arguments to this effect, see Gary Gardner, *Invoking the Spirit: Religion and Spirituality in the Quest for a Sustainable World*, Worldwatch Paper 164 (Washington, DC: Worldwatch Institute, 2002); John T. Houghton, *Global Warming: The Complete Briefing*, 3rd ed. (Cambridge, UK: Cambridge University Press, 2004); Stephen M. Johnson, "Is Religion the Environment's Last Best Hope? Targeting Change in Individual Behavior Through Personal Norm Activation," *Journal of Environmental Law and Litigation* 24, no. 1 (2009): 119–164; Matthew C. Nisbet, "Communicating Climate Change: Why Frames Matter for Public Engagement," *Environment* 51, no. 2 (2009): 12–23; Max Oelschlaeger, *Caring for Creation: An Ecumenical Approach to the Environmental Crisis* (New Haven, CT: Yale University Press, 1994); James Gustave Speth, *Red Sky at Morning: America and the Crisis of the Global Environment* (New Haven, CT: Yale University Press, 2004); James Gustave Speth, *The Bridge at the Edge of the World: Capitalism, the Environment, and Crossing from Crisis to Sustainability* (New Haven, CT: Yale University Press, 2008); Edward O. Wilson, *The Future of Life* (New York: Knopf, 2002); E. O. Wilson, *The Creation: An Appeal to Save Life on Earth* (New York: W.W. Norton, 2006).

5. Riley E. Dunlap and Aaron M. McCright, "A Widening Gap: Republican and Democratic Views on Climate Change," *Environment* 50, no. 5 (2008): 26–35; Aaron M. McCright and Riley E. Dunlap, "The Politicization of Climate Change and Polarization in the American Public's Views of Global Warming, 2001–2010," *The Sociological Quarterly* 52 (2011): 155–194.

6. Anthony Leiserowitz, *Public Perception, Opinion, and Understanding of Climate Change: Current Patterns, Trends, and Limitations* (New York: United Nations Development Program, 2007), http://hdr.undp.org/en/reports/global/hdr2007-2008/papers/leiserowitz_anthony.pdf (accessed June 1, 2011); Susanne C. Moser, "Toward a Deeper Engagement of the US Public on Climate Change: An Open Letter to the 44th President of the United States of America," *International Journal of Sustainability Communication* 3 (2008): 119–132; Susanne C. Moser and Lisa Dilling, introduction to *Creating a Climate for Change: Communicating Climate Change and Facilitating Social Change*, eds. Susanne C. Moser and Lisa Dilling (New York: Cambridge University Press, 2007), 1–27; Matthew C. Nisbet and Teresa Myers, "Trends: Twenty Years of Public Opinion about Global Warming," *Public Opinion Quarterly* 71, no. 3 (2007): 444–470.

7. Roger S. Gottlieb, introduction to *The Oxford Handbook of Religion and Ecology*, ed. Roger S. Gottlieb (Oxford, UK: Oxford University Press, 2006), 3–22, 12.

8. Mary Evelyn Tucker, "Religion and Ecology," in *The Oxford Handbook of the Sociology of Religion*, ed. Peter Clarke (Oxford, UK: Oxford University Press, 2009), 819–835, 820.

9. For more on the religion-environment intersection, see also Bron R. Taylor, ed., *The Encyclopedia of Religion and Nature* (London: Continuum, 2005).

10. Mary Evelyn Tucker, *Worldly Wonder: Religions Enter Their Ecological Phase* (Chicago: Open Court, 2004).

11. See Roger S. Gottlieb, ed., *The Oxford Handbook of Religion and Ecology* (Oxford, UK: Oxford University Press, 2006); Tucker, "Religion and Ecology"; Mary Evelyn Tucker and John Grim, eds., World Religions and Ecology Series (Cambridge, MA: Harvard University Press, 1997–2004).

12. Bill McKibben, "The Gospel of Green: Will Evangelicals Help Save the Earth?" *OnEarth*, Fall 2006.

13. See Hackett and Lindsay, "Measuring Evangelicalism"; Christian Smith, *Christian America? What Evangelicals Really Want* (Berkeley: University of California Press, 2000).

14. See John C. Green, Mark J. Rozell, and Clyde Wilcox, eds., *The Values Campaign? The Christian Right and the 2004 Elections* (Washington, DC: Georgetown University Press, 2006); Clyde Wilcox and Carin Larson, *Onward Christian Soldiers? The Religious Right in American Politics*, 3rd ed. (Boulder, CO: Westview, 2006).

15. D. Michael Lindsay, "Ties That Bind and Divisions That Persist: Evangelical Faith and the Political Spectrum," *American Quarterly* 59, no. 3 (2007): 883–909, 901.

16. Lindsay, "Ties That Bind." John Green and Steve Waldman developed the term *free-style evangelicals* to describe this growing trend, used in a variety of pieces published on Beliefnet.com.

17. Tracy Miller, ed., *US Religious Landscape Survey 2008* (Washington, DC: Pew Forum on Religion and Public Life, 2008), http://religions.pewforum.org/pdf/report-religious-landscape-study-full.pdf (accessed June 1, 2011).

18. See Gregory E. Hitzhusen, "Judeo-Christian Theology and the Environment: Moving Beyond Skepticism to New Sources for Environmental Education in the United States," *Environmental Education Research* 13, no. 1 (2007): 55–74.

19. See John C. Dernbach, "Harnessing Individual Behavior to Address Climate Change: Options for Congress," *Virginia Environmental Law Journal* 26, no. 1 (2008): 107–156.

20. Michael P. Vandenbergh and Anne C. Steinemann, "The Carbon-Neutral Individual," *New York University Law Review* 82 (2007): 101–168.

21. Roger E. Olson, *The Westminster Handbook to Evangelical Theology* (Louisville, KY: Westminster John Knox, 2004), 1.

22. Others use the term more narrowly, to identify only the subset of conservative Protestants who broke away from fundamentalism in the "neoevangelical" movement of the mid-twentieth century. See chapter 1.

23. David W. Bebbington, *Evangelicalism in Modern Britain: A History from the 1730s to the 1980s* (London: Unwin Hyman, 1989), 1–19.

24. Mark A. Noll, *American Evangelical Christianity: An Introduction* (Oxford, UK: Blackwell, 2001).

25. Scholars use a variety of operationalization strategies to demarcate American evangelicals. Most employ one of three methods to determine evangelical constituencies or research subjects: (1) using affiliation with historically evangelical denominations to classify people; (2) relying on people to identify themselves as evangelical; and (3) defining people according to their subscription to a set of theological beliefs or convictions deemed evangelical. These different strategies—affiliation, self-identification, and subscription—and the variations therein can lead to different results in defining the evangelical population and, thus, different profiles of and attribution of characteristics to evangelicals or evangelicalism. See Hackett and Lindsay, "Measuring Evangelicalism"; Noll, *American Evangelical Christianity*; Smith, *Christian America*.

26. Susan Solomon, Dahe Qin, Martin Manning, Melinda Marquis, Kristen Averyt, Melinda M. B. Tignor, Henry LeRoy Miller, and Zhenlin Chin, eds., *Climate Change 2007: The Physical Science Basis* (Cambridge, UK: Cambridge University Press, 2007), 51, 60.

27. See Houghton, *Global Warming*; Solomon et al., *Climate Change 2007*; Nicholas Stern, *The Economics of Climate Change: The Stern Review* (Cambridge, UK: Cambridge University Press, 2007).

28. UNFCCC, article 2. For the full text, see http://unfccc.int/resource/docs/convkp/conveng.pdf (accessed June 1, 2011).

29. Amy L. Luers, Michael D. Mastrandrea, Katharine Hayhoe, and Peter C. Frumhoff, *How to Avoid Dangerous Climate Change: A Target for US Emissions Reductions* (Cambridge, MA: Union of Concerned Scientists, 2007); Johan Rockström, Will Steffen, Kevin Noone, ÅsaPersson, F. Stuart Chapin III, Eric F. Lambin, Timothy M. Lenton, Marten Scheffer, Carl Folke, Hans Joachim Schellnhuber, Björn Nykvist, Cynthia A. de Wit, Terry Hughes, Sander van der Leeuw, Henning Rodhe, Sverker Sörlin, Peter K. Snyder, Robert Costanza, Uno Svedin, Malin Falkenmark, Louise Karlberg, Robert W. Corell, Victoria J. Fabry, James Hansen, Brian Walker, Diana Liverman, Katherine Richardson, Paul Crutzen, and Jonathan A. Foley, "A Safe Operating Space for Humanity," *Nature* 461 (2009): 472–475; Solomon et al., *Climate Change 2007*; Stern, *Stern Review*; Nicholas Stern, "The Economics of Climate Change," *American Economic Review* 98, no. 2 (2008): 1–37; United Nations Environment Program, *Bridging the Emissions Gap* (Nairobi, Kenya: UNEP, 2011). CO_2eq, or carbon dioxide equivalent, is a universal measurement that can be used to express the heat-trapping capacity of all greenhouse gases in terms of carbon dioxide.

30. See Luers et al., *Dangerous Climate Change*; Stern, "Economics of Climate Change"; Stern, *Stern Review*; UNEP, *Bridging the Emissions Gap*.

31. See Hannah Choi Granade, Jon Creyts, Anton Derkach, Philip Farese, Scott Nyquist, Ken Ostrowski, *Unlocking Energy Efficiency in the US Economy* (New York: McKinsey and Company, 2009); Stephen Pacala and Robert Socolow, "Stabilization Wedges: Solving the Climate Problem for the Next 50 Years with Current Technologies," *Science* 305, no. 5686 (2004): 968–972; Solomon et al., *Climate Change 2007*.

32. Stern, "Economics of Climate Change"; Stern, *Stern Review*.

33. See Harriet Bulkeley and Michele Betsill, *Cities and Climate Change: Urban Sustainability and Global Environmental Governance* (London:Routledge, 2003); Barry Rabe, *Statehouse and Greenhouse: The Emerging Politics of American Climate Change Policy* (Washington, DC: Brookings Institution, 2004).

34. J. Robert Cox, *Environmental Communication and the Public Sphere*, 2nd ed. (Thousand Oaks, CA: Sage, 2010), 20.

35. For more on the significance of environmental language and discourse, see Loren R. Cass and Mary E. Pettenger, "Conclusion: The Constructions of Climate Change," in *The Social Construction of Climate Change: Power, Knowledge, Norms, Discourses*, ed. Mary E. Pettenger (Aldershot, UK: Ashgate, 2007), 235–246; John S. Dryzek, *The Politics of the Earth: Environmental Discourses*, 2nd ed. (Oxford, UK: Oxford University Press, 2005); Hajer, *Politics of Environmental Discourse*; John A. Hannigan, "Environmental Discourse," in *Environmental Sociology*, 2nd ed. (London: Routledge, 2006); Susanne C. Moser and Lisa Dilling, eds., *Creating a Climate for Change: Communicating Climate Change and Facilitating Social Change* (New York: Cambridge University Press, 2007). For two other treatments of creation care discourse, see Lawrence J. Prelli and Terri S. Winters, "Rhetorical

Features of Green Evangelicalism," *Environmental Communication* 3, no. 2 (2009): 224–243; J. Arjan Wardekker, Arthur C. Petersen, and Jeroen P. van der Sluijs, "Ethics and Public Perception of Climate Change: Exploring Christian Voices in the US Public Debate," *Global Environmental Change* 19 (2009): 512–521.

36. Marteen Hajer and Wytske Versteeg, "A Decade of Discourse Analysis of Environmental Politics: Achievements, Challenges, Perspectives," in *Journal of Environmental Policy and Planning* 7, no. 3 (2005): 175–184, 176.

37. See Mike Hulme, *Why We Disagree about Climate Change: Understanding Controversy, Inaction, and Opportunity* (Cambridge, UK: Cambridge University Press, 2009).

38. Hulme puts it this way: "One of the reasons we disagree about climate change is because we believe different things about our duty to others, to nature, and to our deities." See Hulme, *Why We Disagree*, 144.

39. Much climate communication to date has been based on the notion that a knowledge deficit underlies the lack of public concern about climate change (attitudes) and action in response (behavior), and so pursued information transmission as the prime solution. But this "deficit model" has proved inadequate, as public interpretations of scientific information are mediated by personal and contextual factors and constraints. Therefore, the how of communication is equally as important as the what. See Paul M. Kellstedt, Sammy Zahran, and Arnold Vedlitz, "Personal Efficacy, the Information Environment, and Attitudes Toward Global Warming and Climate Change in the United States," *Risk Analysis* 28, no. 1 (2008): 113–126; Anja Kollmuss and Julian Agyeman, "Mind the Gap: Why Do People Act Environmentally and What Are the Barriers to Pro-Environmental Behavior?" *Environmental Education Research* 8, no. 3 (2002): 239–260; Moser, "Toward a Deeper Engagement"; Patrick Sturgis and Nick Allum, "Science in Society: Re-evaluating the Deficit Model of Public Attitudes," *Public Understanding of Science* 13, no. 1 (2004): 55–74.

40. For more on the promise of religion for climate communication, see Sally Bingham, "Climate Change: A Moral Issue," in *Creating a Climate for Change: Communicating Climate Change and Facilitating Social Change*, eds. Susanne C. Moser and Lisa Dilling (New York: Cambridge University Press, 2007), 153–166; Cathleen Fogel, "Constructing Progressive Climate Change Norms: The US in the Early 2000s," in *The Social Construction of Climate Change: Power, Knowledge, Norms, Discourses*, ed. Mary E. Pettenger (Aldershot, UK: Ashgate, 2007), 99–120; Dale Jamieson, "The Moral and Political Challenges of Climate Change," in *Creating a Climate for Change: Communicating Climate Change and Facilitating Social Change*, eds. Susanne C. Moser and Lisa Dilling (New York: Cambridge University Press, 2007), 475–482; Anthony Leiserowitz, "Communicating the Risks of Global Warming: American Risk Perceptions, Affective Images, and Interpretive Communities," in *Creating a Climate for Change: Communicating Climate Change and Facilitating Social Change*, eds. Susanne C. Moser and Lisa Dilling (New York: Cambridge University Press, 2007), 44–63; Nisbet, "Communicating Climate Change."

Hulme, on the other hand, is less convinced. "Religious beliefs often do not wield the power needed to bridge differences that exist in our views of science, economics, and…politics," he argues. "[A]ppeals to religion—to arguably, or hopefully, common spiritual and human values—may also be a long way from reconciling a fragmented and argumentative world." See Hulme, *Why We Disagree*, 155, 175.

CHAPTER I

1. This account is based primarily on my conversations with Cizik and Houghton: John Houghton, former chairman, Scientific Working Group of the Intergovernmental Panel on Climate Change, chairman, John Ray Initiative, phone interview with the author, June 5, 2007; Richard Cizik, former vice president for governmental affairs, National Association of Evangelicals, founder, New Evangelical Partnership for the Common Good, phone interview with the author, September 25, 2008.

2. Richard Cizik, interview for *The Great Warming*, http://www.thegreatwarming. com/revrichardcizik.html (accessed June 1, 2011).

3. Cizik, interview with the author. For an account of Wesley's experience, see Stephen Tomkins, *John Wesley: A Biography* (Grand Rapids, MI: Eerdmans, 2003).

4. Alexis de Tocqueville, *Democracy in America*, trans. Henry Reeve (London: Saunders and Otley, 1835), 229.

5. Christian Smith, *American Evangelicalism: Embattled and Thriving* (Chicago: University of Chicago Press, 1998), 2, emphasis in original.

6. The twelve volumes of *The Fundamentals: A Testimony To The Truth* were edited by A. C. Dixon and later by R. A. Torrey and published between 1910 and 1915.

7. For more on the Great Reversal, see George M. Marsden, *Fundamentalism and American Culture: The Shaping of Twentieth Century Evangelicalism, 1870–1925* (New York: Oxford University Press, 1980); David O. Moberg, *The Great Reversal: Evangelism and Social Concern* (Philadelphia: Lippincott, 1977); Mark D. Regnerus and Christian Smith, "Selective Deprivatization among American Religious Traditions: The Reversal of the Great Reversal," *Social Forces* 76, no. 4 (1998): 1,347–1,372.

8. Smith, *American Evangelicalism*, 10.

9. Carl F. H. Henry, *The Uneasy Conscience of Modern Fundamentalism* (Grand Rapids, MI: Eerdmans, 1947).

10. For more on neoevangelicalism, see George M. Marsden, *Reforming Fundamentalism: Fuller Seminary and the New Evangelicalism* (Grand Rapids, MI: Eerdmans, 1995).

11. Robert Wuthnow, "The Political Rebirth of American Evangelicals," in *The New Christian Right: Mobilization and Legitimation*, eds. Robert C. Liebman and Robert Wuthnow (New York: Aldine, 1983), 167–185, 184.

12. "Born Again! The Year of the Evangelicals," *Newsweek*, October 25, 1976; "Counting Souls," *Time*, October 4, 1976.

13. According to political scientists Clyde Wilcox and Carin Larson, "The Christian Right is a social movement that attempts to mobilize evangelical Protestants and

other orthodox Christians into conservative political action." Though white evangelicals are "the core potential constituency of the Christian Right," "some oppose [it], many are neutral toward the movement, a sizeable minority are supportive, and a much smaller number are active members." See Wilcox and Larson, *Onward Christian Soldiers*, 6–7.

14. Noll, *American Evangelical Christianity*, 23.

15. Regnerus and Smith, "Selective Deprivatization."

16. Smith, *American Evangelicalism*, 10.

17. Michael O. Emerson and Christian Smith, *Divided by Faith: Evangelical Religion and the Problem of Race in America* (New York: Oxford University Press, 2000), 3.

18. John C. Green, "Evangelical Protestants and Civic Engagement: An Overview," in *A Public Faith: Evangelicals and Civic Engagement*, ed. Michael Cromartie (Lanham, MD: Rowman and Littlefield, 2003), 11–29, 12, emphasis in original.

19. See, for example, Laurie Goodstein, "Evangelical Leaders Swing Influence Behind Effort to Combat Global Warming," *New York Times*, March 10, 2005; Laurie Goodstein, "Evangelical Leaders Join Global Warming Initiative," *New York Times*, February 8, 2006; Laurie Goodstein, "Evangelical's Focus on Climate Draws Fire of Christian Right," *New York Times*, March 3, 2007; Laurie Goodstein, "At Home with Jim Ball; Living Day to Day by a Gospel of Green," *New York Times*, March 8, 2007.

20. See David Larsen, "God's Gardeners: American Protestant Evangelicals Confront Environmentalism, 1967–2000" (Ph.D. diss., University of Chicago, 2001).

21. See Calvin B. DeWitt, "The Scientist and the Shepherd: The Emergence of Evangelical Environmentalism," in *The Oxford Handbook of Religion and Ecology*, ed. Roger S. Gottlieb (Oxford, UK: Oxford University Press, 2006), 568–587.

22. White, "Historical Roots."

23. White, "Historical Roots," 1206, 1207. White spends the latter part of his article promoting St. Francis of Assisi as a promising model for Christian environmental concern.

24. Francis A. Schaeffer, *Pollution and the Death of Man: The Christian View of Ecology* (Wheaton, IL: Tyndale House, 1970).

25. Schaeffer, *Pollution and the Death of Man*, 47. Rather than abandoning the term *dominion* in favor of "stewardship," Schaeffer emphasizes the biblical meaning of dominion as a kind of caring rule imbued with responsibility to those less powerful, similar to a proper relationship between king and subjects.

26. National Association of Evangelicals, "Resolution on Ecology," 1970, http://www.nae.net/resolutions/131-ecology-1970 (accessed June 1, 2011).

27. National Association of Evangelicals, "Resolution on Environment and Ecology," 1971, http://www.nae.net/resolutions/137-environment-and-ecology-1971 (accessed June 1, 2011).

28. Robert Booth Fowler, *The Greening of Protestant Thought* (Chapel Hill: University of North Carolina Press, 1995), 39.

29. Loren Wilkinson, ed., *Earthkeeping: Christian Stewardship of Natural Resources* (Grand Rapids, MI: Eerdmans, 1980).

30. Loren Wilkinson, ed., *Earthkeeping in the Nineties: Stewardship and the Renewal of Creation* (Grand Rapids, MI: Eerdmans, 1991), vii.

31. Larsen, "God's Gardeners," 190.

32. Wesley Granberg-Michaelson, ed., *Tending the Garden: Essays on the Gospel of the Earth* (Grand Rapids, MI: Eerdmans, 1987).

33. "An Open Letter to the Religious Community," January 1990, http://nrpe.org/interaith/statements/open-letter-religious-community (accessed June 1, 2011).

34. National Association of Evangelicals, "Resolution on Stewardship: All for God's Glory," 1990, http://www.nae.net/resolutions/313-stewardship-all-for-gods-glory-1990 (accessed June 1, 2011).

35. Mark J. Thomas, "Evangelicals and the Environment: Theological Foundations for Christian Environmental Stewardship," *Evangelical Review of Theology* 17, no. 2 (1993): 119–286.

36. "It's Not Easy Being Green: But the Time Has Come for Evangelicals to Confront the Environmental Crisis," *Christianity Today*, May 18, 1992, 14.

37. While other faith traditions have umbrella organizations with the authority to speak for their constituents and set overarching, top-down policy, the nonhierarchical nature of evangelicalism precludes that. The NAE and the SBC are the closest approximations to such structures, but they also epitomize evangelicalism's inherent decentralization: The United States' largest evangelical denomination, the SBC, is not one of the member denominations of the NAE.

38. See http://www.nrpe.org/ (accessed June 1, 2011).

39. EEN, "Let the Earth Be Glad: A Starter Kit for Evangelical Churches to Care for God's Creation" (Monrovia, CA: World Vision, 1994).

40. David P. Gushee, *The Future of Faith in American Politics: The Public Witness of the Evangelical Center* (Waco, TX: Baylor University Press, 2008), 175–176. For other work on this period of evangelical environmental engagement, see Jim Ball, "Evangelical Protestants, the Ecological Crisis, and Public Theology" (Ph.D. diss., Drew University, 1997); Jim Ball, "The Use of Ecology in the Evangelical Protestant Response to the Ecological Crisis," *Perspectives on Science and Christian Faith* 50 (1998): 32–40; Laurel Kearns, "Saving the Creation: Christian Environmentalism in the United States," *Sociology of Religion* 57, no. 1 (1996): 55–70; Laurel Kearns, "Saving the Creation: Religious Environmentalism" (Ph.D. diss., Emory University, 1994).

41. Peter Steinfels, "Evangelical Group Defends Laws Protecting Endangered Species as a Modern 'Noah's Ark,'" *New York Times*, January 31, 1996.

42. For more on the Noah's Ark campaign, see Laurel Kearns, "Noah's Ark Goes to Washington: A Profile of Evangelical Environmentalism," *Social Compass* 44, no. 3 (1997): 349–366.

43. Jo Anne Lyon, founder and former CEO, World Hope International, general superintendent, Wesleyan Church, interview with the author, Duluth, GA, May 14, 2009.

44. Jim Ball, executive vice president for policy and climate campaign, former president, Evangelical Environmental Network, interview with the author, Duluth, GA, May 13, 2009; Albert Gore, *Earth in the Balance: Ecology and the Human Spirit* (New York: Houghton Mifflin, 1992).

45. Ball, interview with the author.

46. Ball, interview with the author.

47. Gushee, *Future of Faith*, 176.

48. The origin of this slogan is somewhat unclear, as Bill McKibben claims he and Dan Smith first developed "What Would Jesus Drive?" while protesting outside a sport utility vehicle (SUV) dealership in Boston: "[W]e liked the emphasis on personal responsibility—and we guessed that the newspapers might like it too." Regardless of its beginnings, Ball's activism integrated "what would Jesus drive?" into public discourse. See McKibben, "Gospel of Green," 36.

49. Jim Ball, "From the Publisher's Desk," *Creation Care*, Fall 2004.

50. Ball, interview with the author.

51. Neela Banerjee, "Accused of Gay Liaison, Head of Evangelical Group Resigns," *New York Times*, November 3, 2006; Neela Banerjee and Laurie Goodstein, "Pastor Dismissed for 'Sexually Immoral Conduct,'" *New York Times*, November 5, 2006.

52. National Association of Evangelicals, "For the Health of the Nation: An Evangelical Call to Civic Responsibility," 2004, http://www.nae.net/images/content/For_The_Health_Of_The_Nation.pdf (accessed June 1, 2011).

53. Gushee, *Future of Faith*.

54. Megachurches are Protestant churches with more than 2,000 attendees at weekend services. See Scott Thumma and Dave Travis, *Beyond Megachurch Myths: What We Can Learn from America's Largest Churches* (San Francisco: Jossey-Bass, 2007).

55. Joel Hunter quoted in Goodstein, "Evangelical Leaders Swing Influence."

CHAPTER 2

1. US Senate Committee on the Environment and Public Works, testimony of Jim Ball, Evangelical Climate Initiative, June 7, 2007, http://epw.senate.gov/public/index.cfm?FuseAction=Files.View&FileStore_id=b430cae6–9164–472a-b979-d2e1d75ad5ca (accessed June 1, 2011).

2. Ball's Senate testimony, emphasis added. Here, Ball's scriptural quotation deviates from the *NIV* translation.

3. Hulme, *Why We Disagree*, xxvi.

4. For a hardcopy of the formatted document, contact the EEN. The imagery of the "Call to Action" is extensive and strategic. The document's visual components support and enrich its verbal dimensions, subtly interweaving theological aspects

among the written words and strengthening the case for religiously grounded engagement with climate change.

5. John T. Houghton, L. G. Meira Filho, B. A. Callander, N. Harris, A. Kattenberg, and K. Maskell, eds., *Climate Change 1995: The Science of Climate Change* (Cambridge, UK: Cambridge University Press, 1995), 39.

6. John T. Houghton, Y. Ding, D. J. Griggs, M. Noguer, P. J. Van der Linden, X. Dai, K. Maskell, and C. A. Johnson, eds., *Climate Change 2001: The Scientific Basis* (Cambridge, UK: Cambridge University Press, 2001), 10. The IPCC subsequently published its "Fourth Assessment Report" in 2007. See Solomon et al., *Climate Change 2007*.

7. Dunlap and McCright, "Widening Gap," 33. For an inventory of sources on and an analysis of the topic, see Aaron M. McCright and Riley E. Dunlap, "Anti-Reflexivity: The American Conservative Movement's Success in Undermining Climate Science and Policy," *Theory, Culture & Society* 27, no. 2–3 (2010): 100–133. For one example, see Robert F. Kennedy Jr., *Crimes Against Nature: How George W. Bush and His Corporate Pals Are Plundering the Country and High-Jacking Our Democracy* (New York: HarperCollins, 2004).

8. Overtones of Pascal's Wager are evident in this section of the "Call to Action." While the existence of God cannot be definitively proved through reason, Blaise Pascal argued, to act as though God exists is the wiser course. If one believes in God, but God does not exist, nothing is lost; if God exists, however, one has everything to gain. But if one does not believe and God exists, the losses are immense. Andy Crouch has compared this wager to the climate debate: "Likewise, we have little to lose, and much technological progress, energy security, and economic efficiency to gain, if we act on climate change now—even if the worst predictions fail to come to pass. But if we choose inaction and are mistaken, we will leave our descendants a blighted world." See Andy Crouch, "Environmental Wager," *Christianity Today*, June 29, 2005, http://www.christianitytoday.com/ct/2005/august/22.66.html (accessed June 1, 2011).

9. See, for example, John M. Broder, "Climate Change Seen as Threat to US Security," *New York Times*, August 8, 2009a; Andy Revkin, "The Sky Is Falling! Say Hollywood and, Yes, the Pentagon," *New York Times*, February 29, 2004.

10. Peter Schwartz and Doug Randall, "An Abrupt Climate Change Scenario and Its Implications for United States National Security," Prepared for the Defense Department, October 2003, http://www.gbn.com/articles/pdfs/Abrupt%20Climate%20Change%20February%202004.pdf (accessed June 1, 2011).

11. For a treatment of the spatial and temporal concerns raised by climate change, see Garvey, *Ethics of Climate Change*.

12. For a recent evangelical treatment of Genesis 1 from a creation care perspective, see Steven Bouma-Prediger, *For the Beauty of the Earth: A Christian Vision for Creation Care* (Grand Rapids, MI: Baker Academic, 2006).

13. Oelschlaeger, *Caring for Creation*, 130, emphasis in original.

14. White, "Historical Roots."

15. See Bouma-Prediger, *Beauty of the Earth.*

16. See, for example, Jim Ball, *Global Warming and the Risen Lord: Christian Discipleship and Climate Change* (Washington, DC: Evangelical Environmental Network, 2010); Jonathan Merritt, *Green Like God: Unlocking the Divine Plan for Our Planet* (New York: FaithWords, 2010); Tri Robinson, *Saving God's Green Earth: Rediscovering the Church's Responsibility to Environmental Stewardship* (Norcross, GA: Ampelon, 2006); J. Matthew Sleeth, *The Gospel According to the Earth: Why the Good Book Is a Green Book* (New York: HarperCollins, 2010).

17. J. Aaron Simmons, "Evangelical Environmentalism: Oxymoron or Opportunity?" *Worldviews* 13, no. 1 (2009): 40–71, 47.

18. UNFCCC, article 2.

19. Historical responsibility is rooted in the "polluter pays principle," which suggests that more developed countries are largely to blame for causing the climate problem and thus have the responsibility to ameliorate it. A related but less prevalent concept is distributive justice: More developed countries' have disproportionately used a common resource—carbon sinks—also implying greater responsibility to amend this iniquity. See Garvey, *Ethics of Climate Change.*

20. The Byrd-Hagel (1997) and Domenici-Bingaman (2005) resolutions were nonbinding Sense of the Senate statements, presenting the Senate's opinion but not creating legislation. See Sense of the Senate on UNFCCC, S.RES.98, 105th Congress, 1st Session, 1997, http://frwebgate.access.gpo.gov/cgi-bin/getdoc.cgi?dbname=105_cong_bills&docid=f:sr98ats.txt.pdf (accessed June 1, 2011); Sense of the Senate on Climate Change, SEC.1612., H.R.6.EAS., 109th Congress, 1st Session, 2005, http://frwebgate.access.gpo.gov/cgi-bin/getdoc.cgi?dbname=109_cong_bills&docid=f:h6eas.txt.pdf (accessed June 1, 2011).

21. For a current list, see http://christiansandclimate.org/ signatories/(accessed June 1, 2011).

22. Hulme, *Why We Disagree.*

23. Oelschlaeger, *Caring for Creation*, 123.

CHAPTER 3

1. The story reconstructed here is based primarily on Ball's own account, which he shared during his interview; quotations are his recollection. Citing Michael Cromartie, columnist David Brooks notes, "if evangelicals could elect a pope, Stott is the person they would likely choose." Stott passed away on July 27, 2011, leaving a legacy of evangelical leadership. He was a noted theologian; a prolific author and speaker; the framer of the Lausanne Covenant, "a crucial organizing document for modern evangelicalism"; and the founder of Langham Partnership International, an organization aimed at cultivating evangelical Christian leaders in the developing

world and based out of Stott's church, All Souls, Langham Place, in London. See David Brooks, "Who Is John Stott?" *New York Times*, November 30, 2004.

2. For more on A Rocha see http://www.arocha.org/ (accessed June 1, 2011).

3. Here, Marteen Hajer's concept of discourse coalitions is instructive. He explains that story lines unite the actors that employ them: "Discourse coalitions are defined as the ensemble of (1) a set of story-lines; (2) the actors who utter these story-lines; and (3) the practices in which this discursive activity is based." Though discourse coalitions are comprised by people who share discursive utterances, they may or may not have met. Story liness, as opposed to interaction or institutions, cement them as a unit. See Hajer, *Politics of Environmental Discourse*, 65.

4. David Gushee, professor of Christian ethics, Mercer University, founder, New Evangelical Partnership for the Common Good, interview with the author, Atlanta, GA, September 23, 2008.

5. Ball, interview with the author.

6. Alexei Laushkin, senior director of communications, EEN, interview with the author, Arlington, VA, September 19, 2008.

7. D. Michael Lindsay, "Evangelicals in the Power Elite: Elite Cohesion Advancing a Movement," *American Sociological Review* 73 (2008): 60–82, 75.

8. Ball, interview with the author.

9. Ball, interview with the author.

10. Rusty Pritchard, former national outreach director, EEN, founder and president, Flourish, interview with the author, Atlanta, GA, September 23, 2008.

11. For a copy of Houghton's NAE address, "Climate Change: A Christian Challenge and Opportunity," contact the EEN.

12. David Neff, editor-in-chief, *Christianity Today*, interview with the author, Carol Stream, IL, November 4, 2008.

13. Ron Sider, professor of theology, Eastern University, founder and director, Evangelicals for Social Action, interview with the author, Wynnewood, PA, September 17, 2008. See Ron Sider, *Rich Christians in an Age of Hunger* (Downers Grove, IL: InterVarsity, 1977).

14. Scott Sabin, executive director, Plant with Purpose (formerly Floresta USA), interview with the author, Duluth, GA, May 14, 2009.

15. John Phelan, former president, North Park Theological Seminary, interview with the author, Chicago, IL, November 5, 2008.

16. Dan Boone, president, Trevecca Nazarene University, phone interview with the author, January 8, 2009.

17. Tri Robinson, senior pastor, Vineyard Boise, interview with the author, Duluth, GA, May 14, 2009.

18. See Robinson, *Saving God's Green Earth*; Tri Robinson, *Small Footprint, Big Handprint: How to Live Simply and Love Extravagantly* (Norcross, GA: Ampelon, 2008).

19. Ball, interview with the author.

20. See Sleeth, Gospel According to the Earth.

21. Sleeth, Gospel According to the Earth, xii–xiii.

22. Matthew Sleeth, executive director, Blessed Earth, interview with the author, Duluth, GA, May 14, 2009. See J. Matthew Sleeth, *Serve God, Save the Planet: A Christian Call to Action* (Grand Rapids, MI: Zondervan, 2007); Sleeth, *Gospel According to the Earth*.

23. Sleeth's wife, Nancy, and daughter, Emma, have also penned books about their religious-environmental experiences and lessons learned. See Emma Sleeth, *It's Easy Being Green: One Student's Guide to Serving God and Saving the Planet* (Grand Rapids, MI: Zondervan, 2008); Nancy Sleeth, *Go Green, Save Green: A Simple Guide to Saving Time, Money, and God's Green Earth* (Carol Stream, IL: Tyndale House, 2009).

24. Wilson attended this retreat at the encouragement of Bert Waggoner, national director of the Association of Vineyard Churches and an ECI signatory. For the press release, see http://creationcareforpastors.com/PDF_files/creationcarestatement.pdf (accessed June 1, 2011).

25. Ken Wilson, senior pastor, Ann Arbor Vineyard, phone interview with the author, June 10, 2009.

26. See also Speth, *Red Sky at Morning*; Speth, *Bridge at the Edge*.

27. Wilson made these comments at a Friendship Collaborative Workshop, March 20, 2009, in Ann Arbor, Michigan. See http://www.friendshipcollaborative.org/wp-content/uploads/2009/05/fc_orientation-to-evangelicalism.doc (accessed June 1, 2011).

28. Cizik, interview with the author.

29. Jim Jewell, former campaign director, ECI, former chief operating officer, EEN, board chair and founder, Flourish, interview with the author, Suwanee, GA, September 24, 2008.

30. Phelan, interview with the author.

31. Neff, interview with the author.

32. Duane Litfin, former president, Wheaton College, Wheaton, IL, October 31, 2008.

33. Ball, interview with author.

34. Andy Crouch, author, editor, and producer, interview with the author, Swarthmore, PA, September 17, 2008. See Andy Crouch, *Culture Making: Recovering Our Creative Calling* (Downers Grove, IL: InterVarsity, 2008).

35. Wilson, interview with the author.

36. Sleeth, interview with the author.

37. Robinson, interview with the author.

38. Sleeth, interview with the author.

39. Robinson, interview with the author.

40. Laushkin, interview with the author.

41. Jewell, interview with the author.

42. Paul Corts, president, CCCU, interview with the author, Washington, DC, September 18, 2008.

43. Lyon, interview with the author.

44. Joel Hunter, senior pastor, Northland, A Church Distributed, phone interview with the author, January 7, 2009.

45. Sabin, interview with the author.

46. Crouch, interview with the author.

47. Crouch, *Culture Making*, 34.

48. Wilson, interview with the author.

49. Boone, interview with the author.

50. Corts, interview with the author.

51. Hunter, interview with the author.

52. Robinson, interview with the author.

53. Wilson, interview with the author.

54. See Evangelicals and Scientists United to Protect Creation, "Creation Care: An Introduction for Busy Pastors," http://creationcareforpastors.com/PDF_files/CreationCare_02-08.pdf (accessed June 1, 2011); http://www.creationcareforpastors.com/ (accessed June 1, 2011).

55. Sleeth, interview with the author. For instance, see Blessed Earth's new *Hope for Creation* and *Hope for Humanity* DVDs.

56. Boone, interview with the author.

57. Steve Timmermans, president, Trinity Christian College, interview with the author, Palos Heights, IL, November 4, 2008.

58. For more examples of campus-based creation care, see Renewal's 2010 "Green Awakenings Report," http://www.renewingcreation.org/resources/green-awakenings-report (accessed June 1, 2011).

59. Corts, interview with the author.

60. See Buster G. Smith and Bryan Johnson, "The Liberalization of Young Evangelicals: A Research Note," *Journal for the Scientific Study of Religion* 49, no. 2 (2010): 351–360.

61. Phelan, interview with the author.

62. For more on the student wing of the movement, see Ben Lowe, *Green Revolution: Coming Together to Care for Creation* (Downers Grove, IL: InterVarsity, 2009); http://renewingcreation.org/ (accessed June 1, 2011).

63. Corts, interview with the author.

64. Laushkin, interview with the author.

65. Lindsay, "Evangelicals in the Power Elite," 79; Peter L. Berger, *The Sacred Canopy: Elements of a Sociological Theory of Religion* (Garden City, NJ: Doubleday, 1967).

66. Justice concerns have not been nearly as widespread as those around abortion, but they have a long and rich tradition among the evangelical Left—what Phelan called the "Sojourners side" of American evangelicalism, referencing Jim Wallis's organization. See http://www.sojo.net/ (accessed June 1, 2011). For an exploration of Sojourners' place within evangelical politics, see Peter G. Heltzel, "Prophetic

Evangelicals: Toward a Politics of Hope," in *The Sleeping Giant Has Awoken: The New Politics of Religion in the United States*, eds. Jeffrey W. Robbins and Neal Magee (New York: Continuum, 2008), 25–40.

67. Blaine Harden, "The Greening of Evangelicals: Christian Right Turns, Sometimes Warily, to Environmentalism," *Washington Post*, February 6, 2005.

68. Lyon, interview with the author.

69. Phelan, interview with the author.

70. Gushee, interview with the author.

71. Harry O. Maier, "Green Millennialism: American Evangelicals, Environmentalism, and the Book of Revelation," in *Ecological Hermeneutics: Biblical, Historical, and Theological Perspectives*, eds. David G. Horrell, Cherryl Hunt, Christopher Southgate, and Francesca Stavrakopoulou (London: T&T Clark International, 2010), 246–265, 247. See also Janel Curry, "Christians and Climate Change: A Social Framework of Analysis," *Perspectives on Science and Christian Faith* 60, no. 3 (2008): 156–164; Janel M. Curry-Roper, "Contemporary Christian Eschatologies and Their Relation to Environmental Stewardship," *The Professional Geographer* 42, no. 2 (1990): 157–169.

72. Al Truesdale, "Last Things First: The Impact of Eschatology on Ecology," *Perspectives on Science and Christian Faith* 46 (1994): 116–122.

73. Harry O. Maier and J. Aaron Simmons both suggest that dispensationalism does not necessarily imply antienvironmentalism. In particular, progressive dispensationalism, a more recent theological development, challenges some of the tenets of classical dispensationalism and creates more space for an ethic of creation care. Simmons also argues that evangelical creation care advocates are not trying to supplant premillennialism but, rather, make a case for the former position; belief in the rapture and environmental concern are not incompatible. Nonetheless, my interviews with evangelical leaders suggest that many are trying to debunk dispensationalism. See Maier, "Green Millennialism"; Simmons, "Evangelical Environmentalism."

74. Tim LaHaye and Jerry B. Jenkins, *Left Behind* (Carol Stream, IL: Tyndale House, 1995–2007); Hal Lindsey, *The Late Great Planet Earth* (Grand Rapids, MI: Zondervan, 1970). For an exploration of apocalyptic fiction and the phenomenon of rapture culture, see Amy Johnson Frykholm, *Rapture Culture: Left Behind in Evangelical America* (New York: Oxford University Press, 2004).

75. Phelan, interview with the author.

76. Boone, interview with the author.

77. Larry Lloyd, former president, Crichton College, interview with the author, Memphis, TN, September 5, 2008. Romans 8:19–22: "The creation waits in eager expectation for the sons of God to be revealed. For the creation was subjected to frustration, not by its own choice, but by the will of the one who subjected it, in hope that the creation itself will be liberated from its bondage to decay and brought

into the glorious freedom of the children of God. We know that the whole creation has been groaning as in the pains of childbirth right up to the present time."

78. Ball, interview with the author. Here, Ball's scriptural quotation deviates from the *NIV* translation.

79. Timmermans, interview with the author.

80. Gushee, interview with the author.

81. The covers of the "Call to Action" subtly communicate this eschatology of renewal. The front cover is comprised solely of red, orange, and yellow tones. A horizon glows intensely marigold, sharing its color with the radiating sun and creating a palpable sense of high temperature. In striking contrast, soothing blue and green tones dominate the back cover. The Earth seems cool and restored to its proper balance. Paired with text from Colossians 1:16, the sense here is that creation has not been destroyed but renewed. This is a new heaven, a new Earth—a redeemed creation.

82. Robinson, interview with the author.

83. Sleeth, interview with the author.

84. Cizik, interview with the author.

85. Sleeth, interview with the author.

86. Robinson, interview with the author.

87. Cizik, interview with the author.

88. See Lindsay, *Faith in the Halls of Power*, 211.

89. Lyon, interview with the author.

90. Boone, interview with the author.

91. Ball, interview with the author.

92. Litfin, interview with the author.

93. Simmons, "Evangelical Environmentalism," 50.

94. Sabin, interview with the author.

95. Phelan, interview with the author.

96. Corts, interview with the author.

97. Ball, interview with the author.

98. Corts, interview with the author.

99. Robinson, interview with the author.

CHAPTER 4

1. Lydia DePillis, "What Would Jesus Drive?" *The New Republic*, September 22, 2009.

2. The program for the 2009 Values Voters Summit was previously available on the organization's website.

3. Larsen, "God's Gardeners."

4. E. Calvin Beisner, *Where Garden Meets Wilderness: Evangelical Entry into the Environmental Debate* (Grand Rapids, MI: Acton Institute for the Study of Religion and Liberty, 1997).

5. Cornwall Alliance, "The Cornwall Declaration on Environmental Stewardship" (Burke, VA: Cornwall Alliance, 2000), http://www.cornwallalliance.org/docs/the-cornwall-declaration-on-environmental-stewardship.pdf (accessed June 1, 2011).

6. Cizik, interview with the author.

7. Karen Breslau and Martha Brant, "God's Green Soldiers," *Newsweek*, February 13, 2006; John Tierney, "And on the Eighth Day, God Went Green," *New York Times*, February 11, 2006; Marc Gunther, "Strange Bedfellows," *Fortune*, February 8, 2006.

8. See http://www.cornwallalliance.org/docs/an-open-letter-to-the-signers-of-climate-change-an-evangelical-call-to-action-and-others-concerned-about-global-warming.pdf (accessed June 1, 2011).

9. E. Calvin Beisner, Paul K. Driessen, R. McKitrick, and Roy W. Spencer, "A Call to Truth, Prudence, and Protection of the Poor: An Evangelical Response to Global Warming" (Burke, VA: Cornwall Alliance, 2006).

10. Cited in Peter G. Heltzel, *Jesus and Justice: Evangelicals, Race, and American Politics* (New Haven, CT: Yale University Press, 2009), 154.

11. This letter was previously available on Focus on the Family's CitizenLink website.

12. Gushee, *Future of Faith*, 95–97; Heltzel, *Jesus and Justice*, 156–157.

13. See Gushee, *Future of Faith*; Laurel Kearns, "Cooking the Truth: Faith, Science, the Market, and Global Warming," in *EcoSpirit: Religions and Philosophies for the Earth*, eds. Laurel Kearns and Catherine Keller (New York: Fordham University Press, 2007), 97–124; Brian McCammack, "Hot Damned America: Evangelicalism and the Climate Change Policy Debate," *American Quarterly* 59, no. 3 (2007): 645–668; John C. Nagle, "The Evangelical Debate over Climate Change," *University of St. Thomas Law Journal* 5, no. 1 (2008): 52–86. Scholars debate which factor is chief. Gushee argues "these forces are fundamentally theological, not economic or political, though these latter factors do play a major part" (178). Nagle, on the other hand, suggests theology is frequently a space of agreement between Cornwall and the ECI and instead suggests different perspectives on the use of law are the major space of contention. Alternatively, Kearns argues that the most significant factor in these debates is "economics and the support of free enterprise and capitalism" (114).

14. See, for example, E. Calvin Beisner, Barrett Duke, and Stephen Livesay, eds., "The Cornwall Stewardship Agenda" (Burke, VA: Cornwall Alliance, 2008); Cornwall Alliance, "Cornwall Declaration."

15. See, for example, Beisner et al., "Call to Truth"; Beisner, Duke, and Livesy, "Cornwall Stewardship Agenda."

16. See, for example, Beiser et al., "Call to Truth"; Beisner, Duke, and Livesy, "Cornwall Stewardship Agenda."

17. Riley E. Dunlap and Aaron M. McCright, "Organized Climate Change Denial," in *The Oxford Handbook of Climate Change and Society*, eds. John S. Dryzek, Richard

B. Norgaard, and David Schlosberg (Oxford, UK: Oxford University Press, 2011), 144–160, 144. See also Naomi Oreskes and Erik M. Conway, *Merchants of Doubt* (New York: Bloomsbury Press, 2010).

18. See http://www.we-get-it.org/declaration/ (June 1, 2011).

19. Inhofe made this claim in a floor speech given on July 28, 2003, when he was chair of the Senate Committee on Environment and Public Works. See http://inhofe.senate.gov/pressreleases/climate.htm (June 1, 2011).

20. See http://www.resistingthegreendragon.com/ (June 1, 2011).

21. Here, the scriptural quotation deviates from the *NIV* translation.

22. Think Progress, an investigative reporting project of the liberal Center for American Progress Action Fund, has delved at length into the ties between Cornwall and the conservative antienvironmental countermovement, chiefly responsible for generating doubt about the science of climate change. See Lee Feng, "Exclusive: The Oily Operators Behind the Religious Climate Change Denial Front Group, Cornwall Alliance," *The Wonk Room*, June 15, 2010, http://wonkroom.thinkprogress.org/2010/06/15/cornwall-alliance-frontgroup/ (accessed June 1, 2011).

23. See http://www.jamespartnership.org/ (accessed June 1, 2011).

24. See http://cdrcommunications.com/about/clients/ (accessed June 1, 2011); Marc J. Ambinder, "Inside the Council for National Policy," *ABC News*, May 2, 2008, http://abcnews.go.com/Politics/story?id=121170 (accessed June 1, 2011); David D. Kirkpatrick, "Club of the Most Powerful Gathers in Strictest Privacy," *New York Times*, August 28, 2004.

25. Dunlap and McCright, "Organized Climate Change Denial," 149. See, for example, http://allpainnogain.cfact.org/ (accessed June 1, 2011).

26. See Feng, "Oily Operators"; http://www.cfact.org/about/1551/CFACT-Board-of-Advisors (accessed June 1, 2011).

27. Leith Anderson, "*Time* 100 Scientists and Thinkers: Eric Chivian and Richard Cizik," *Time*, May 12, 2008. For more on the documentary *God and Global Warming*, see http://www.pbs.org/now/shows/343/ (accessed June 1, 2011).

28. Richard Cizik, "Rev. Richard Cizik on God and Global Warming," interview with Terry Gross, *Fresh Air*, National Public Radio, WHYY, December 2, 2008. For a transcript, see http://www.npr.org/templates/transcript/transcript.php?storyId=97690760 (accessed June 1, 2011).

29. Sarah Pulliam, "Richard Cizik Resigns from the National Association of Evangelicals," *Christianity Today*, December 11, 2008, http://www.christianitytoday.com/ct/2008/decemberweb-only/150-42.0.html (June 1, 2011).

30. Sarah Pulliam, "Interview: NAE President Leith Anderson on Richard Cizik's Resignation," *Christianity Today*, December 11, 2008, http://www.christianitytoday.com/ct/2008/decemberweb-only/150-41.0.html (June 1, 2011).

31. Others, as well as Cizik, have interpreted this series of events somewhat differently. In a blog post, Perkins blamed Cizik's "environmentalism" for, in his own estimation, the misguided views expressed in the interview and cited Cizik's resignation

as a repudiation of an environmental agenda. "This is the risk of walking through the green door of environmentalism and global warming," he wrote. "You risk being blinded by the green light and losing your sense of direction." In an interview with Gross on July 28, 2010, Cizik explained: "I think it was the sum total, according to the president of the NAE, who asked for my resignation. It was the sum total of everything. It was speaking out on behalf of creation care, climate change, a broader agenda, speaking out on a host of levels that just offended the old guard. And civil unions, well, that was just one part of it." See Tony Perkins, "If NAE's Rich Cizik Doesn't Speak for Them, Who Does He Speak For?" FRC Blog, December 8, 2008, http://www.frcblog.com/2008/12/if-naes-rich-cizik-doesnt-speak-for-them-who-does-he-speak-for/ (June 1, 2011); Richard Cizik, "Ousted Evangelical Reflects on Faith, Future," interview with Terry Gross, *Fresh Air*, National Public Radio, WHYY, July 28, 2010. For a transcript, see http://www.npr.org/templates/transcript/transcript.php?storyId=128776382 (June 1, 2011).

32. Michelle A. Vu, "Evangelical Richard Cizik Re-emerges for Green Cause," *Christian Post*, April 20, 2009, http://www.christianpost.com/article/20090420/evangelical-richard-cizik-re-emerges-for-green-cause/index.html (June 1, 2011).

33. See "Dear Colleague" letter from Senator John Kerry and Senator Richard Lugar, November 10, 2009, http://chge.med.harvard.edu/programs/unite/documents/ScientistsEvangelicalsSenateDearColleague.pdf (June 1, 2011).

34. Adelle M. Banks, "For Cizik, It's Suddenly a Lot Easier Being Green," *Religion News Service*, May 7, 2009, http://www.religionnews.com/index.php?/rnspremiumtext/for_cizik_its_suddenly_a_lot_easier_being_green/ (June 1, 2011).

35. See http://www.newevangelicalpartnership.org/ (June 1, 2011).

36. See http://www.christianitytoday.com/ct/special/cizik_letter121608.pdf (June 1, 2011).

37. NAE, "Press Release: Galen Carey Named Director of Government Affairs of the NAE," June 24, 2009, http://www.nae.net/news/40-news-item-4 (June 1, 2011).

38. Sarah Pulliam, "The NAE Chooses Government Affairs Director," *Christianity Today*, June 24, 2009, http://www.christianitytoday.com/ct/2009/juneweb-only/125-31.0.html (June 1, 2011).

39. Wilson, interview with the author.

40. Heltzel, "Prophetic Evangelicals."

41. Lyon, interview with the author.

42. Cizik, interview with the author.

43. Phelan, interview with the author.

44. Brian McLaren, author and theologian, founding pastor, Cedar Ridge Community Church, interview with the author, Laurel, MD, September 18, 2008.

45. Cizik, interview with the author.

46. Sleeth, interview with the author.

47. Robinson, interview with the author.

48. Cizik, interview with the author.

49. Robin Rogers and Peter Goodwin Heltzel, "The New Evangelical Politics," *Society* 45 (2008): 412–414, 413, emphasis in original.

50. Lindsay, "Ties That Bind."

51. Lyon, interview with the author.

52. See http://reformnow.wordpress.com/ (accessed June 1, 2011).

53. Cizik, interview with the author.

54. Litfin, interview with the author.

55. Smith, *American Evangelicalism*, 10.

56. Lindsay, *Faith in the Halls of Power*, 216.

57. Lindsay, *Faith in the Halls of Power*, 217.

58. Lindsay, *Faith in the Halls of Power*, 226.

59. Hunter, interview with the author.

60. Cizik, interview with the author.

61. Gushee, interview with the author.

62. Ball, interview with the author.

63. See http://www.friendshipcollaborative.org/ (accessed June 1, 2011).

64. Wilson wrote his book *The Creation* as a series of letters to a Southern Baptist pastor, arguing that religious believers and secular humanists, like Wilson himself, can and should collaborate to save this place of mutual concern. See Wilson, *The Creation*.

65. For a list of scientists involved, see http://www.creationcareforpastors.com/about/advisors (accessed June 1, 2011).

66. Wilson, interview with the author.

67. Ball, interview with the author.

68. See, for example, Tom Strode, "Pro-abortion Foundation Aided Evangelical Climate Effort," *Baptist Press*, March 1, 2006, http://www.bpnews.net/bpnews.asp?id=22753 (accessed June 1, 2011).

69. Gushee, *Future of Faith*.

70. Heltzel, *Jesus and Justice*, 133.

71. Ball, interview with the author.

72. Cited in Heltzel, *Jesus and Justice*, 147.

73. Lyon, interview with the author.

74. Phelan, interview with the author.

75. McLaren, interview with the author.

76. Timmermans, interview with the author.

77. Robinson, interview with the author.

78. John Dominic Crossan, *The Birth of Christianity* (New York: HarperCollins, 1998), xxiii.

79. For more on white evangelicals' engagement with civil rights, see Curtis J. Evans, "White Evangelical Protestant Responses to the Civil Rights Movement," *Harvard Theological Review* 102, no. 2 (2009): 245–273.

80. Martin Luther King Jr., "Letter from Birmingham City Jail," in *A Testament of Hope: The Essential Writings and Speeches of Martin Luther King Jr.*, ed. James M. Washington (New York: HarperCollins, 1986), 289–302.

81. Kelly Brown Douglas and Wendell Berry make related claims. Douglas argues that such a binary understanding also functioned in "slaveholding Christianity," allowing the "master" to neglect any obligation to his or her "holdings," for this "dust" warranted no real concern. Berry proposes a similar critique of the sarcophobic dualism at work in American Christianity for contributing and failing to respond to environmental degradation. He argues that these hierarchical binaries have significant, negative social and environmental impacts and thus profound moral and religious implications. Berry states, "If we divide reality into two parts, spiritual and material, and hold…that only the spiritual is good or desirable, then our relation to the material Creation becomes arbitrary." See Kelly Brown Douglas, *The Black Christ* (Maryknoll, NY: Orbis, 1994); Berry, "Christianity and Survival," 109.

82. Gushee, *Future of Faith*, 176.

83. See "Global Warming: Who Said What and When," *Wall Street Journal*, March 24, 2008, http://online.wsj.com/article/SB120605552237153199.html?mod=googlewsj (accessed June 1, 2011).

84. See http://www.coloribus.com/adsarchive/tv-commercials/alliance-for-climate-protection-sharpton-robertson-512542/ (accessed June 1, 2011).

85. Harry R. Jackson Jr. and Tony Perkins, *Personal Faith, Public Policy* (Lake Mary, FL: FrontLine, 2008).

CHAPTER 5

1. J. Lester Feder, "The Floral Majority," *The New Republic*, December 30, 2008, http://www.tnr.com/article/politics/the-floral-majority (accessed June 1, 2011).

2. Raymond Randall, "Confessions of a Closet Environmentalist," Northland blog, comment posted on February 27, 2009, http://www.northlandchurch.net/blogs/confessions_of_a_closet_environmentalist/ (accessed June 1, 2011).

3. For more on the documentary *The Great Warming*, see http://www.thegreatwarming.com/ (accessed June 1, 2011).

4. Randall, "Closet Environmentalist."

5. Feder, "Floral Majority."

6. See ABC News, Planet Green, and Stanford University, "Fuel Costs Boost Conservation Efforts; 7 in 10 Reducing 'Carbon Footprint,'" August 9, 2008, http://abcnews.go.com/images/PollingUnit/1067a1Environment2008.pdf (accessed June 1, 2011); ABC News, *Time*, and Stanford University, "Intensity Spikes Concern on Warming; Many See a Change in Weather Patterns," March 25, 2006, http://woods.stanford.edu/docs/surveys/GW_Woods_ABC_Release_on_2006_GW_poll.pdf (accessed June 1, 2011); Barna Group, "Born Again Christians Remain Skeptical, Divided about Global Warming," September 17, 2007, http://www.barna.org/

barna-update/article/20-donorscause/95-born-again-christians-remain-skeptical-divided-about-global-warming (accessed June 1, 2011); Barna Group, "Evangelicals Go 'Green' with Caution," September 22, 2008, http:// www.barna.org/barna-update/article/13-culture/23-evangelicals-go-qgreenq-with-caution (accessed June 1, 2011); Ellison Research, "Nationwide Survey Shows Concerns of Evangelical Christians over Global Warming," prepared for the EEN, February 8, 2006, http:// www.npr.org/documents/2006/feb/evangelical/newsrelease.pdf (accessed June 1, 2011); Greenberg Quinlan Rosner Research, "America's Evangelicals Questionnaire," prepared for *Religion and Ethics Newsweekly*, April 5, 2004, http://www.pbs.org/ wnet/religionandethics/week733/questionnaire.pdf (accessed June 1, 2011); Cathy Lynn Grossman, "Evangelicals Less Worried about Global Climate Change," *USA Today*, September 18, 2008, http://www.usatoday.com/news/religion/2008–09-18-baylor-environment_N.htm (accessed June 1, 2011); Edward Maibach, Connie Roser-Renouf, and Anthony Leiserowitz, *Global Warming's Six Americas 2009: An Audience Segmentation Analysis* (New Haven, CT and Fairfax, VA: Yale Project on Climate Change and the George Mason University Center for Climate Change Communication, 2009); Pew Research Center for the People and the Press and Pew Forum on Religion and Public Life, "Many Americans Uneasy with Mix of Religion and Politics," August 24, 2006, http://pewforum.org/uploadedfiles/ Topics/Issues/Politics_and_Elections/religion-politics-06.pdf (accessed June 1, 2011); Pew Research Center for the People and the Press and Pew Forum on Religion and Public Life, "Religious Groups' Views on Global Warming," April 16, 2009, http://pewforum.org/Science-and-Bioethics/Religious-Groups-Views-on-Global-Warming.aspx (accessed June 1, 2011); Public Religion Research, "Key Religious Groups Want Government to Address Climate Change and Its Impact on World's Poor," prepared for Faith in Public Life and Oxfam America, March 27, 2009, http://www.faithinpubliclife.org/tools/polls/climate-change/ (accessed June 1, 2011).

7. While evangelicals in the Southeast may not be fully representative of evangelicals in other regions of the country, triangulation with polling data and the evangelical leaders I interviewed suggests these results have wider geographical applicability.

8. To maintain confidentiality of the churches and their members who participated in these discussion groups, I use pseudonyms.

9. Despite personal agreement with scholarly critiques of gendered theological language, in particular pairing "God" with male pronouns, I seek to echo, to the greatest extent possible, the theology of and language employed by church goers themselves, which included such gendered usage. (For further exploration of such debates, see, for example, the work of feminist theologians Rosemary Radford Ruether and Sallie McFague.)

10. White, "Historical Roots." A plethora of social-scientific studies have investigated the White thesis, particularly the relationship between American Christianity and environmental concern. They have led to a variety of disparate conclusions: Some

early ones find that religious belief correlates with low environmental concern; others identify a weak religion-environment relationship; and still others refute White, often suggesting the positive influence of a religious stewardship ethic. Within these broad trends, some identify a link between conservative Christianity—identified as fundamentalism, biblical literalism, or conservative eschatology—and low environmental concern, while others strongly dispute such claims. Further findings posit complicating factors: primarily that political ideology is actually the main determinant of environmental attitudes. As the debate currently stands, then, findings generally indicate that a link between religion and environmental concerns exists but is weak, likely but not clearly positive, and complicated by other demographic and ideological factors. Though the White thesis has not been decisively confirmed or refuted, as social scientific conclusions about this relationship remain unsettled and methodologically disputed, it is clear that, as Gregory Hitzhusen puts it, the definitive "specter of biblical anti-environmentalism is largely a myth." See Hitzhusen, "Theology and the Environment," 62. See also Heather Hartwig Boyd, "Christianity and the Environment in the American Public," *Journal for the Scientific Study of Religion* 38, no. 1 (1999): 36–44; Paul Dekker, Peter Ester, and Masja Nas, "Religion, Culture, and Environmental Concern: An Empirical Cross-National Analysis," *Social Compass* 44, no. 3 (1997): 443–458; Douglas Lee Eckberg and T. Jean Blocker, "Varieties of Religious Involvement and Environmental Concerns: Testing the Lynn White Thesis," *Journal for the Scientific Study of Religion* 28, no. 4 (1989): 509–517; Douglas Lee Eckberg and T. Jean Blocker, "Christianity, Environmentalism, and the Theoretical Problem of Fundamentalism," *Journal for the Scientific Study of Religion* 35, no. 4 (1996): 343–355; Andrew Greeley, "Religion and Attitudes Toward the Environment," *Journal for the Scientific Study of Religion* 32, no. 1 (1993): 19–28; James L. Guth, John C. Green, Lyman A. Kellstedt, and Corwin E. Smidt, "Faith and the Environment: Religious Beliefs and Attitudes on Environmental Policy," *American Journal of Political Science* 39, no. 2 (1995): 364–382; James L. Guth, Lyman A. Kellstedt, Corwin E. Smidt, and John C. Green, "Theological Perspectives and Environmentalism among Religious Activists," *Journal for the Scientific Study of Religion* 32, no. 4 (1993): 373–382; Carl M. Hand and Kent D. Van Liere, "Religion, Mastery-over-Nature, and Environmental Concern," *Social Forces* 63, no. 2 (1984): 555–570; Bernadette C. Hayes and Manussos Marangudakis, "Religion and Environmental Issues Within Anglo-American Democracies," *Review of Religious Research* 42, no. 2 (2000): 159–174; Conrad L. Kanagy and Hart M. Nelsen, "Religion and Environmental Concern: Challenging the Dominant Assumptions," *Review of Religious Research* 37, no. 1 (1995): 33–45; Conrad L. Kanagy and Fern K. Willits, "A 'Greening' of Religion? Some Evidence from a Pennsylvania Sample," *Social Science Quarterly* 74 (1993): 674–683; Willit M. Kempton, James S. Boster, and Jennifer A. Hartley, *Environmental Values in American Culture* (Cambridge, MA: MIT Press, 1995); P. Wesley Schultz, Lynnette Zelezny, and Nancy J. Dalrymple, "A Multinational Perspective on the Relation

Between Judeo-Christian Religious Beliefs and Attitudes of Environmental Concern," *Environmental Behavior* 32, no. 4 (2000): 576–591; Ronald G. Shaiko, "Religion, Politics, and Environmental Concern: A Powerful Mix of Passions," *Social Science Quarterly* 68, no. 2 (1987): 244–262; Darrren E. Sherkat and Christopher G. Ellison, "Structuring the Religion-Environment Connection: Identifying Religious Influences on Environmental Concern and Activism," *Journal for the Scientific Study of Religion* 46, no. 1 (2007): 71–85; Mark A. Shibley and Jonathon L. Wiggins, "The Greening of Mainline American Religion: A Sociological Analysis of the Environmental Ethics of the National Religious Partnership for the Environment," *Social Compass* 44, no. 3 (1997): 333–348; Michelle Wolkomir, Michael Futreal, Eric Woodrum, and Thomas Hoban, "Denominational Subcultures of Environmentalism," *Review of Religious Research* 38, no. 4 (1997): 325–343; Michelle Wolkomir, Michael Futreal, Eric Woodrum, and Thomas Hoban, "Substantive Religious Belief and Environmentalism," *Social Science Quarterly* 78, no. 1 (1997): 96–108; Eric Woodrum and Thomas Hoban, "Theology and Religiosity Effects on Environmentalism," *Review of Religious Research* 35, no. 3 (1994): 193–206; Eric Woodrum and Michelle J. Wolkomir, "Religious Effects on Environmentalism," *Sociological Spectrum* 17, no. 2 (1997): 223–234.

11. See, for example, Gushee, "Faith, Science, and Climate"; Simmons, "Evangelical Environmentalism"; Loren Wilkinson, "The Making of the Declaration," in *The Care of Creation: Focusing Concern and Action*, ed. R. J. Berry (Downers Grove, IL: InterVarsity, 2000), 50–59.

12. See, for example, James Lovelock, *Gaia: A New Look at Life on Earth* (Oxford, UK: Oxford University Press, 2000).

13. Bill Moyers, acceptance remarks for the Global Environmental Citizen Award, given by the Harvard University Center for Health and the Global Environment, New York, NY, December 1, 2004, http://chge.med.harvard.edu/events/documents/Moyerstranscript.pdf (accessed June 1, 2011).

14. Glenn Scherer, "The Godly Must Be Crazy," *Grist*, October 27, 2004, http://www.grist.org/article/scherer-christian/ (accessed June 1, 2011).

15. John C. Green quoted in Harden, "Greening of Evangelicals."

16. Cody's comments, and those of other skeptics in the group discussions, misstate fundamental climate science. For clarification of the peer-reviewed science of climate change, see Houghton, *Global Warming*; Solomon et al., *Climate Change 2007*.

17. David P. Gushee, "Faith, Science, and Climate Change," paper presented at the annual conference of the Christian Life Commission, Baptist General Convention of Texas, San Antonio, TX, March 3–4, 2008.

18. Crouch, "Environmental Wager."

19. For an account of the competing views of special creationist theism, theistic evolution, and progressive creationism, see Olson, *Handbook to Evangelical Theology*.

20. William R. Freudenburg, "Social Constructions and Social Constrictions: Toward Analyzing the Social Construction of 'the Naturalized' as well as 'the Natural,'" in *Environment and Global Modernity*, eds. Gert Spaargaren, Arthur P. J. Mol, and Frederick H. Buttel (London: Sage, 2000), 103–119, 106.

21. For treatments of the antienvironmental countermovement and its role in organized climate change denial, see Andrew Austin, "Advancing Accumulation and Managing Its Discontents: The US Anti-Environmental Countermovement," *Sociological Spectrum* 22, no. 1 (2002): 71–105; Riley E. Dunlap and Aaron M. McCright, "Climate Change Denial: Sources, Actors, and Strategies," in *Routledge Handbook of Climate Change and Society*, ed. Constance Lever-Tracy (New York: Routledge, 2010), 240–259; Dunlap and McCright, "Organized Climate Change Denial"; Aaron M. McCright and Riley E. Dunlap, "Challenging Global Warming as a Social Problem: An Analysis of the Conservative Movement's Counter-Claims," *Social Problems* 47, no. 4 (2000): 499–522; Oreskes and Conway, *Merchants of Doubt*.

22. Frank Luntz, "The Environment: A Cleaner, Safer, Healthier America," in *Straight Talk* (Alexandria, VA: The Luntz Research Companies, 2002), 131–146.

23. Luntz, "Cleaner, Safer, Healthier America," 137, emphasis in original.

24. McCright and Dunlap, "Politicization of Climate Change."

25. See Crossan, *Birth of Christianity*.

26. McCright and Dunlap, "Challening Global Warming," 510.

27. Aaron M. McCright and Riley E. Dunlap, "Defeating Kyoto: The Conservative Movement's Impact on US Climate Change Policy," *Social Problems* 50, no. 3 (2003): 348–373, 353. See also Dunlap and McCright, "Climate Change Denial"; Dunlap and McCright, "Organized Climate Change Denial"; Oreskes and Conway, *Merchants of Doubt*.

28. Dunlap and McCright, "Widening Gap."

29. McCright and Dunlap, "Politicization of Climate Change."

30. Emerson and Smith, *Divided by Faith*, 75.

31. Emerson and Smith, *Divided by Faith*, 76. See Ann Swidler, "Culture in Action: Symbols and Strategies," *American Sociological Review* 51, no. 2 (1986): 273–286.

32. Emerson and Smith, *Divided by Faith*, 76.

33. Emerson and Smith, *Divided by Faith*, 80.

34. Emerson and Smith, *Divided by Faith*, 70.

35. A historian of American religion, Curtis Evans argues, however, that individualism is an insufficient explanation for evangelicals' perspectives on race, as they "have selectively applied an individualist ethic primarily to social practices with which they have disagreed." Following this line of thought, selective application may also be at work in regard to the issue of climate change, allowing some evangelicals "to oppose legislation that differ[s] from their conception of the social good by denying its efficacy." See Evans, "Evangelical Protestant Responses," 250, 259.

36. Gushee has begun to do so. In 2009, he critiqued theological individualism at a creation care conference at Mercer University and in an opinion piece for the *Associated Baptist Press*. Instead, he recommended structural thinking and ethics: "Hyper-personalized theology leads to hyper-personalized ethics. Most everyday Christians understand their ethical responsibilities in terms of the purity of their inner lives and the integrity of their interpersonal relationships. These are laudable qualities, but this vision blocks attention to issues arising at the social, structural, economic, or global level. We need to nurture Christians who understand the ethical significance of, say, their own economic and environmental decisions as well as those of their churches, communities, businesses, and nations." See David P. Gushee, "Urgency, Creation Care, and Theological Advance," *Associated Baptist Press*, October 26, 2009, http://www.abpnews.com/index.php?option=com_content&task=view& id=4511&Itemid=9 (accessed June 1, 2011); Mark Vanderhoek, "Merritt, Gushee: On Creation Care, Evangelicals Must Move Toward 'We,'" *Associated Baptist Press*, November 3, 2009, http://www.abpnews.com/index.php?option=com_content& task=view&id=4538&Itemid=53 (accessed June 1, 2011).
37. Feder, "Floral Majority."

CHAPTER 6

1. This account is based primarily on Sabin's comments during his interview.
2. Sleeth, interview with the author.
3. Boone, interview with the author.
4. See John M. Broder, "With Something for Everyone, Climate Bill Passed," *New York Times*, June 30, 2009; Paul Krugman, "Betraying the Planet," *New York Times*, June 28, 2009.
5. See Ryan Lizza, "As the World Burns," *The New Yorker*, October 11, 2010.
6. See http://flourishonline.org/about/history/ (accessed June 1, 2011).
7. See http://flourishonline.org/about/ (accessed June 1, 2011).
8. Jewell, interview with the author; Pritchard, interview with the author.
9. Jonathan Merritt, founder and spokesperson, Southern Baptist Environment and Climate Initiative, director of church programs, Flourish, interview with the author, Duluth, GA, September 23, 2008.
10. See http://www.baptistcreationcare.org/node/1 (accessed June 1, 2011).
11. See http://www.baptistcreationcare.org/sites/default/files/SBE_CI_News_Release. pdf (accessed June 1, 2011); http://www.baptistcreationcare.org/node/2 (accessed June 1, 2011).
12. Interestingly, though Land and the ERLC have been a core part of climate care's opposition, in 1992 he published an edited volume titled *The Earth Is the Lord's: Christians and the Environment*, which indicates a commitment to stewardship. This seeming discrepancy suggests a perceived differentiation between stewardship

and climate change. See Richard D. Land and Louis A. Moore, eds., *The Earth Is the Lord's: Christians and the Environment* (Nashville, TN: Broadman, 1992).

13. Jonathan Merritt, welcome address at the Flourish conference, Duluth, GA, May 13, 2009.

14. Rusty Pritchard, keynote address at the Flourish conference, Duluth, GA, May 13, 2009.

15. Rusty Pritchard, "A Funny Thing Happened on the Way to the Conference," SustainLane Blog, comment posted on May 20, 2009, http://www.sustain-lane.com/reviews/a-funny-thing-happened-on-the-way-to-the-conference/FBHIPQTHJLLVUA9A3D1B1K7C13QB (accessed June 1, 2011).

16. Rusty Pritchard, "I'm No Environmentalist," SustainLane blog, comment posted on July 15, 2009, http://www.sustainlane.com/reviews/im-no-environmentalist/JXP4KTTI74W9H7MDY4R8NAVYY78J (accessed June 1, 2011).

17. In his own commentary, Neff has deemed Flourish's approach a separation of creation care from "political action" and "creation care without the baggage." See David Neff, "Can We Separate Creation Care from Political Action?" *Christianity Today* blog, comment posted on April 24, 2009, http://blog.christianitytoday.com/ctliveblog/archives/2009/04/can_we_separate.html (accessed June 1, 2011); David Neff, "Creation Care Without the Baggage," *Christianity Today* blog, comment posted on May 17, 2009, http://blog.christianitytoday.com/ctliveblog/archives/2009/05/creation_care_w.html (accessed June 1, 2011).

18. Jim Jewell, "Environmental Words," Flourish blog, comment posted in June 2009, http://flourishonline.org/2009/06/environmental-words/ (accessed June 1, 2011).

19. Jim Ball, comments at the Flourish conference, Duluth, GA, May 13, 2009.

20. Alexei Laushkin, comments at the Flourish conference, Duluth, GA, May 13, 2009.

21. Angela M. Smith and Simone Pulver, "Ethics-Based Environmentalism in Practice: Religious-Environmental Organizations in the United States," *Worldviews* 13, no. 2 (2009): 145–179, 146.

22. Pritchard, keynote address.

23. Jewell, interview with the author.

24. Matthew Sleeth, address at the Flourish conference, Duluth, GA, May 15, 2009.

25. J. Matthew Sleeth, "God's Mental Health Prescription," *Creation Care*, Summer 2008, 41.

26. Jonathan Merritt, "Green Means Growing Churches," *Flourish*, Spring 2009, 8. For a reposting online, see http://flourishonline.org/2009/06/green-means-growing-churches/ (accessed June 1, 2011).

27. Tri Robinson, address at the Flourish conference, Duluth, GA, May 14, 2009.

28. Smith and Pulver, "Ethics-Based Environmentalism," 166.

29. Robert J. Brulle, *Agency, Democracy, and Nature: The US Environmental Movement from a Critical Theory Perspective* (Cambridge, MA: MIT Press, 2000).

30. Ball, interview with the author.

31. Sabin, interview with the author.

32. Pritchard, interview with the author.

33. David S. Meyer, "Building Social Movements," in *Creating a Climate for Change: Communicating Climate Change and Facilitating Social Change*, eds. Susanne C. Moser and Lisa Dilling (New York: Cambridge University Press, 2007), 451–461, 452.

34. Wilson, interview with the author.

35. Barrett Duke, comments at the Flourish Conference, Duluth, GA, May 15, 2009.

36. Cornwall Alliance, press release on "Evangelicals Say Poor, Minorities Will Be Hardest Hit by Climate Legislation," May 26, 2009, http://www.cornwallalliance.org/docs/evangelicals-say-poor-minorities-will-be-hardes-hit-by-climate-legislation.pdf (accessed June 1, 2011); Richard Land, "House Votes for Cap and Trade," Ethics and Religious Liberty Commission blog, comment posted on June 26, 2009, http://erlc.com/article/cap-and-trade-vote-today/ (accessed June 1, 2011).

37. Robinson, interview with the author.

38. Wilson, interview with the author.

39. Tri Robinson and Ken Wilson, "Vineyard Churches: Seven Year Plan for American Evangelicalism," in *Many Heavens, One Earth: Faith Commitments to Protect the Living Planet*, eds. Mary Colwell, Victoria Finlay, Alison Hilliard, and Susie Weldon (Bath, UK: Alliance of Religions and Conservation, 2009), 135–137.

40. For more on this engagement, see Sharon Gramby-Sobukwe and Tim Hoiland, "The Rise of Mega-Church Efforts in International Development: A Brief Analysis and Areas for Further Research," *Transformation* 26, no. 2 (2009): 104–117.

41. See http://www.aerdo.net/aboutus.php (accessed June 1, 2011).

42. See https://worldrelief.org/SSLPage.aspx?pid=1444 (accessed June 1, 2011); http://www.worldvision.org/content.nsf/about/our-mission (accessed June 1, 2011).

43. Ball, interview with the author.

44. The fourth claim of the "Call to Action" briefly addresses the issue of adaptation: "[W]hile we must reduce our global warming pollution to help mitigate the impacts of climate change, as a society and as individuals we must also help the poor adapt to the significant harm that global warming will cause."

45. See http://www.aerdo.net/innerloop/ClimateChangeStatementApril2009.pdf (accessed June 1, 2011).

46. Wilson, interview with the author.

47. ESUPC, *Creation Care*, 12–14.

48. Alex Kirby, *Climate in Peril* (Arendal, Norway: UNEP/GRID-Arendal, 2009).

49. See Brulle, *Agency, Democracy, and Nature*, 256.

CONCLUSION

1. See Hitzhusen, "Theology and the Environment," 62.
2. Christian Smith, "Correcting a Curious Neglect, or Bringing Religion Back In," in *Disruptive Religion: The Force of Faith in Social Movement Activism*, ed. Christian Smith (New York: Routledge, 1996), 1–25, 1. This perspective represents a significant shift from the long-held structural-functional view, as promoted by Émile Durkheim and others, which emphasizes religion's role in building and sustaining social consensus and integration. Instead, it draws more on Weberian notions about religion's contribution to social innovation.
3. See Randall Balmer, *Mine Eyes Have Seen the Glory: A Journey into the Evangelical Subculture in America*, 4th ed. (New York: Oxford University Press, 2006).
4. Hulme, *Why We Disagree,* 322.
5. Hulme, *Why We Disagree*, 358.
6. McCright and Dunlap, "Politicization of Climate Change," 178.
7. Anthony A. Leiserowitz, Edward W. Maibach, Connie Roser-Renouf, Nicholas Smith, and Erica Dawson, *Climate Gate, Public Opinion, and the Loss of Trust* (New Haven, CT: Yale Project on Climate Change Communication, 2010), http:// environment.yale.edu/climate/publications/climategate-public-opinion-and-the-loss-of-trust/ (accessed June 1, 2011).
8. See, for example, John M. Broder, "Climate Change Doubt Is Tea Party Article of Faith," *New York Times*, October 20, 2010; John Collins Rudolph, "Climate Skeptic Seeks Energy Committee Chairmanship," *New York Times*, November 16, 2010. For a transcript of Beisner and Beck's conversation, see http://www.foxnews.com/story/0,2933,601962,00.html (accessed June 1, 2011).
9. See, for example, Mark Galli, "Judgment in the Gulf," *Christianity Today*, June 1, 2010, http://www.christianitytoday.com/ct/2010/juneweb-only/32–22.0.html (June 1, 2011); Russell D. Moore, "Ecological Catastrophe and the Uneasy Evangelical Conscience," Moore to the Point blog, June 1, 2010, http://www.russellmoore. com/2010/06/01/ecological-catastrophe-and-the-uneasy-evangelical-conscience/ (June 1, 2011). On Mountain Top Removal, see the work of Peter Illyn and Restoring Eden, http://restoringeden.org/ (June 1, 2011), as well as that of Judy Bonds and Christians for the Mountains, http://www.christiansforthemountains.org/ (June 1, 2011).

APPENDIX H

1. BFM stands for the Baptist Faith and Message—the confession of faith of the Southern Baptist Convention.

Bibliography

ABC News, Planet Green, and Stanford University. "Fuel Costs Boost Conservation Efforts; 7 in 10 Reducing 'Carbon Footprint,'" August 9, 2008. Accessed June 1, 2011. http://abcnews.go.com/images/PollingUnit/1067a1Environment2008.pdf.

ABC News, *Time*, and Stanford University. "Intensity Spikes Concern on Warming; Many See a Change in Weather Patterns," March 25, 2006. Accessed June 1, 2011. http://woods.stanford.edu/docs/surveys/GW_Woods_ABC_Release_on_2006_GW_poll.pdf.

Ambinder, Marc J. "Inside the Council for National Policy." *ABC News*, May 2, 2008. Accessed June 1, 2011. http://abcnews.go.com/Politics/story?id=121170.

Anderson, Leith. "*Time* 100 Scientists and Thinkers: Eric Chivian and Richard Cizik." *Time*, May 12, 2008.

Austin, Andrew. "Advancing Accumulation and Managing Its Discontents: The US Anti-Environmental Countermovement." *Sociological Spectrum* 22, no. 1 (2002): 71–105.

Ball, Jim. "Evangelical Protestants, the Ecological Crisis, and Public Theology." Ph.D. diss., Drew University, 1997.

Ball, Jim. "From the Publisher's Desk." *Creation Care*, Fall 2004.

Ball, Jim. *Global Warming and the Risen Lord: Christian Discipleship and Climate Change*. Washington, DC: Evangelical Environmental Network, 2010.

Ball, Jim. "The Use of Ecology in the Evangelical Protestant Response to the Ecological Crisis." *Perspectives on Science and Christian Faith* 50 (1998): 32–40.

Balmer, Randall. *Mine Eyes Have Seen the Glory: A Journey into the Evangelical Subculture in America*, 4th ed. New York: Oxford University Press, 2006.

Ban, Ki-moon. Speech given at the Celebration of Faiths and the Environment, Windsor, UK, November 3, 2009, transcript. Accessed June 1, 2011. http://www.windsor2009.org/ARC-UNDPWindsor2009-SpeechBanKi-moon.pdf.

Banerjee, Neela. "Accused of Gay Liaison, Head of Evangelical Group Resigns." *New York Times*, November 3, 2006.

Banerjee, Neela and Laurie Goodstein. "Pastor Dismissed for 'Sexually Immoral Conduct.'" *New York Times*, November 5, 2006.

Banks, Adelle M. "For Cizik, It's Suddenly a Lot Easier Being Green." *Religion News Service*, May 7, 2009. Accessed June 1, 2011. http://www.religionnews.com/index. php?/rnspremiumtext/for_cizik_its_suddenly_a_lot_easier_being_green/.

Barna Group. "Born Again Christians Remain Skeptical, Divided about Global Warming," September 17, 2007. Accessed June 1, 2011. http://www.barna.org/barna-update/article/20-donorscause/95-born-again-christians-remain-skeptical-divided-about-global-warming.

Barna Group. "Evangelicals Go 'Green' with Caution," September 22, 2008. Accessed June 1, 2011. http://www.barna.org/barna-update/article/13-culture/23-evangelicals-go-qgreenq-with-caution.

Bebbington, David W. *Evangelicalism in Modern Britain: A History from the 1730s to the 1980s*. London: Unwin Hyman, 1989.

Beisner, E. Calvin. *Where Garden Meets Wilderness: Evangelical Entry into the Environmental Debate*. Grand Rapids, MI: Acton Institute for the Study of Religion and Liberty, 1997.

Beisner, E. Calvin, Paul K. Driessen, R. McKitrick, and Roy W. Spencer. "A Call to Truth, Prudence, and Protection of the Poor: An Evangelical Response to Global Warming." Burke, VA: Cornwall Alliance, 2006.

Beisner, E. Calvin, Barrett Duke, and Stephen Livesay, eds. "The Cornwall Stewardship Agenda." Burke, VA: Cornwall Alliance, 2008.

Berger, Peter L. *The Sacred Canopy: Elements of a Sociological Theory of Religion*. Garden City, NJ: Doubleday, 1967.

Berry, R. J., ed. *The Care of Creation: Focusing Concern and Action*. Downers Grove, IL: InterVarsity, 2000.

Berry, Wendell. "Christianity and the Survival of Creation." In *Sex, Economy, Freedom, and Community*. New York: Pantheon, 1993.

Bingham, Sally. "Climate Change: A Moral Issue." In *Creating a Climate for Change: Communicating Climate Change and Facilitating Social Change*, Susanne C. Moser and Lisa Dilling, eds., 153–166. New York: Cambridge University Press, 2007.

"Born Again! The Year of the Evangelicals." *Newsweek*, October 25, 1976.

Bouma-Prediger, Steven. *For the Beauty of the Earth: A Christian Vision for Creation Care*. Grand Rapids, MI: Baker Academic, 2006.

Boyd, Heather Hartwig. "Christianity and the Environment in the American Public." *Journal for the Scientific Study of Religion* 38, no. 1 (1999): 36–44.

Breslau, Karen and Martha Brant. "God's Green Soldiers." *Newsweek*, February 13, 2006.

Broder, John M. "Climate Change Doubt Is Tea Party Article of Faith." *New York Times*, October 20, 2010.

Broder, John M. "Climate Change Seen as Threat to US Security." *New York Times*, August 8, 2009.

Broder, John M. "With Something for Everyone, Climate Bill Passed." *New York Times*, June 30, 2009.

Brooks, David. "Who Is John Stott?" *New York Times*, November 30, 2004.

Brulle, Robert J. *Agency, Democracy, and Nature: The US Environmental Movement from a Critical Theory Perspective.* Cambridge, MA: MIT Press, 2000.

Bulkeley, Harriet and Michele Betsill. *Cities and Climate Change: Urban Sustainability and Global Environmental Governance.* London: Routledge, 2003.

Cass, Loren R. Cass and Mary E. Pettenger. "Conclusion: The Constructions of Climate Change." In *The Social Construction of Climate Change: Power, Knowledge, Norms, Discourses*, Mary E. Pettenger, ed., 235–246. Aldershot, UK: Ashgate, 2007.

Cizik, Richard. "Ousted Evangelical Reflects on Faith, Future." Interview with Terry Gross, *Fresh Air*, National Public Radio, WHYY, July 28, 2010, transcript. Accessed June 1, 2011. http://www.npr.org/templates/transcript/transcript.php?storyId=128776382.

Cizik, Richard. "Rev. Richard Cizik on God and Global Warming." Interview with Terry Gross, *Fresh Air*, National Public Radio, WHYY, December 2, 2008, transcript. Accessed June 1, 2011. http://www.npr.org/templates/transcript/transcript.php?storyId=97690760.

Colwell, Mary, Victoria Finlay, Alison Hilliard, and Susie Weldon, eds. *Many Heavens, One Earth: Faith Commitments to Protect the Living Planet.* Bath, UK: Alliance of Religions and Conservation, 2009.

Cornwall Alliance. "The Cornwall Declaration on Environmental Stewardship." Burke, VA: Cornwall Alliance, 2000. Accessed June 1, 2011. http://www.cornwallalliance.org/docs/the-cornwall-declaration-on-environmental-stewardship.pdf.

Cornwall Alliance. Press release on "Evangelicals Say Poor, Minorities Will Be Hardest Hit by Climate Legislation," May 26, 2009. Accessed June 1, 2011. http://www.cornwallalliance.org/docs/evangelicals-say-poor-minorities-will-be-hardes-hit-by-climate-legislation.pdf.

"Counting Souls." *Time*, October 4, 1976.

Cox, J. Robert. *Environmental Communication and the Public Sphere.* 2nd ed. Thousand Oaks, CA: Sage, 2010.

Crossan, John Dominic. *The Birth of Christianity.* New York: HarperCollins, 1998.

Crouch, Andy. *Culture Making: Recovering Our Creative Calling.* Downers Grove, IL: InterVarsity, 2008.

Crouch, Andy. "Environmental Wager." *Christianity Today*, June 29, 2005. Accessed June 1, 2011. http://www.christianitytoday.com/ct/2005/august/22.66.html.

Curry, Janel. "Christians and Climate Change: A Social Framework of Analysis." *Perspectives on Science and Christian Faith* 60, no. 3 (2008): 156–164.

Curry-Roper, Janel M. "Contemporary Christian Eschatologies and Their Relation to Environmental Stewardship." *The Professional Geographer* 42, no. 2 (1990): 157–169.

Dekker, Paul, Peter Ester, and Masja Nas. "Religion, Culture, and Environmental Concern: An Empirical Cross-National Analysis." *Social Compass* 44, no. 3 (1997): 443–458.

Dernbach, John C. "Harnessing Individual Behavior to Address Climate Change: Options for Congress." *Virginia Environmental Law Journal* 26, no. 1 (2008): 107–156.

DePillis, Lydia. "What Would Jesus Drive?" *The New Republic*, September 22, 2009.

DeWitt, Calvin B. "The Scientist and the Shepherd: The Emergence of Evangelical Environmentalism." In *The Oxford Handbook of Religion and Ecology*, Roger S. Gottlieb, ed., 568–587. Oxford, UK: Oxford University Press, 2006.

Douglas, Kelly Brown. *The Black Christ*. Maryknoll, NY: Orbis, 1994.

Dryzek, John S. *The Politics of the Earth: Environmental Discourses*. 2nd ed. Oxford, UK: Oxford University Press, 2005.

Dunlap, Riley E. and Aaron M. McCright. "Climate Change Denial: Sources, Actors, and Strategies." In *Routledge Handbook of Climate Change and Society*, Constance Lever-Tracy, ed., 240–259. New York: Routledge, 2010.

Dunlap, Riley E. and Aaron M. McCright. "Organized Climate Change Denial." In *The Oxford Handbook of Climate Change and Society*, John S. Dryzek, Richard B. Norgaard, and David Schlosberg, eds., 144–160. Oxford, UK: Oxford University Press, 2011.

Dunlap, Riley E. and Aaron M. McCright. "A Widening Gap: Republican and Democratic Views on Climate Change." *Environment* 50, no. 5 (2008): 26–35.

Eckberg, Douglas Lee and T. Jean Blocker. "Christianity, Environmentalism, and the Theoretical Problem of Fundamentalism." *Journal for the Scientific Study of Religion* 35, no. 4 (1996): 343–355.

Eckberg, Douglas Lee and T. Jean Blocker. "Varieties of Religious Involvement and Environmental Concerns: Testing the Lynn White Thesis." *Journal for the Scientific Study of Religion* 28, no. 4 (1989): 509–517.

Ellison Research. "Nationwide Survey Shows Concerns of Evangelical Christians over Global Warming." Prepared for the EEN, February 8, 2006. Accessed June 1, 2011. http://www.npr.org/documents/2006/feb/evangelical/newsrelease.pdf.

Emerson, Michael O. and Christian Smith. *Divided by Faith: Evangelical Religion and the Problem of Race in America*. New York: Oxford University Press, 2000.

Evangelical Environmental Network. "Let the Earth Be Glad: A Starter Kit for Evangelical Churches to Care for God's Creation." Monrovia, CA: World Vision, 1994.

Evangelicals and Scientists United to Protect Creation. "Creation Care: An Introduction for Busy Pastors". Accessed June 1, 2011. http://creationcareforpastors.com/PDF_files/CreationCare_02–08.pdf.

Evans, Curtis J. "White Evangelical Protestant Responses to the Civil Rights Movement." *Harvard Theological Review* 102, no. 2 (2009): 245–273.

Feder, J. Lester. "The Floral Majority." *The New Republic*, December 30, 2008. Accessed June 1, 2011. http://www.tnr.com/article/politics/the-floral-majority.

Feng, Lee. "Exclusive: The Oily Operators Behind the Religious Climate Change Denial Front Group, Cornwall Alliance." *The Wonk Room*, June 15, 2010. Accessed June 1, 2011. http://wonkroom.thinkprogress.org/2010/06/15/cornwall-alliance-frontgroup/.

Fogel, Cathleen. "Constructing Progressive Climate Change Norms: The US in the Early 2000s." In *The Social Construction of Climate Change: Power, Knowledge, Norms, Discourses*, Mary E. Pettenger, ed., 99–120. Aldershot, UK: Ashgate, 2007.

Fowler, Robert Booth. *The Greening of Protestant Thought*. Chapel Hill, NC: University of North Carolina Press, 1995.

Freudenburg, William R. "Social Constructions and Social Constrictions: Toward Analyzing the Social Construction of 'the Naturalized' as well as 'the Natural.'" In *Environment and Global Modernity*, Gert Spaargaren, Arthur P. J. Mol, and Frederick H. Buttel, eds., 103–119. London: Sage, 2000.

Frykholm, Amy Johnson. *Rapture Culture: Left Behind in Evangelical America*. New York: Oxford University Press, 2004.

Galli, Mark. "Judgment in the Gulf." *Christianity Today*, June 1, 2010. Accessed November 14, 2010. http://www.christianitytoday.com/ct/2010/juneweb-only/32-22.0.html.

Gardiner, Stephen M. "Ethics and Global Climate Change." *Ethics* 114, no. 3 (2004): 555–600.

Gardner, Gary. *Invoking the Spirit: Religion and Spirituality in the Quest for a Sustainable World*. Worldwatch Paper 164. Washington, DC: Worldwatch Institute, 2002.

Garvey, James. *The Ethics of Climate Change: Right and Wrong in a Warming World*. London: Continuum, 2008.

"Global Warming: Who Said What and When." *Wall Street Journal*, March 24, 2008. Accessed June 1, 2011. http://online.wsj.com/article/SB120605552237153199.html?mod=googlewsj.

Goodstein, Laurie. "At Home with Jim Ball; Living Day to Day by a Gospel of Green." *New York Times*, March 8, 2007.

Goodstein, Laurie. "Evangelical Leaders Join Global Warming Initiative." *New York Times*, February 8, 2006.

Goodstein, Laurie. "Evangelical Leaders Swing Influence Behind Effort to Combat Global Warming." *New York Times*, March 10, 2005.

Goodstein, Laurie. "Evangelical's Focus on Climate Draws Fire of Christian Right." *New York Times*, March 3, 2007.

Gore, Albert. *Earth in the Balance: Ecology and the Human Spirit*. New York: Houghton Mifflin, 1992.

Gottlieb, Roger S. Introduction to *The Oxford Handbook of Religion and Ecology*, Roger S. Gottlieb, ed., 3–22. Oxford, UK: Oxford University Press, 2006.

Gottlieb, Roger S., ed. *The Oxford Handbook of Religion and Ecology*. Oxford, UK: Oxford University Press, 2006.

Gramby-Sobukwe, Sharon and Tim Hoiland. "The Rise of Mega-Church Efforts in International Development: A Brief Analysis and Areas for Further Research." *Transformation* 26, no. 2 (2009): 104–117.

Granade, Hannah Choi, Jon Creyts, Anton Derkach, Philip Farese, Scott Nyquist, and Ken Ostrowski. *Unlocking Energy Efficiency in the US Economy*. New York: McKinsey and Company, 2009.

Granberg-Michaelson, Wesley, ed. *Tending the Garden: Essays on the Gospel of the Earth*. Grand Rapids, MI: Eerdmans, 1987.

Greeley, Andrew. "Religion and Attitudes toward the Environment." *Journal for the Scientific Study of Religion* 32, no. 1 (1993): 19–28.

Green, John C. "Evangelical Protestants and Civic Engagement: An Overview." In *A Public Faith: Evangelicals and Civic Engagement*, Michael Cromartie, ed., 11–29. Lanham, MD: Rowman and Littlefield, 2003.

Green, John C., Mark J. Rozell, and Clyde Wilcox, eds. *The Values Campaign? The Christian Right and the 2004 Elections*. Washington, DC: Georgetown University Press, 2006.

Greenberg Quinlan Rosner Research. "America's Evangelicals Questionnaire." Prepared for *Religion and Ethics Newsweekly*, April 5, 2004. Accessed June 1, 2011. http://www.pbs.org/wnet/religionandethics/week733/questionnaire.pdf.

Griffith, R. Marie. *God's Daughters: Evangelical Women and the Power of Submission*. Berkeley: University of California Press, 1997.

Grossman, Cathy Lynn Grossman. "Evangelicals Less Worried about Global Climate Change." *USA Today*, September 18, 2008. Accessed June 1, 2011. http://www.usa-today.com/news/religion/2008-09-18-baylor-environment_N.htm.

Gunther, Marc. "Strange Bedfellows." *Fortune*, February 8, 2006.

Gushee, David P. "Urgency, Creation Care, and Theological Advance." *Associated Baptist Press*, October 26, 2009. Accessed June 1, 2011. http://www.abpnews.com/index.php?option=com_content&task=view&id=4511&Itemid=9.

Gushee, David P. "Faith, Science, and Climate Change." Paper presented at the annual conference of the Christian Life Commission, Baptist General Convention of Texas, San Antonio, TX, March 3–4, 2008.

Gushee, David P. *The Future of Faith in American Politics: The Public Witness of the Evangelical Center*. Waco, TX: Baylor University Press, 2008.

Guth, James L., John C. Green, Lyman A. Kellstedt, and Corwin E. Smidt. "Faith and the Environment: Religious Beliefs and Attitudes on Environmental Policy." *American Journal of Political Science* 39, no. 2 (1995): 364–382.

Guth, James L., Lyman A. Kellstedt, Corwin E. Smidt, and John C. Green. "Theological Perspectives and Environmentalism among Religious Activists." *Journal for the Scientific Study of Religion* 32, no. 4 (1993): 373–382.

Hackett, Conrad and D. Michael Lindsay. "Measuring Evangelicalism: Consequences of Different Operationalization Strategies." *Journal for the Scientific Study of Religion* 47, no. 3 (2008): 499–514.

Hajer, Maarten A. *The Politics of Environmental Discourse: Ecological Modernization and the Policy Process*. Oxford, UK: Oxford University Press, 1995.

Hajer, Marteen and Wytske Versteeg. "A Decade of Discourse Analysis of Environmental Politics: Achievements, Challenges, Perspectives." In *Journal of Environmental Policy and Planning* 7, no. 3 (2005): 175–184.

Hand, Carl M. and Kent D. Van Liere. "Religion, Mastery-over-nature, and Environmental Concern." *Social Forces* 63, no. 2 (1984): 555–570.

Hannigan, John A. "Environmental Discourse." In *Environmental Sociology*. 2nd ed. London: Routledge, 2006.

Harden, Blaine. "The Greening of Evangelicals: Christian Right Turns, Sometimes Warily, to Environmentalism." *Washington Post*, February 6, 2005.

Hayes, Bernadette C. and Manussos Marangudakis. "Religion and Environmental Issues within Anglo-American Democracies." *Review of Religious Research* 42, no. 2 (2000): 159–174.

Heltzel, Peter G. "Prophetic Evangelicals: Toward a Politics of Hope." In *The Sleeping Giant Has Awoken: The New Politics of Religion in the United States*, Jeffrey W. Robbins and Neal Magee, eds., 25–40. New York: Continuum, 2008.

Heltzel, Peter G. *Jesus and Justice: Evangelicals, Race, and American Politics*. New Haven, CT: Yale University Press, 2009.

Henry, Carl F. H. *The Uneasy Conscience of Modern Fundamentalism*. Grand Rapids, MI: Eerdmans, 1947.

Hitzhusen, Gregory E. "Judeo-Christian Theology and the Environment: Moving Beyond Skepticism to New Sources for Environmental Education in the United States." *Environmental Education Research* 13, no. 1 (2007): 55–74.

Houghton, John T. *Global Warming: The Complete Briefing*. 3rd ed. Cambridge, UK: Cambridge University Press, 2004.

Houghton, John T., L. G. Meira Filho, B. A. Callander, N. Harris, A. Kattenberg, and K. Maskell, ed. *Climate Change 1995: The Science of Climate Change*. Cambridge, UK: Cambridge University Press, 1995.

Houghton, John T., Y. Ding, D. J. Griggs, M. Noguer, P. J. Van der Linden, X. Dai, K. Maskell, and C. A. Johnson, ed. *Climate Change 2001: The Scientific Basis*. Cambridge, UK: Cambridge University Press, 2001.

Hulme, Mike. *Why We Disagree about Climate Change: Understanding Controversy, Inaction, and Opportunity*. Cambridge, UK: Cambridge University Press, 2009.

"It's Not Easy Being Green: But the Time Has Come for Evangelicals to Confront the Environmental Crisis." *Christianity Today*, May 18, 1992.

Jackson, Harry R., Jr., and Tony Perkins. *Personal Faith, Public Policy*. Lake Mary, FL: FrontLine, 2008.

Jamieson, Dale. "The Moral and Political Challenges of Climate Change." In *Creating a Climate for Change: Communicating Climate Change and Facilitating Social Change*, Susanne C. Moser and Lisa Dilling, eds., 475–482. New York: Cambridge University Press, 2007.

Jewell, Jim. "Environmental Words." Flourish Blog, comment posted in June 2009. Accessed June 1, 2011. http://flourishonline.org/2009/06/environmental-words/.

Johnson, Stephen M. "Is Religion the Environment's Last Best Hope? Targeting Change in Individual Behavior Through Personal Norm Activation." *Journal of Environmental Law and Litigation* 24, no. 1 (2009): 119–164.

Kanagy, Conrad L. and Fern K. Willits. "A 'Greening' of Religion? Some Evidence from a Pennsylvania Sample." *Social Science Quarterly* 74 (1993): 674–683.

Kanagy, Conrad L. and Hart M. Nelsen. "Religion and Environmental Concern: Challenging the Dominant Assumptions." *Review of Religious Research* 37, no. 1 (1995): 33–45.

Kearns, Laurel. "Cooking the Truth: Faith, Science, the Market, and Global Warming." In *EcoSpirit: Religions and Philosophies for the Earth*, Laurel Kearns and Catherine Keller, eds., 97–124. New York: Fordham University Press, 2007.

Kearns, Laurel. "Noah's Ark Goes to Washington: A Profile of Evangelical Environmentalism." *Social Compass* 44, no. 3 (1997): 349–366.

Kearns, Laurel. "Saving the Creation: Christian Environmentalism in the United States." *Sociology of Religion* 57, no. 1 (1996): 55–70.

Kearns, Laurel. "Saving the Creation: Religious Environmentalism." Ph.D. diss., Emory University, 1994.

Kellstedt, Paul M., Sammy Zahran, and Arnold Vedlitz. "Personal Efficacy, the Information Environment, and Attitudes Toward Global Warming and Climate Change in the United States." *Risk Analysis* 28, no. 1 (2008): 113–126.

Kempton, Willit M., James S. Boster, and Jennifer A. Hartley. *Environmental Values in American Culture*. Cambridge, MA: MIT Press, 1995.

Kennedy, Robert F., Jr. *Crimes Against Nature: How George W. Bush and His Corporate Pals Are Plundering the Country and High-Jacking Our Democracy*. New York: HarperCollins, 2004.

King, Martin Luther, Jr. "Letter from Birmingham City Jail." In *A Testament of Hope: The Essential Writings and Speeches of Martin Luther King Jr.*, James M. Washington, ed., 289–302. New York: HarperCollins, 1986.

Kirby, Alex. *Climate in Peril*. Arendal, Norway: UNEP/GRID-Arendal, 2009.

Kirkpatrick, David D. "Club of the Most Powerful Gathers in Strictest Privacy." *New York Times*, August 28, 2004.

Kollmuss, Anja and Julian Agyeman. "Mind the Gap: Why Do People Act Environmentally and What Are the Barriers to Pro-Environmental Behavior?" *Environmental Education Research* 8, no. 3 (2002): 239–260.

Krugman, Paul. "Betraying the Planet." *New York Times*, June 28, 2009.

LaHaye, Tim and Jerry B. Jenkins. *Left Behind*. Carol Stream, IL: Tyndale House, 1995–2007.

Land, Richard D. and Louis A. Moore, eds. *The Earth Is the Lord's: Christians and the Environment*. Nashville, TN: Broadman, 1992.

Land, Richard. "House Votes for Cap and Trade." Ethics and Religious Liberty Commission blog, comment posted on June 26, 2009. Accessed June 1, 2011. http://erlc.com/article/cap-and-trade-vote-today/.

Larsen, David. "God's Gardeners: American Protestant Evangelicals Confront Environmentalism, 1967–2000." Ph.D. diss., University of Chicago, 2001.

Leiserowitz, Anthony. "Communicating the Risks of Global Warming: American Risk Perceptions, Affective Images, and Interpretive Communities." In *Creating a Climate for Change: Communicating Climate Change and Facilitating Social Change*, Susanne C. Moser and Lisa Dilling, eds., 44–63. New York: Cambridge University Press, 2007.

Leiserowitz, Anthony. *Public Perception, Opinion, and Understanding of Climate Change: Current Patterns, Trends, and Limitations*. New York: United Nations Development Program, 2007. Accessed June 1, 2011. http://hdr.undp.org/en/reports/global/hdr2007–2008/papers/leiserowitz_anthony.pdf.

Leiserowitz, Anthony A., Edward W. Maibach, Connie Roser-Renouf, Nicholas Smith, and Erica Dawson. *Climate Gate, Public Opinion, and the Loss of Trust*. New Haven, CT: Yale Project on Climate Change Communication, 2010. Accessed June 1, 2011. http://environment.yale.edu/climate/publications/climategate-public-opinion-and-the-loss-of-trust/.

Lindsay, D. Michael. "Evangelicals in the Power Elite: Elite Cohesion Advancing a Movement." *American Sociological Review* 73 (2008): 60–82.

Lindsay, D. Michael. "Ties That Bind and Divisions That Persist: Evangelical Faith and the Political Spectrum." *American Quarterly* 59, no. 3 (2007): 883–909.

Lindsay, D. Michael. *Faith in the Halls of Power: How Evangelicals Joined the American Elite*. New York: Oxford University Press, 2007.

Lindsey, Hal. *The Late Great Planet Earth*. Grand Rapids, MI: Zondervan, 1970.

Lizza, Ryan. "As the World Burns." *The New Yorker*, October 11, 2010.

Lovelock, James. *Gaia: A New Look at Life on Earth*. Oxford, UK: Oxford University Press, 2000.

Lowe, Ben. *Green Revolution: Coming Together to Care for Creation*. Downers Grove, IL: InterVarsity, 2009.

Luers, Amy L., Michael D. Mastrandrea, Katharine Hayhoe, and Peter C. Frumhoff. *How to Avoid Dangerous Climate Change: A Target for US Emissions Reductions*. Cambridge, MA: Union of Concerned Scientists, 2007.

Luntz, Frank. "The Environment: A Cleaner, Safer, Healthier America." In *Straight Talk*, 131–146. Alexandria, VA: The Luntz Research Companies, 2002.

Maibach, Edward, Connie Roser-Renouf, and Anthony Leiserowitz. *Global Warming's Six Americas 2009: An Audience Segmentation Analysis*. New Haven, CT and Fairfax, VA: Yale Project on Climate Change and the George Mason University Center for Climate Change Communication, 2009.

Maier, Harry O. "Green Millennialism: American Evangelicals, Environmentalism, and the Book of Revelation." In *Ecological Hermeneutics: Biblical, Historical, and Theological Perspectives*, David G. Horrell, Cherryl Hunt, Christopher Southgate, and Francesca Stavrakopoulou, eds., 246–265. London: T&T Clark International, 2010.

Marsden, George M. *Fundamentalism and American Culture: The Shaping of Twentieth Century Evangelicalism, 1870–1925.* New York: Oxford University Press, 1980.

Marsden, George M. *Reforming Fundamentalism: Fuller Seminary and the New Evangelicalism.* Grand Rapids, MI: Eerdmans, 1995.

McCammack, Brian. "Hot Damned America: Evangelicalism and the Climate Change Policy Debate." *American Quarterly* 59, no. 3 (2007): 645–668.

McCright, Aaron M. and Riley E. Dunlap. "Anti-Reflexivity: The American Conservative Movement's Success in Undermining Climate Science and Policy." *Theory, Culture & Society* 27, nos. 2–3 (2010): 100–133.

McCright, Aaron M. and Riley E. Dunlap. "Challenging Global Warming as a Social Problem: An Analysis of the Conservative Movement's Counter-Claims." *Social Problems* 47, no. 4 (2000): 499–522.

McCright, Aaron M. and Riley E. Dunlap. "Defeating Kyoto: The Conservative Movement's Impact on US Climate Change Policy." *Social Problems* 50, no. 3 (2003): 348–373.

McCright, Aaron M. and Riley E. Dunlap. "The Politicization of Climate Change and Polarization in the American Public's Views of Global Warming, 2001–2010." *The Sociological Quarterly* 52 (2011): 155–194.

McKibben, Bill. "The Gospel of Green: Will Evangelicals Help Save the Earth?" *OnEarth*, Fall 2006.

Merritt, Jonathan. *Green Like God: Unlocking the Divine Plan for Our Planet.* New York: FaithWords, 2010.

Merritt, Jonathan. "Green Means Growing Churches." *Flourish*, Spring 2009.

Meyer, David S. "Building Social Movements." In *Creating a Climate for Change: Communicating Climate Change and Facilitating Social Change*, Susanne C. Moser and Lisa Dilling, eds., 451–461. New York: Cambridge University Press, 2007.

Moberg, David O. *The Great Reversal: Evangelism and Social Concern.* Philadelphia: Lippincott, 1977.

Moore, Russell D. "Ecological Catastrophe and the Uneasy Evangelical Conscience." Moore to the Point blog, comment posted on June 1, 2010. Accessed June 1, 2011. http://www.russellmoore.com/2010/06/01/ecological-catastrophe-and-the-uneasy-evangelical-conscience/.

Moser, Susanne C. "Toward a Deeper Engagement of the US Public on Climate Change: An Open Letter to the 44th President of the United States of America." *International Journal of Sustainability Communication* 3 (2008): 119–132.

Moser, Susanne C. and Lisa Dilling, eds. *Creating a Climate for Change: Communicating Climate Change and Facilitating Social Change.* New York: Cambridge University Press, 2007.

Moser, Susanne C. and Lisa Dilling. Introduction to *Creating a Climate for Change: Communicating Climate Change and Facilitating Social Change*, Susanne C. Moser and Lisa Dilling, eds., 1–27. New York: Cambridge University Press, 2007.

Nagle, John C. "The Evangelical Debate over Climate Change." *University of St. Thomas Law Journal* 5, no. 1 (2008): 52–86.

National Association of Evangelicals. "For the Health of the Nation: An Evangelical Call to Civic Responsibility." Washington, DC: National Association of Evangelicals, 2004. Accessed June 1, 2011. http://www.nae.net/images/content/For_The_Health_Of_The_Nation.pdf.

National Association of Evangelicals. "Press Release: Galen Carey Named Director of Government Affairs of the NAE," June 24, 2009. Accessed June 1, 2011. http://www.nae.net/news/40-news-item-4.

Neff, David. "Can We Separate Creation Care from Political Action?" *Christianity Today* blog, comment posted on April 24, 2009. Accessed June 1, 2011. http://blog.christianitytoday.com/ctliveblog/archives/2009/04/can_we_separate.html.

Neff, David. "Creation Care Without the Baggage." *Christianity Today* Blog, comment posted on May 17, 2009. Accessed June 1, 2011. http://blog.christianitytoday.com/ctliveblog/archives/2009/05/creation_care_w.html.

Nisbet, Matthew C. "Communicating Climate Change: Why Frames Matter for Public Engagement." *Environment* 51, no. 2 (2009): 12–23.

Nisbet, Matthew C. and Teresa Myers. "Trends: Twenty Years of Public Opinion about Global Warming." *Public Opinion Quarterly* 71, no. 3 (2007): 444–470.

Noll, Mark A. *American Evangelical Christianity: An Introduction*. Oxford, UK: Blackwell, 2001.

Oelschlaeger, Max. *Caring for Creation: An Ecumenical Approach to the Environmental Crisis*. New Haven, CT: Yale University Press, 1994.

Olson, Roger E. *The Westminster Handbook to Evangelical Theology*. Louisville, KY: Westminster John Knox, 2004.

Oreskes, Naomi and Erik M. Conway. *Merchants of Doubt*. New York: Bloomsbury Press, 2010.

Pacala, Stephen and Robert Socolow. "Stabilization Wedges: Solving the Climate Problem for the Next 50 Years with Current Technologies." *Science* 305, no. 5686 (2004): 968–972.

Perkins, Tony. "If NAE's Rich Cizik Doesn't Speak for Them, Who Does He Speak For?" FRC blog, comment posted on December 8, 2008. Accessed June 1, 2011. http://www.frcblog.com/2008/12/if-naes-rich-cizik-doesnt-speak-for-them-who-does-he-speak-for/.

Pew Research Center for the People and the Press and Pew Forum on Religion and Public Life. "Many Americans Uneasy with Mix of Religion and Politics," August 24, 2006. Accessed June 1, 2011. http://pewforum.org/uploadedfiles/Topics/Issues/Politics_and_Elections/religion-politics-06.pdf.

Pew Research Center for the People and the Press and Pew Forum on Religion and Public Life. "Religious Groups' Views on Global Warming," April 16, 2009. Accessed June 1, 2011. http://pewforum.org/Science-and-Bioethics/Religious-Groups-Views-on-Global-Warming.aspx.

Prelli, Lawrence J. and Terri S. Winters. "Rhetorical Features of Green Evangelicalism." *Environmental Communication* 3, no. 2 (2009): 224–243.

Pritchard, Rusty. "A Funny Thing Happened on the Way to the Conference." SustainLane blog, comment posted on May 20, 2009. Accessed June 1, 2011. http://www.sustainlane.com/reviews/a-funny-thing-happened-on-the-way-to-the-conference/FBHIPQTHJLLVUA9A3D1B1K7C13QB.

Pritchard, Rusty. "I'm No Environmentalist." SustainLane blog, comment posted on July 15, 2009. Accessed June 1, 2011. http://www.sustainlane.com/reviews/im-no-environmentalist/JXP4KTTI74W9H7MDY4R8NAVYY78J.

Public Religion Research. "Key Religious Groups Want Government to Address Climate Change and Its Impact on World's Poor." Prepared for Faith in Public Life and Oxfam America, March 27, 2009. Accessed June 1, 2011. http://www.faithinpubliclife.org/tools/polls/climate-change/.

Pulliam, Sarah. "Interview: NAE President Leith Anderson on Richard Cizik's Resignation." *Christianity Today*, December 11, 2008. Accessed June 1, 2011. http://www.christianitytoday.com/ct/2008/decemberweb-only/150-41.0.html.

Pulliam, Sarah. "The NAE Chooses Government Affairs Director." *Christianity Today*, June 24, 2009. Accessed June 1, 2011. http://www.christianitytoday.com/ct/2009/juneweb-only/125-31.0.html.

Pulliam, Sarah. "Richard Cizik Resigns from the National Association of Evangelicals." *Christianity Today*, December 11, 2008. Accessed June 1, 2011. http://www.christianitytoday.com/ct/2008/decemberweb-only/150-42.0.html.

Rabe, Barry. *Statehouse and Greenhouse: The Emerging Politics of American Climate Change Policy*. Washington, DC: Brookings Institution, 2004.

Randall, Raymond. "Confessions of a Closet Environmentalist." Northland blog, comment posted on February 27, 2009. Accessed June 1, 2011. http://www.northland-church.net/blogs/confessions_of_a_closet_environmentalist/.

Regnerus, Mark D. and Christian Smith. "Selective Deprivatization among American Religious Traditions: The Reversal of the Great Reversal." *Social Forces* 76, no. 4 (1998): 1,347–1,372.

Revkin, Andy. "The Sky Is Falling! Say Hollywood and, Yes, the Pentagon." *New York Times*, February 29, 2004.

Robinson, Tri. *Saving God's Green Earth: Rediscovering the Church's Responsibility to Environmental Stewardship*. Norcross, GA: Ampelon, 2006.

Robinson, Tri. *Small Footprint, Big Handprint: How to Live Simply and Love Extravagantly*. Norcross, GA: Ampelon, 2008.

Robinson, Tri and Ken Wilson. "Vineyard Churches: Seven Year Plan for American Evangelicalism." In *Many Heavens, One Earth: Faith Commitments to Protect the Living Planet*, Mary Colwell, Victoria Finlay, Alison Hilliard, and Susie Weldon, eds., 135–137. Bath, UK: Alliance of Religions and Conservation, 2009.

Rockström, Johan, Will Steffen, Kevin Noone, Åsa Persson, F. Stuart Chapin III, Eric F. Lambin, Timothy M. Lenton, Marten Scheffer, Carl Folke, Hans Joachim Schellnhuber, Björn Nykvist, Cynthia A. de Wit, Terry Hughes, Sander van der Leeuw, Henning Rodhe, Sverker Sörlin, Peter K. Snyder, Robert Costanza, Uno Svedin, Malin Falkenmark, Louise Karlberg, Robert W. Corell, Victoria J. Fabry, James Hansen, Brian Walker, Diana Liverman, Katherine Richardson, Paul Crutzen, and Jonathan A. Foley. "A Safe Operating Space for Humanity." *Nature* 461 (2009): 472–475.

Rogers, Robin and Peter Goodwin Heltzel. "The New Evangelical Politics." *Society* 45 (2008): 412–414.

Rudolph, John Collins. "Climate Skeptic Seeks Energy Committee Chairmanship." *New York Times*, November 16, 2010.

Schaeffer, Francis A. *Pollution and the Death of Man: The Christian View of Ecology.* Wheaton, IL: Tyndale House, 1970.

Scherer, Glenn. "The Godly Must Be Crazy." *Grist*, October 27, 2004. Accessed June 1, 2011. http://www.grist.org/article/scherer-christian/.

Schultz, P. Wesley, Lynnette Zelezny, and Nancy J. Dalrymple. "A Multinational Perspective on the Relation between Judeo-Christian Religious Beliefs and Attitudes of Environmental Concern." *Environmental Behavior* 32, no. 4 (2000): 576–591.

Schwartz, Peter and Doug Randall. "An Abrupt Climate Change Scenario and Its Implications for United States National Security." Prepared for the Defense Department, October 2003. Accessed June 1, 2011. http://www.gbn.com/articles/pdfs/Abrupt%20Climate%20Change%20February%202004.pdf.

Shaiko, Ronald G. "Religion, Politics, and Environmental Concern: A Powerful Mix of Passions." *Social Science Quarterly* 68, no. 2 (1987): 244–262.

Sherkat, Darrren E. and Christopher G. Ellison. "Structuring the Religion-Environment Connection: Identifying Religious Influences on Environmental Concern and Activism." *Journal for the Scientific Study of Religion* 46, no. 1 (2007): 71–85.

Shibley, Mark A. and Jonathon L. Wiggins. "The Greening of Mainline American Religion: A Sociological Analysis of the Environmental Ethics of the National Religious Partnership for the Environment." *Social Compass* 44, no. 3 (1997): 333–348.

Sider, Ronald J. *Rich Christians in an Age of Hunger.* Downers Grove, IL: InterVarsity, 1977.

Simmons, J. Aaron. "Evangelical Environmentalism: Oxymoron or Opportunity?" *Worldviews* 13, no. 1 (2009): 40–71.

Sleeth, Emma. *It's Easy Being Green: One Student's Guide to Serving God and Saving the Planet.* Grand Rapids, MI: Zondervan, 2008.

Sleeth, J. Matthew. "God's Mental Health Prescription." *Creation Care*, Summer 2008.

Sleeth, J. Matthew. *The Gospel According to the Earth: Why the Good Book Is a Green Book.* New York: HarperCollins, 2010.

Sleeth, J. Matthew. *Serve God, Save the Planet: A Christian Call to Action*. Grand Rapids, MI: Zondervan, 2007.

Sleeth, Nancy. *Go Green, Save Green: A Simple Guide to Saving Time, Money, and God's Green Earth*. Carol Stream, IL: Tyndale House, 2009.

Smith, Angela M. and Simone Pulver. "Ethics-Based Environmentalism in Practice: Religious-Environmental Organizations in the United States." *Worldviews* 13, no. 2 (2009): 145–179.

Smith, Buster G. and Bryan Johnson. "The Liberalization of Young Evangelicals: A Research Note." *Journal for the Scientific Study of Religion* 49, no. 2 (2010): 351–360.

Smith, Christian. *American Evangelicalism: Embattled and Thriving*. Chicago: University of Chicago Press, 1998.

Smith, Christian. *Christian America? What Evangelicals Really Want*. Berkeley: University of California Press, 2000.

Smith, Christian. "Correcting a Curious Neglect, or Bringing Religion Back In." In *Disruptive Religion: The Force of Faith in Social Movement Activism*, Christian Smith, ed., 1–25. New York: Routledge, 1996.

Solomon, Susan, Dahe Qin, Martin Manning, Melinda Marquis, Kristen Averyt, Melinda M. B. Tignor, Henry LeRoy Miller, and Zhenlin Chin, eds. *Climate Change 2007: The Physical Science Basis*. Cambridge, UK: Cambridge University Press, 2007.

Speth, James Gustave. *The Bridge at the Edge of the World: Capitalism, the Environment, and Crossing from Crisis to Sustainability*. New Haven, CT: Yale University Press, 2008.

Speth, James Gustave. *Red Sky at Morning: America and the Crisis of the Global Environment*. New Haven, CT: Yale University Press, 2004.

Steinfels, Peter. "Evangelical Group Defends Laws Protecting Endangered Species as a Modern 'Noah's Ark.'" *New York Times*, January 31, 1996.

Stern, Nicholas. "The Economics of Climate Change." *American Economic Review*, 98, no. 2 (2008): 1–37.

Stern, Nicholas. *The Economics of Climate Change: The Stern Review*. Cambridge, UK: Cambridge University Press, 2007.

Strode, Tom. "Pro-Abortion Foundation Aided Evangelical Climate Effort." *Baptist Press*, March 1, 2006. Accessed June 1, 2011. http://www.bpnews.net/bpnews. asp?id=22753.

Sturgis, Patrick and Nick Allum. "Science in Society: Re-Evaluating the Deficit Model of Public Attitudes." *Public Understanding of Science* 13, no. 1 (2004): 55–74.

Swidler, Ann. "Culture in Action: Symbols and Strategies." *American Sociological Review* 51, no. 2 (1986): 273–286.

Taylor, Bron R., ed. *The Encyclopedia of Religion and Nature*. London: Continuum, 2005.

Thomas, Mark J. "Evangelicals and the Environment: Theological Foundations for Christian Environmental Stewardship." *Evangelical Review of Theology* 17, no. 2 (1993): 119–286.

Thumma, Scott and Dave Travis. *Beyond Megachurch Myths: What We Can Learn from America's Largest Churches.* San Francisco: Jossey-Bass, 2007.

Tierney, John. "And on the Eighth Day, God Went Green." *New York Times*, February 11, 2006.

Tocqueville, Alexis de. *Democracy in America*, Henry Reeve, trans. London: Saunders and Otley, 1835.

Tomkins, Stephen. *John Wesley: A Biography.* Grand Rapids, MI: Eerdmans, 2003.

Tracy Miller, ed. *US Religious Landscape Survey 2008.* Washington, DC: Pew Forum on Religion and Public Life, 2008. Accessed June 1, 2011. http://religions.pewforum.org/pdf/report-religious-landscape-study-full.pdf.

Truesdale, Al. "Last Things First: The Impact of Eschatology on Ecology." *Perspectives on Science and Christian Faith* 46 (1994): 116–122.

Tucker, Mary Evelyn and John Grim, eds. *World Religions and Ecology Series.* Cambridge, MA: Harvard University Press, 1997–2004.

Tucker, Mary Evelyn. "Religion and Ecology." In *The Oxford Handbook of the Sociology of Religion*, Peter Clarke, ed., 819–835. Oxford, UK: Oxford University Press, 2009.

Tucker, Mary Evelyn. *Worldly Wonder: Religions Enter Their Ecological Phase.* Chicago: Open Court, 2004.

United Nations Environment Program. *Bridging the Emissions Gap.* Nairobi, Kenya: UNEP, 2011.

US Senate Committee on the Environment and Public Works. Testimony of Jim Ball, Evangelical Climate Initiative, June 7, 2007. Accessed June 1, 2011. http://epw.senate.gov/public/index.cfm?FuseAction=Files.View&FileStore_id=b430cae6-9164-472a-b979-d2e1d75ad5ca.

Vandenbergh, Michael P. and Anne C. Steinemann. "The Carbon-Neutral Individual." *New York University Law Review* 82 (2007): 101–168.

Vanderhoek, Mark. "Merritt, Gushee: On Creation Care, Evangelicals Must Move Toward 'We.'" *Associated Baptist Press*, November 3, 2009. Accessed June 1, 2011. http://www.abpnews.com/index.php?option=com_content&task=view&id=4538&Itemid=53.

Vu, Michelle A. "Evangelical Richard Cizik Re-Emerges for Green Cause." *Christian Post*, April 20, 2009. Accessed June 1, 2011. http://www.christianpost.com/article/20090420/evangelical-richard-cizik-re-emerges-for-green-cause/index.html.

Wardekker, J. Arjan, Arthur C. Petersen, and Jeroen P. van der Sluijs. "Ethics and Public Perception of Climate Change: Exploring Christian Voices in the US Public Debate." *Global Environmental Change* 19 (2009): 512–521.

White, Lynn. "The Historical Roots of our Ecologic Crisis." *Science* 155, no. 3767 (1967): 1,203–1,207.

Wilcox, Clyde and Carin Larson. *Onward Christian Soldiers? The Religious Right in American Politics.* 3rd ed. Boulder, CO: Westview, 2006.

Wilkinson, Loren, ed. *Earthkeeping in the Nineties: Stewardship and the Renewal of Creation.* Grand Rapids, MI: Eerdmans, 1991.

Wilkinson, Loren, ed. *Earthkeeping: Christian Stewardship of Natural Resources.* Grand Rapids, MI: Eerdmans, 1980.

Wilkinson, Loren. "The Making of the Declaration." In *The Care of Creation: Focusing Concern and Action*, edited R. J. Berry, 50–59. Downers Grove, IL: InterVarsity, 2000.

Wilson, E. O. *The Creation: An Appeal to Save Life on Earth.* New York: W. W. Norton, 2006.

Wilson, Edward O. *The Future of Life.* New York: Knopf, 2002.

Wolkomir, Michelle, Michael Futreal, Eric Woodrum, and Thomas Hoban. "Denominational Subcultures of Environmentalism." *Review of Religious Research* 38, no. 4 (1997): 325–343.

Wolkomir, Michelle, Michael Futreal, Eric Woodrum, and Thomas Hoban. "Substantive Religious Belief and Environmentalism." *Social Science Quarterly* 78, no. 1 (1997): 96–108.

Woodrum, Eric and Thomas Hoban. "Theology and Religiosity Effects on Environmentalism." *Review of Religious Research* 35, no. 3 (1994): 193–206.

Woodrum, Eric and Michelle J. Wolkomir. "Religious Effects on Environmentalism." *Sociological Spectrum* 17, no. 2 (1997): 223–234.

Wuthnow, Robert. "The Political Rebirth of American Evangelicals." In *The New Christian Right: Mobilization and Legitimation*, Robert C. Liebman and Robert Wuthnow, eds., 167–185. New York: Aldine, 1983.

Index